Disciplines of Education

Are the disciplines of education ghosts of a productive past or creative and useful forms of inquiry? Are they in a demographic and organisational crisis today?

The contribution of the 'foundation disciplines' of sociology, psychology, philosophy, history and economics to the study of education has always been contested in the UK and in much of the English-speaking world. Such debates are now being brought to a head in education by the demographic crisis. Recent research has shown that, with an ageing population of education academics, in 10 years' time there could be very few disciplinary specialists left working in faculties of education within British universities. But does that matter and is the UK no more than a special case? How does this 'crisis' look from Europe where the disciplines of education are more embedded, and from the USA with its more diverse higher education system?

In this book, leading scholars – including A.H. Halsey, David Bridges, John Furlong, Hugh Lauder, Martin Lawn and Sheldon Rothblatt – consider the changing fortunes of each discipline as education moved away from the dominance of psychology in the 1930s, 1940s and 1950s as a result of the growing importance of the other disciplines and new social questions, and how the changing epistemological and political debates of the last 20 years have resulted in their progressive demise. Finally, the book confronts the question as to whether the disciplines have a place in education in the twenty-first century.

The book brings the coming crisis into the public view and explores the issue of the past, current and future relevance of the disciplines to the study of education. It will be of interest to all international academics and researchers in the field of education and the contributory disciplines and to students on educational research methods courses.

John Furlong is a Professor in the Department of Education at the University of Oxford, UK.

Martin Lawn is a Professorial Research Fellow at the Department of Education, University of Oxford, UK.

Disciplines of Education

Their role in the future of education research

Edited by John Furlong and Martin Lawn

Routledge
Taylor & Francis Group

LONDON AND NEW YORK

First edition published 2011
by Routledge
2 Park Square, Milton Park, Abingdon, Oxon OX14 4RN

Simultaneously published in the USA and Canada
by Routledge
270 Madison Avenue, New York, NY 10016

Routledge is an imprint of the Taylor & Francis Group, an informa business

© 2011 Selection and editorial matter, John Furlong and Martin Lawn; individual chapters, the contributors

Typeset in Garamond by Wearset Ltd, Boldon, Tyne and Wear
Printed and bound in Great Britain by TJ International Ltd, Padstow, Cornwall

British Library Cataloguing in Publication Data
A catalogue record for this book is available from the British Library

Library of Congress Cataloging-in-Publication Data
Disciplines of education: their role in the future of education research/[edited by] John Furlong and Martin Lawn. – 1st ed.
p. cm.
Includes bibliographical references and index.
1. Education–Study and teaching (Higher)–Great Britain. 2. Education–Research–Great Britain. I. Furlong, John, 1947– II. Lawn, Martin.

LB2326.3.D57 2010
370.7'20941–dc22

2010008824

ISBN13: 978-0-415-58205-6 (hbk)
ISBN13: 978-0-415-58206-3 (pbk)
ISBN13: 978-0-203-84413-7 (ebk)

Contents

Introduction

John Furlong and Martin Lawn

This book is about the 'disciplines of education', what in the USA are often referred to as the 'foundations of education' – the sociology, psychology, history and philosophy of education. Our aim and that of our contributing authors is to assess the current 'health' of the disciplines of education in the modern university: their current institutional position, their major achievements – theoretical, practical and methodological – and their potential for further contributions in the future.

In the UK, a recent Economic and Social Research Council (ESRC) *Demographic Review* (Mills *et al.*, 2006) has highlighted the profound demographic difficulties facing the field of education. With more than one-third of education academics now in their late 50s, the challenge of securing the future of education is more problematic than almost any other social science discipline. Within education, the position of academics with specialist expertise in the 'disciplines of education' is particularly problematic. Significant numbers of such specialists were recruited into higher education (and education remains a major 'importer' from other social science disciplines (Mills *et al.*, 2006)) in the 1970s and 1980s in the move to make education a 'degree-worthy' subject. Following what Hoyle described in the 1980s as 'the turn to the practical' (Hoyle, 1982) in teacher-education policy, practice and research, such specialists have not been replaced as they have left or retired from higher education. The current nature of teacher-education courses in the UK – both initial and in-service – means that very few institutions are now in a position to recruit the next generation of disciplinary specialists.

Of course, the contribution of the disciplines and of theory more generally to research in education has always been contested. In the last 20 years, as Barnett has argued (Barnett, 1990) many forms of university-based professional education have experienced both an 'epistemological' and a 'sociological' undermining. Such debates are now being brought to a head in education by the demographic crisis. In ten years' time, there could be very few such disciplinary specialists left working within faculties of education in UK universities. But does that matter? The aim of this book is to bring this coming crisis into the public view. By encouraging education researchers to research themselves, we aim to explore the past, current and future relevance of the disciplines to the field.

The book is therefore an opportunity for education researchers and the non-specialist reader to engage in a series of disciplinary-based conversations about what each discipline's major contributions in the past have been and what they should be in the future. We also asked each contributor to describe and assess their discipline's 'sociological' position – its mechanisms and sites of production, its journals, places, projects and development – and its 'epistemological' strengths – substantive, methodological and theoretical developments which have contemporary relevance and value.

The majority of the chapters we have included focus primarily on the issues raised within UK higher education; nevertheless it is clear that the challenges we and our various contributors consider have far wider resonances internationally – particularly within the anglophone world. That is why we have also included two reflective pieces: from the USA with its more diverse conception of 'the modern university', and from mainland Europe where the 'disciplines of education' are more often securely embedded.

The disciplines we have chosen to include illustrate a range of different positions in relation to what we in the opening chapter describe as the 'disciplinary project': the political struggle to establish a secure place for a discipline. We have included contributions on the four foundation disciplines of the earlier period of the 1960s to the 1980s – philosophy (Oancea and Bridges), sociology (Lauder *et al.*), psychology (Crozier) and history (Goodman and Grosvenor) – in that they have the greatest historical claim. However, as we will see, they vary in their epistemological coherence and some are more sociologically challenged than in the past. To these we have added economics (Dearden *et al.*). Though highly influential in recent years, the economics of education never was part of the main 'canon', at least in a sociological sense; it has never had a secure institutional base within mainstream departments of education – nor in economics for that matter. We have also included a contribution on comparative and international education (Crossley and Watson). Some might claim that this is not a discipline at all, in an epistemological sense; yet it has established itself as a very important 'perspective' and perhaps in sociological terms has many of the hallmarks of a sub-disciplinary field. We have also included geography (Taylor) – what might perhaps be considered an emergent sub-discipline within education, though at present it has neither institutional status nor epistemological certainty. We then have two contributions from outside the UK context – Sheldon Rothblatt from the USA and Edwin Keiner from Germany – to give their reflections on the issues raised by our UK contributors. In the final chapter we ourselves reflect on what we have learned about the contribution of the nature of disciplines per se and their potential for the future of education research.

Our hope is that through these contemporary conversations, the reader will be in a better position to assess the current and future contribution of disciplinary-based perspectives to research, teaching and scholarship in education.

References

Barnett, R. (1990) *The Idea of Higher Education*. Buckingham: SRHE/Open University Press.

Hoyle, E. (1982) 'The professionalization of teachers: A paradox', *British Journal of Educational Studies* 30(2): 161–171.

Mills, D., A. Jepson, T. Coxon, M. Easterby-Smith, P. Hawkins and J. Spencer (2006) *Demographic Review of the Social Sciences*. Swindon: ESRC.

1   The disciplines of education

Between the ghost and the shadow

Martin Lawn and John Furlong

> The air was filled with phantoms, wandering hither and thither in restless haste, and moaning as they went.... The misery with them all was, clearly, that they sought to interfere, for good, in human matters, and had lost the power for ever.
>
> Charles Dickens, A Christmas Carol (1843); quoted in Kenway et al. (2006)

Introduction

In their evocatively titled book *Haunting the Knowledge Economy*, Kenway *et al*. (2006) ask: How we can learn to live with the ghosts of our past, to think about them, even find ways to 'converse' with them and, in doing so, understand where we are and how the future is shaped?

Kenway and her colleagues use Dickens to conjure a powerful image, but does that image provide an appropriate metaphor with which to begin a discussion of the contemporary position of the disciplines of education in 2010? In the UK, have they fallen into desuetude, so much so that they are now no more than ghosts? Has the policy context of the last 20 years, that has increasingly come to influence our teaching and the funding of our research with its pressure on the production of knowledge which stresses use value, has this external force squeezed out the power of disciplinary contributions to the study of education? Do the remnants of the past now only live on in the routines of method, not in the analytical strength of disciplines? Does the absence of reference back in much that is published, the absence of conceptual communities or disciplinary-based theorization, do these now mean that the (disciplinary) past is another country?

That 'other country' we are referring to here is the period of the 1960s to the 1980s which came about as a result of the Robbins Report (1963). The Robbins Report, probably the UK's last full expression of liberal higher education, saw university education in more than just instrumental terms; knowledge was an end in itself. The subsequent 'search for degree worthiness' in teacher-education courses meant that the 'foundation' disciplines of philosophy, sociology, psychology and history of education came to the fore, dominating both teacher education and educational research in the UK and much of the English-speaking world. This was the period, albeit relatively short-lived, when, as Bridges (2006) reminds us, the foundation disciplines appeared to offer a secure way forward for education. They offered:

> a *differentiation* between different kinds of enquiry [R.S. Peters had recently complained of the current condition of educational theory as 'undifferentiated mush']; *coherence* in terms of internal consistency of any one of these forms and the *'systematic'* or rigor of enquiry which raised such enquiry above the level of popular or received opinion – the discipline of the discipline.
>
> (p. 259)

Those days of certainty are long gone; but does that mean that sociology, psychology, philosophy, history (and indeed the whole range of disciplinary-based perspectives), economics and geography have nothing to offer research, scholarship and university teaching in education now and in the future? What can and should those contributions be and what is the current institutional position of those disciplines within the academy? These are the questions that we want to begin to address in this volume. An earlier and somewhat shorter version of this edited collection of papers on the disciplines of education first appeared as a special edition of the *Oxford Review of Education* in 2009 (Furlong and Lawn, 2009); in fact, the idea of this book had a much longer genesis. It began in 2005 with British Educational Research Association seminars on the social organization of educational research with scholars from the US Social Science Research Council/National Academy of Education on educational research (Lawn and Furlong, 2007; Humes, 2007; Rees and Power, 2007; Gardner and Gallagher, 2007).

A further stimulus was the Economic and Social Research Council (ESRC) *Demographic Review of the Social Sciences* (Mills *et al.*, 2006), which highlighted the profound demographic difficulties facing the field of education in the UK. With more than one-third of education academics now in their late 50s, the challenge of securing the future of education is more problematic than almost any other social science discipline.

While we, and all of our contributors, fully recognize that university departments of education, which now include most of the once-independent teachers' colleges, are not the only place where educational research, scholarship and teaching takes place, they are an important part of the picture. If education departments faced a general demographic crisis with an ageing population, we feared that the position of those working explicitly within the disciplines of education was likely to be even worse. At the very least, those individuals specifically employed in the earlier period to teach 'the foundation disciplines', many of whom helped to shape educational research and scholarship for over a generation, were now either retired or on the verge of it. The 2008 Research Assessment Exercise (RAE) was, for many of them, probably their last.

Of course, the contribution of the disciplines and of theory more generally has always been contested. Our sense, though, has been that such internal debates are now being brought to a head in education by the demographic crisis. But our questions were not merely demographic (who was or was not employed specifically to 'profess' the sociology or psychology of education, etc). Rather we were concerned to understand the current strength of the disciplines of education as forms of academic practice. If in ten years' time there were very few disciplinary specialists left working within faculties of education within British universities, would that be a cause for concern?

Our aim in producing this volume was therefore to bring these questions into the public view and to explore the issue of the past, current and future relevance of the disciplines to the field. Interestingly, what we have found is that the story is not as straightforward as we had imagined. While there are real problems of power, of supply and of effect, most of the contributors to this volume are optimistic about what has been achieved and what will be achieved in the future in their own specialist areas. Driven by their close affiliation with their disciplinary work, their sense of what is being produced and how it is being produced is positive. Our aim in this chapter is therefore to explore the puzzling position of disciplines in education in the UK and their ghostly or material futures.

What's in a discipline?

> Amongst the many beliefs that modernity legitimised and underwrote was the general conviction that social progress depended on making our social practices and institutions less dependent on custom, habit, dogma and tradition and more firmly based on knowledge that met universal standards of objectivity and conformed to impersonal criteria of rationality and truth.
>
> (Carr, 2006, p. 138)

There are a range of competing views of what disciplines do. The view described in the quotation above, which sees disciplines as (uncontested) carriers of theory and standards, is still present in discourses of education. So is its corollary, that scholars working within disciplinary boundaries produce a bounded academic identity, which is constantly reconfirmed. That is, those who support the same theories and standards cluster together, using department-buildings, publications, courses, procedures, appointments, journals and conferences to maintain their intellectual community (Spani *et al.*, 2002). There is a stronger 'European' notion of discipline, in which community-created standards and qualifications protect the borders of the discipline, which can be contrasted with a 'weaker' UK version in which 'being interested' is treated as the equivalent of being qualified. In this more pragmatic UK version, policy influence upon the academy is stronger, and the impact of 'movement' and 'associational' activity is also more marked. Working in the discipline can mean absorption and socialization into skills, hierarchies and the canon, or a more social and equal activity of like-minded enthusiasts, working with or against policy and funding pressure. The classical European version still expects a significant effect from disciplinary processes, for example, its capacity to break down public problems into its own disciplinary logics, while the pragmatic UK version has to be convinced that they still have a significant or functional place in the business of education, even if it is reduced to knowledge about methods. Educational studies in the UK might have lost the powerful disciplinary claims and procedures of the classical European model while retaining only the sociality and intensification of pragmatism under pressure.

A different view of disciplines in social science refers to them as a 'project'. From this perspective, a discipline does not have clear boundaries; rather, its ideas are sharply contested and legitimacy is something that has to be struggled for. A discipline is, then, a continuous struggle to occupy a field and yet it 'always involves the projection of a world of possibilities within which things gain their meaning' (Ross, 2006, p. 208). Bourdieu's work takes the notion of field further: it involves a 'critical mediation between the practice of those who partake of it and the surrounding social and economic conditions' (Bourdieu and Wacquant, 1992, p. 105). Here is the idea of a project, a community of knowledge determined less by its extensive and defended disciplinary procedures, standards and artefacts than a determination to contest and create, in which the production of ideas and methods reflect its engagement with the social world both within the discipline as well as outside it.

This view, of an active and contested discipline, as an intellectual and practical project, is probably more closely linked to the numbers of subfields and groups of fragmented enthusiasts in the UK who are able to organize seminars and create websites and eJournals without reference to disciplinary boundaries. Post-disciplinary elements and actors may network or be sustained by a university department without reference back to any common project, nor, indeed, with any necessity for contestation as they work only within micro-communities.

The rise of the disciplines

Broadly speaking, two approaches to the idea of a discipline can be seen here, a consolidating and powerful community and a knowledge project, constantly engaging and reforming through argument. Neither seems fully to characterize the current situation of educational disciplines in the UK at the moment. Critical mass appears to be replaced by micro-communities; common disciplinary work and accumulated insight seems either unknown or impossible; skill is replaced by willingness or audit, and intellectual engagement with requisite publication.

What these broadly different disciplinary approaches have in common, however, is that each of them recognizes the importance of both an 'epistemological' dimension (questions of theory and of method, debates about the nature of evidence and how it should be represented and defended) and a political or 'sociological' dimension which examines their struggle to establish themselves witin their field. Interestingly, Kuhn (1977) argues that both of these different dimensions are essential for intellectual progress to be made. Progress, he suggests, requires a context where there is relatively close agreement on theories and methods of enquiry, and where there is sufficient institutional certainty so that newcomers can be inducted into the discipline.

Put like that, it is clear that even in the 1980s in the UK these conditions did not fully exist. As Bridges (2006) reminds us, during that period (and indeed ever since) the disciplines of education were seriously divided within themselves: 'The sociology of education for example contained everything from traditional hard data survey people through ethnographers, neo Marxists and critical theorists to post modernists and socal relativists. Psychology spanned neurophysiology, behaviourism, cognitivism and constructivism through to psychoanalysis' (p. 260). But it remains the case that whatever their internal intellectual differences, they did exist institutionally in the 1970s and 1980s in the UK. They were enshrined in course curricula and in dedicated jobs; there was a growth of specialist conferences, of journals and of specialist Master's programmes which served to induct newcomers into these disciplines, newcomers who eventually found employment either in the UK or overseas as an intellectual diaspora.

But how had that been achieved? A rough sketch would suggest the following: from the 1920s to the 1950s, the main discipline in education was psychology; subjects of study, training, careers and publications were defined by the dominance of psychology in education. From the 1960s to the 1970s, the disciplines in education grew in range and scale. History and philosophy were the most active disciplines and thus established an 'opposite pole based in the humanities to the quasi-scientific approach that was already established in educational psychology' (McCulloch, 2002, p. 106). Sociology of education then grew out of clusters of researchers in the London School of Economics, defining itself through questions of class and stratification, and working with survey data.

> By the mid 1970s then the disciplines were well established both in terms of their general rationale for contributing to the study of education as a whole, and also increasingly as clearly defined and discrete disciplinary communities in their own right.
>
> (McCulloch, 2002, pp. 111–112)

From the 1970s to the 1980s, a rapid massification and expansion of universities and teacher-training colleges saw a range of new subjects of study and ways of understanding or defining them. The Open University's influence in redefining educational studies (particularly in the sociology and psychology of education, and in new areas like educational administration and management and curriculum studies) was crucial in the expansion. Both macro theoretical and micro case-study research crossed the borders of the disciplines and even fostered the growth of determinedly non-disciplinary-based study. The identity of the British Educational Research Association, founded in 1974, was shaped by the growing fields of action research and 'teachers as researchers' rather than disciplinary division.

McCulloch's analysis of the more recent period of educational history is more cursory. Although he notes the serious challenges faced by the disciplines in the 1990s and beyond, he concludes on a very positive note, arguing that:

> Over the past 50 years, the disciplines separately and together have made a significant contribution to the study of education ... having successfully established themselves and survived in difficult conditions, the disciplines continue in the 21st century to represent central pillars of educational studies and research.
>
> (McCulloch, 2002, p. 117)

We would take a different view and suggest that the more recent period deserves more careful analysis. At an institutional level, by the 1980s the position of the disciplines began to be seriously undermined; from then on, there was a 'falling from grace'.

Charting the fall from grace

At one level, the reasons for this significant change in fortunes within British higher education are not hard to find; they are the result of what, as early as 1982, Hoyle was describing the 'turn to the practical' both in teacher education and research. Perhaps too much has already been written about this 'turn' and the struggles behind it (Adams and Tulasiewicz, 1995; Wilkin, 1996; Furlong et al., 2000; Mahony and Hextall, 2000; Whitty, 2002). Suffice it to say that of particular significance in England (and to a lesser extent elsewhere in the UK) was the establishment of the Training and Development Agency (TDA) for Schools with its emphasis on competences and 'standards' in initial teacher education; the rapid expansion of employment-based routes into teaching where higher education was no longer seen as essential; the development of school-based continuing professional development (CPD) and the end of full-time funded higher degree programmes for teachers; the increasing interest in practitioner research with only weak links to higher education; and differentiation of research capacity in universities as a result of successive research assessment exercises (the RAE). Each one of these moves has served progressively to either undermine or reform the contribution of disciplinary-based knowledge to research and teaching in education.

However, we would suggest that in order to understand these changes they need to be contextualized within wider movements in higher education. Education as a field of study is (no more than) a particularly acute example of changes that have overtaken higher education more broadly. Those changes, as Barnett (1990) pointed out 20 years ago, are both 'sociological' and 'epistemological' in origin. At the 'sociological' level, the main challenge has been as a consequence of universities increasingly coming under the influence of neo-liberal policies. As Marginson (2007) has observed, the result has been a redefined internal economy for universities, in which under-funding drives a 'pseudo-market' in fee incomes, soft budget allocations for special purposes and contested earnings for new enrolments and research grants. Increasingly, therefore, higher education 'managers' (including deans of education) have found themselves having to compete in internal and external markets in order to maintain the position of their departments. This has had major implications for both teaching and research.

In terms of teaching, university managers have increasingly found themselves having to compete for external funding in a highly competitive environment. And the dominant 'market' in terms of teaching for university departments of education in England has been TDA-funded forms of teacher education with its increasingly instrumental focus. In departments where all of the teaching is funded by the TDA, there have been major consequences for the staff that are recruited (mostly practitioners recruited directly from schools) and for the professional development opportunities they are offered (often professionally rather than theoretically led), as well as the teaching that they undertake. In a market where they need to compete for funding, universities have been keen to take on government-funded programmes and, with them, government agendas. As Marginson comments: 'The paradox of this new openness to outside funding and competition is a process of "isomorphic closure" through which universities with diverse histories choose from an increasingly restricted menu of commercial options and strategies' (Marginson, 2007, p. 4).

It is in this 'sociological' context that the disciplines of education have fared badly in the last 20 years. As the chapters in this volume testify, small numbers of individuals have managed to maintain their personal commitment to disciplinary-based teaching and research – for example, with funding from the ESRC. However, at an institutional level the story is different. It is only those institutions that have access to alternative sources of funding – for example, through non-vocational undergraduate education degrees or through the international postgraduate market – that have had any significant opportunities to maintain a degree of independence in terms of the courses they offer and in the appointment of disciplinary-based staff. It is only they who have been able to decide *for themselves* what contribution disciplinary-based knowledge should make to their teaching and research.

But why has this externally imposed agenda been so explicitly instrumentalist? Intellectually, why have most of the disciplines of education been so marginalized? In order to answer this question we need to turn to the second of Barnett's dimensions – the 'epistemological'.

From the 1980s onwards, a much wider repertoire of methodologies and theories started to come into education. Literary theory, cultural studies, activity theory, feminism, postcolonial theory – all of these and many more began to make their claims for a space in the analysis of educational questions. In a very short period of time, they began to undermine (or 'enrich', as some might put it (Bridges, 2006)) the theoretical hegemony of sociology, psychology, history and philosophy.

But by the 1990s there were also growing doubts at a more fundamental level. What Barnett (1990) then described as the 'end of certainty' was something that was experienced throughout higher education:

> The idea of objective knowledge is central to Higher Education. But from various theoretical quarters – philosophy of science, sociology of knowledge, epistemology, critical theory and post-structuralism – the idea of objective knowledge and truth has come under a massive assault. What if anything is to replace objective knowledge is unclear. Pragmatism, relativism, 'meta-criticism' and even 'anything goes' are all proposed. The very diversity of the alternative options is testimony to the collapse of some of our basic epistemological tenets.
>
> (Barnett, 1990, p. 11)

Epistemological self-doubt was particularly acute in the field of professional education – the economic base of many university departments of education. There was an increasing recognition that there was much more to professional knowledge than had been traditionally captured in disciplinary-based theory. In the 1980s and 1990s, writers such as Schön (1983, 1987) and Eraut (1994) began to argue that, because groups like teachers inhabited 'the swampy lowlands' of professional life, much of their knowledge was implicit and therefore could not by definition be represented by abstract, disciplinary-based knowledge. As Eraut said at the time, there was 'increasing acceptance that important aspects of professional competence and experience can not be represented in propositional form and embedded in a publicly accessible knowledge base' (Eraut, 1994, p. 15).

If theoretical, disciplinary-based knowledge was uncertain and if key aspects of professional knowledge were by definition *implicit*, then the traditional contribution of the disciplines to understanding in the field of education became increasingly open to question. The widespread development of school-based research, school-based CPD and employment-based initial teacher education – all of which have very little to do with higher education in general and disciplinary-based knowledge in particular – is testament to this epistemological crisis of confidence.

At the same time as this growing marginalization of the disciplines from professional education, there have been significant changes in management of educational research that have served further to challenge their position. This has been particularly marked since the coming to power in 1997 of New Labour with their enthusiasm for 'research informed policy and practice'. In a seminal speech to the ESRC in 2000, David Blunkett, Tony Blair's first Secretary of State for Education, argued for a 'revolution' in the relations between government and the research community (Blunkett, 2000); a revolution that would allow government to harness research to its struggle to re-position Britain's education system in a globally competitive market. This has resulted in a 'new social contract' for research (Demeritt, 2000): significantly increased funding in return for increased accountability. That accountability has meant greater government specification of research topics and methodologies than in the past, with the prioritizing of certain sorts of research that can provide evidence directly to ministers: large-scale evaluation studies, school effectiveness studies and a renewed interest in the economics of education with a narrow focus on 'rates of return'. This is not to criticize these approaches but to note that they are now promoted at the expense of more intellectually driven approaches. Within the neo-liberal university, we would suggest, there has been little option but to follow this lead.

Evidence that there is indeed a 'new social contract' for educational research is apparent from the 2008 RAE. Research funding directly in the field of Education[1] almost doubled compared with the previous RAE period; 60 per cent of that research funding came from government. As the RAE panel comment in their subject overview (RAE, 2008), 'the espousal of evidence informed policy and practice may have been a factor in this increased share from government'. They also note that it was perhaps inevitable that increased funding has resulted in a greater emphasis than in the past on applied work.

While some of this highly applied work was rigorous, drawing on multidisciplinary teams, other work, they suggest, suffered in quality through being too closely tied to shifting government and government agency priorities, tight timescales, a focus on description rather than analysis and limited theorization.

While there was evidence over the last RAE period of 'original high quality theoretical, scholarly and critical works in philosophy, sociology and history of education' that often offered 'challenging new agendas', research of this character, the RAE panel suggest, was very much in the minority. Overall, the evidence-informed movement, they suggest, has 'loosened the links with social sciences'.

And where are we now?

As we noted above, one of the starting points for this volume was the ESRC *Demographic Review of the Social Sciences* (Mills *et al.*, 2006). On Education, the authors state:

> Education is the second largest discipline under consideration, and perhaps one of the most complex. Structural, historical and institutional factors affect all disciplines in different ways but in education their impact has been quite profound.... Despite its size, the field also tends to lack the research autonomy to enable it to engage policy debates confidently and critically.
>
> (Mills *et al.*, 2006)

The picture then is of a large number of professionals working together but, when compared with other social science disciplines, lacking in intellectual autonomy. This complex picture, it would seem, is largely corroborated by the 2008 RAE panel. While high-quality disciplinary-based work continues to be produced, it is very much in the minority and its contribution to the field as a whole seems increasingly problematic, increasingly fragile.

In short, it would seem to us that the earlier post-war foundational model of the patronage of key professors of education and the establishment of key journals has been replaced by a proliferation of professors of education, a disconnection between many of them and older disciplines, with a concentration on useful methods, multiple sources of publication and governmental funding. Neither position seems healthy for a disciplinary project in the twenty-first century.

The danger is that the remnants of the past live on only in the routines of method, not in the analytical strength of disciplines. This is well known to post-structuralists of course, and treated as a fruitful and creative opportunity to insert new theorizations of reflexive modernity. But the effect in education is that many now live with an uncertain relation to the disciplinary-based work. The crucial role of a discipline in education in breaking down problems into its own logics and mediating between public information and problems and public action is in danger of disappearing. It has been short-circuited.

As the ESRC review clearly demonstrated, the material conditions of the production of advanced educational studies largely depends on the arrival in mid-career of neophytes who have to skill themselves quickly, via EdD or PhD programmes, to adapt to the combination of practical and reflective practices of an (in the main) teacher-education-based world of work. To return to our opening metaphor, in the current world, ghosts don't have much time to linger as the speed of reformation, sub-disciplinary groupings, interest-based developments and utilitarian, sponsor-based work re-shapes the field constantly. Journals arrive without a past, reflecting (often creatively) new areas of work and old journals linger on, supplied by the necessity of research audit publication. The internationalization of fields of study and the growth of cross-border study creates hybrids of different disciplinary histories and their production, or micro-studies which avoid the problems of the past while looking to the future and action. Without conversing with the past and recognizing how it was populated, can we recognize our disciplinary responsibilities before we can decide to reject or develop them?

This, then, is how we would suggest the reader engages with the specific contributions to this volume. It is an opportunity for the non-specialist reader to engage in a series of disciplinary-based conversations about what each discipline's major contributions in the past have been and what they should be in the future. We also asked each contributor to describe and assess their discipline's 'sociological' position – its mechanisms and sites of production, its journals, places, projects and development – and its 'epistemological' strengths – substantive, methodological and theoretical developments which have contemporary relevance and value. Our hope is that through these contemporary conversations the reader will be in a better position to assess the current and future potential contribution of disciplinary-based perspectives to research, teaching and scholarship in education, and lay the ghosts to rest.

Note

1 Here we use figures for those researchers returned in the 2008 RAE within the field of Education, acknowledging that academics returned in other disciplinary fields may have received funding to conduct educational research.

References

Adams, A. and Tulasiewicz, W. (1995) *The Crisis in Teacher Education: A European Concern?* London: Falmer Press.

Barnett, R. (1990) *The Idea of Higher Education*. Buckingham: SRHE/Open University Press.

Blunkett, D. (2000) 'Influence or irrelevance: can social science improve government?', *Research Intelligence*, 71: 12–21.

Bourdieu, P. and Wacquant, L. (1992) *An Invitation to Reflexive Sociology*. Chicago: University of Chicago Press.

Bridges, D. (2006) 'The disciplines and discipline of educational research', *Journal of Philosophy of Education*, 40(2): 259–272.

Carr, W. (2006) 'Education without theory', *British Journal of Educational Studies*, 54(2): 136–159.

Demeritt, D. (2000) 'The new Social Contract for Science: accountability, relevance and value in US and UK science and research policy', *Antipode*, 32(3): 308–329.

Eraut, M. (1994) *Developing Professional Knowledge and Competence*. London: Falmer Press.

Furlong, J. and Lawn, M. (eds) (2009) 'The Disciplines of Education: confronting the crisis', *Oxford Review of Education* special edition, 35(5): 541–669.

Furlong, J., Barton, L., Miles, S., Whiting, C. and Whitty, G. (2000) *Teacher Education in Transition: Re-forming Teaching Professionalism*. Buckingham: Open University Press.

Gardner, J. and Gallagher, T. (2007) 'Gauging the deliverable? Educational research in Northern Ireland', *European Educational Research Journal*, 6(1): 101–114.

Hoyle, E. (1982) 'The professionalization of teachers: a paradox', *British Journal of Educational Studies*, 30(2): 161–171.

Humes, W. (2007) 'The infrastructure of educational research in Scotland', *European Educational Research Journal*, 6(1): 71–86.

Kenway, J., Bullen, E., Fahey, J., with Robb, S. (2006) *Haunting the Knowledge Economy*. London: Routledge.

Kuhn, T. (1977) *The Essential Tension*. Chicago: Chicago University Press.

Lawn, M. and Furlong, J. (2007) 'The social organisation of education research in England', *European Educational Research Journal*, 6(1): 55–70.

McCulloch, G. (2002) 'Disciplines contributing to Education? Educational studies and the disciplines', *British Journal of Educational Studies*, 50(1) (March): 100–119.

Mahony, P. and Hextall, I. (2000) *Reconstructing Teaching: Standards, Performance and Accountability*. London: RoutledgeFalmer.

Marginson, S. (2007) 'Are neo-liberal reforms friendly to academic freedom and creativity? Some theoretical and practical reflections on the constituents of academic self-determination in research universities', University of Melbourne Centre for the Study of Higher Education Seminar, *Ideas and Issues in Higher Education*, 28 May 2007.

Mills, D., Jepson, A., Coxon, T., Easterby-Smith, M., Hawkins, P. and Spencer, J. (2006) *Demographic Review of the Social Sciences*. Swindon: ESRC.

RAE (2008) *Sub-panel 45 Education: Subject Overview*. Available online at www.rae.ac.uk/pubs/2009/ov.

Rees, G. and Power, S. (2007) 'Educational research and the restructuring of the state: the impacts of parliamentary devolution in Wales', *European Educational Research Journal*, 6(1): 87–100.

Robbins Report (1963) *Higher Education*. Report of the Committee Appointed by the Prime Minister under the Chairmanship of Lord Robbins, 1961–1963, Cmd 2154. London: HMSO.

Ross, D. (2006) 'Changing contours of the social science disciplines', in T. Porter and D. Ross (eds) *Cambridge History of Science*, vol. 7. Cambridge: Cambridge University Press.

Schön, D. (1983) *The Reflective Practitioner*. London: Temple Smith.

Schön, D. (1987) *Educating the Reflective Practitioner*. San Francisco: Jossey-Bass.

Späni, M., Hofstetter, R. and Schneuwly, B. (2002) 'Interweaving educational sciences and pedagogy with professional education: contrasting configurations at Swiss universities, 1870–1950', *European Educational Research Journal* 1(1): 45–64.

Whitty, G. (2002) *Making Sense of Education Policy*. London: Paul Chapman.

Wilkin, M. (1996) *Initial Teacher Training: The Dialogue of Ideology and Culture*. London: Falmer Press.

2 The sociology of education as 'redemption'

A critical history

Hugh Lauder, Phillip Brown and A.H. Halsey

Introduction

The sociology of education has undergone rapid change since the 1950s, when British sociologists first took an interest in education, through the establishment of a professional discipline in the late 1970s, to the current situation. This development is paradoxical in that the discipline achieved an intellectual standing and political influence in the 1950s that has not been seen since. If we are to consider the future of the discipline then we need to ask why its intellectual and political influence has declined. At a time when we can expect fundamental change to the discipline through retirements and cost-cutting this is a pressing question, but it has been asked before and continues to be asked since reflexivity can be seen as an integral element of the discipline (Dale, 2001a, 2001b; Shain and Ozga, 2001; Ball, 2008; Whitty, 2008).

What makes this decline all the more puzzling is that each of the theoretical, methodological and institutional changes that have occurred in the field over this period can be seen to have addressed, albeit sometimes in new ways, fundamental questions about the nature of education in modern societies. Some of the key questions that have structured the discipline over the past 40 years are these:

1 What role does education play in the life chances of different groups in society?
2 How can we best explain why some groups systematically win and others lose?
3 Is education a means of liberating individuals or is it a means of social control?
4 What is the relationship of educational outcomes to the economy and society?
5 How can educational processes best be understood?
6 What is the purpose of schooling?

Given the importance that is attributed to education by teachers, parents and policy-makers it is, at first sight, hard to understand why these questions are not seen to be at the forefront of academic and policy priorities. After all, we have, since the Enlightenment, seen education as potentially liberating and, with the advent of industrialisation and democracy, indispensable to modern societies because of the understanding, knowledge and skills that it can foster. Perhaps the answer is not so much in the questions themselves but in the way they have been addressed. In order to probe this issue we need first to develop a brief account of the relationship between disciplines, theories, methods and the institutional context in which they are developed. One reason for doing so is that the questions that are asked in sociology of education, for example relating to origins and destinations, child poverty and the nature and determinants of school outcomes, are not necessarily the preserve of sociologists (see, for example, Ridge and Millar, 2000; Feinstein, 2003). Recently, in large part due to their quantitative training, economists and social policy analysts have made significant and/or high-profile contributions to this area and at times have engaged in productive debates with sociologists (e.g. Goldthorpe and McKnight, 2006). This raises fundamental issues about the nature and purpose of sociology of education. In other words, if a discipline cannot be defined by its questions, how should it be understood?

Disciplines, theories and methods

Academic disciplines are often taken to be the epistemological structures within which enquiry takes place and are typically located within institutional practices. However, disciplines cannot be defined by their questions, theories or methods. The theories that comprise the 'discipline' are many and varied and while they have emerged in recognition of new developments in both school and society, it would be difficult and controversial to identify what common basis they have as *sociological* theories. Moreover, theories do not always respect disciplinary boundaries. Frequently, an account of the social is 'colonised' by quite different explanatory structures, as for example in neo-classical economics, Marxism, socio-biology or evolutionary psychology. In all these cases they may appear to be addressing some of the same questions as those we have listed but will 'answer' them with different methods and forms of evidence.

Given these considerations, how can we best understand sociology of education as a discipline? One way of addressing this question is by what Gouldner (1971) calls the infrastructure of social theory, which includes the sentiments and domain assumptions of the discipline and conceptions of reality, all of which have had an influence on theory choice and development.

Gouldner's sentiments and domain assumptions are similar to Lakatos' (1970) notion of a hard core or Kuhn's (1962) world view which stand at the heart of a theory and provide a heuristic for guiding theory development.

However, the focus of analysis for Lakatos and Kuhn is well established theories or paradigms, whereas in the sociology of education it can be argued that these sentiments and domain assumptions have indeed informed the discipline. Here they are bound up with what Dale (2001b) calls a redemptive view of education which seeks to banish inequality and enable individual development. Redemption in the various forms it has taken in the sociology of education over the years could be contrasted with the sentiment taken in neo-classical economics where there is always a cost to 'redemption'.

One of the key tasks, then, of an enquiry into the sociology of education is to map the way this notion of redemption has been understood and utilised as a heuristic within the recent history of the discipline.

However, while such sentiments as 'redemption' can guide and indeed act as an inspiration for progress in addressing the fundamental questions outlined above, the particular meaning it has will be shaped in interaction with the particular theories and methods that have been adopted throughout the history of the discipline.

That history will involve judgements about the questions, theories and methods that at any one time 'count' as part of the discipline. Here, the way a critical community is structured will be crucial because it will make judgements as to the questions and theoretical direction considered most significant, and about the quality of work undertaken. The community will also provide a form of induction, training and networks for young academics. Given these comments we now turn to a recent history of the discipline to chart the relationship between the domain assumptions and the institutional structures, practices and its audience.

A recent history of sociology of education[1]

In the 1950s, the London School of Economics (LSE) became the centre for the emergent discipline of sociology in Britain (Halsey, 2004). Under the leadership of David Glass, some of the young sociologists at the time took an interest in questions relating to social mobility. As Halsey noted, his

> doctorate was an empirical study of the implications of the 1944 Education Act for social mobility. Jean Floud [also at LSE] and he collaborated in the 1950s to give the sociology of education a place in the general development of sociological theory and research. The emphasis was again on egalitarian analysis of social inequality but in their case consciously carrying on the tradition of political arithmetic – marrying a value laden choice of issue with objective methods of data collection and analysis.[2]
>
> (Halsey, 2004, p. 87)

The approach taken by Floud and Halsey (1961) enabled criticism to be made of one of the key elements of the 1944 Act, the tripartite system of education and especially the role of the 11+ exam as a means of selecting pupils for the different kinds of school (grammar, secondary modern and technical). As such, their research was highly influential in the debate over education and life chances and the subsequent change to a more comprehensive system of education. Halsey's focus on origins and destinations remained when moving to Nuffield College, Oxford, where he established the Oxford Mobility Project which is ongoing in the work of John Goldthorpe, Anthony Heath and others.

While the founding methodology for these studies was political arithmetic, by the late 1970s these researchers had become engaged in the major theoretical debates on inequality and had extended the methodology to include narratives as well as numbers (Goldthorpe *et al.*, 1980). However, while the focus on inequality at this time was concerned with social class and in the Goldthorpe *et al.* study gender, the internal processes of schools and their role in contributing to the reproduction of inequalities was not considered.

Indeed, the broader debate in the 1970s on the school–society relationship tended to assume a determinism from the left, in which schools played a passive role relative to wider social forces in the reproduction of inequality (Jencks, 1972; Bowles and Gintis, 1976). At the same time, right-wing psychologists, such as Eysenck (1971) and Jensen (1969), had argued also that schools made little difference because intelligence was relatively fixed and inherited.

In Britain, the focal audience changed during this period from policy-makers to teachers, as did the domain assumptions because the institutional context for the discipline had become that of teacher education. In the 1970s, courses in teacher education included the social science disciplines of sociology, psychology and philosophy. But the determinist conclusions reached by debate over inequalities in education up to that point left teachers in limbo since it implied that they could not make a difference. Not surprisingly, both teachers and students were interested in school processes that could either mitigate or exacerbate social inequalities. While it was the quantitative studies of the 1950s and 1960s that caught the attention of policy-makers, the audience of teachers needed more complex and nuanced understandings of school processes which involved qualitative studies. As Moore (2009) has noted, sociology of education 'thus acquired a much wider constituency and a previously relatively exclusive relationship of a few individuals acting as governmental policy advisors turned into one of many more servicing "front line" professionals' (p. 149). Early ethnographic studies focused on the organisational structures of schools and their implications for inequality. A tradition was developed through the work of Hargreaves (1967), Lacey (1970), Ford (1969) and, latterly, Ball (1981) that sought to understand the effects of grouping on different social classes. This tradition could be seen as consistent with political arithmetic in the sense that they were unpacking the 'black box' of schooling that had been left untouched by quantitative studies but which, nevertheless, could address policy issues such as whether strategies like streaming increased inequalities between groups. In turn, this qualitative tradition branched into a focus on a wider understanding of school and classroom processes in the ethnographies of

Hammersley (1976), Edwards and Furlong (1978), Woods (1979) and in the work of Pollard on the positioning and views of children (1987). These researchers sensitised and challenged teachers as to the nuanced and subtle effects that different kinds of pedagogy, classroom organisation and communication could have on pupils' learning which continues as an important strand within the sociology of education. However, they also pointed up the dilemmas of audience in that, while their research may be seen as supportive of teachers, they did not focus on the question of how social inequalities are implicated in classroom practice and pupil learning.

However, in 1971, *Knowledge and Control*, a collection of papers edited by Michael Young, caused considerable controversy because it marked a turning point in the politics of the sociology of education, as it confronted the way teacher practices may be implicated in reproducing inequalities, while also providing a way forward for them. If, previously, both quantitative and qualitative studies had been focused on questions relevant to policy-makers, Young's volume claimed that school knowledge was the product of power relationships rather than having a secure epistemic justification. The consequence of this position was that the knowledge taught in schools was the product of class dominance and that by changing what was taught teachers could foster greater equality for their students. This account set its face firmly against the views of policy-makers and invited teachers to become radicalised in their understanding of the role of schooling: rather than it being a progressive force for greater equality and personal autonomy, education was seen to be deeply implicated in the reproduction of inequality.

This relativist approach to knowledge not only challenged the orthodoxy of policy-makers but also that of the political arithmeticians who had established the credibility of the discipline. The foundations of political arithmetic were empiricist, implying that 'knowledge' could be established on relatively secure foundations, through the objectivity of its procedures. It led to a fundamental split between quantitative sociologists and those qualitative sociologists that endorsed or presupposed the claims of relativists. There was a further dimension to this debate which related to the development of sophisticated theories concerning the school–society relationship. It was significant that papers by both Pierre Bourdieu and Basil Bernstein were included in the volume and it can be argued that subsequently they provided the core theoretical insights into the school–society relationship. Bourdieu's work was of interest for two reasons. First, and less remarked upon in Britain, was his emphasis on quantitative studies as a way of testing his hypotheses. Second, however, like Young, the papers he contributed to the volume laid the foundation for his concept of what he called the cultural arbitrary; it was a form of class-structured knowledge that provided consistency between socialisation in professional middle-class homes and that of the school. Bourdieu thereby gave impetus to the radical turn in the sociology of education. Bernstein also contributed a now-classic paper to Young's volume which appeared to establish the fundamental problematic of radical sociologists of education: 'How a society selects, classifies, distributes, transmits and evaluates the educational knowledge it considers to be public, reflects both the distribution of power and the principles of social control' (Bernstein, 1971, p. 47). The volume can be seen as raising the possibility of progressive change through an alliance between sociologists of education and teachers, which created a sentiment for radical change.

However, a much more sharply defined account of the radical nature of sociology of education was presented through *Schooling in Capitalist America* by two neo-Marxist American political economists, Sam Bowles and Herb Gintis. The book, which was characterised by historical and quantitative analyses of social-class inequality, provided a determinist account of the role of schooling in capitalist class structures both with respect to the reproduction of inequality and social control. In effect, it filled out and developed the structuralist Marxist account given by Althusser (1972) who was introduced to an education audience in a seminal reader by Cosin, entitled *Education, Structure and Society*.

The response to *Schooling in Capitalist America* was significant for the future development of the discipline. In Britain, as in the work from America by Michael Apple, critics tended to accept the general proposition that capitalist schooling was deeply implicated in the reproduction of inequality and the social control of working-class students but argued over the question of determinism. Here the key issue concerned the spaces in which working-class resistance and degrees of freedom could be achieved. It is important to note that in seeking spaces for resistance the rupture between policy-makers and sociologists of education was further entrenched.

In 1977, Paul Willis published *Learning to Labour*, a neo-Marxist study of the resistance of working-class boys to schooling. It was an engaging ethnography with a strong theoretical analysis providing for the possibility of working-class rejection of the social control imposed by the school and creating a space for working-class agency.

From these developments in the 1970s we can identify three key elements to the dominant radicalism with respect to reproduction in the sociology of education: epistemic relativism, a focus on the processes of inequality within schools through qualitative studies and a search for spaces in which resistance and agency could be established for oppressed groups.

Debate about these seminal publications coincided with two of the key elements in the professionalisation of the discipline, the launch of the *British Journal of Sociology of Education* (BJSE) under the editorship of Len Barton and the holding of a separate annual sociology of education conference at Westhill College, Birmingham. The key identifying elements that gave the discipline its dominant character were carried over into the journal.

The progress of the discipline now largely fell to the recognition that classrooms were not just venues for white working- and middle-class boys with the advent of a strong feminist presence in the work of Madeleine Arnot, Miriam David, Gaby Weiner and Rosemary Deem, followed by recognition that Britain was also a postcolonial society. As the Empire collapsed it had attracted workers from different countries and cultures to the former metropolitan centre, so the focus for questions of inequality and social control widened (see, for example, Centre for Contemporary Cultural Studies, 1982; Mirza, 2005). To an interest in these groups there was also later added a recognition of the importance of sexuality (see, for example, Mac an Ghaill, 1994) and students with disability (Daniels, 1995).

As the recognition of difference between and within these groups developed, the influence of relativist conceptions of postmodernism and post-structuralism built on the early work of Young but focused on the key concept of identity. The emphasis on more fluid accounts of identity replaced that of socialisation. The latter reflected a stable white society in which boys and girls would be inducted into different roles. However, with the breakdown of ascribed roles and the development of negotiated forms of interaction, questions of identity emerged. When linked to the different heritages of a postcolonial society, it became clear that, at the level of school processes, research into the relationship between identity formation, school culture and reproduction assumed importance.

However, at the time when these issues were being placed on the agenda, the Thatcher government sought to break the link between sociologists of education and their audience in two ways: by attacking the Open University which had emerged as the leading centre for the discipline by dint of its range of publications and by removing the foundation disciplines of sociology, philosophy and psychology from the initial teacher-education curriculum. Many of the leading younger sociologists at the Open University moved to new departments or overseas, thereby breaking its seminal influence, while the removal of the discipline from the teacher-education curriculum effectively meant that it no longer had an audience: if the radical turn had divorced the discipline from policy-makers then the neo-liberal turn of Thatcherism severed the tie with teachers.

Despite these setbacks the discipline branched into a series of often-related themes: for example, identity and cultural politics, especially with respect to gender and ethnicity, and the new policy turn in sociology of education, and the development of a theoretically informed quantitative tradition.

However, until recently it was the focus on identity and cultural politics that dominated utilising qualitative studies, often relativist in their epistemological underpinnings and seeking spaces for agency and resistance with little consideration of the structural forces that framed these processes.

Identity and cultural politics

In discussing this cultural turn, Power and Rees (2006, p. 2) noted that

> The sociology of education had changed direction and took what can be characterised as a 'cultural turn'. Perhaps because of the failure of

systemic reform, the focus of empirical research shifted from measuring to deconstructing. The very intractability of educational inequalities forced attention away from issues of access and on to cultural processes. The education system became implicated not only in the unequal distribution of life chances, but in the construction of unequal identities. The investigation of these processes required a very different methodology; one which privileged exposing the processes of dominance and subjugation, revealing how identities are created and unravelling the tyrannies of discourse.

To this should be added a view that held sway in the early 1990s, that processes of individualisation and risk had rendered social class obsolete as an explanatory principle in modern social life (Beck, 1992). It was not just that class was intractable or that postmodern and post-structuralist theorists tended to ignore its effects, rather Beck's thesis proved a beguiling theoretical rationale as to why social class should be relegated in analyses of education.

The consequences of these factors were profound. Power and Rees found that on analysis of articles in the BJSE, over a ten-year period between 1995 and 2004 80 per cent of the 294 research papers published could be seen as falling within the themes of identity and cultural politics.[3]

It should be emphasised that not all these papers were influenced by the sentiment of redemption or indeed the domain assumptions of relativism or the search for agency and the spaces for resistance. For example, while Bernstein, one of the most influential theorists in the discipline, has certainly been co-opted into this framework by some, it is not at all clear that his work reflects these domain assumptions.

Atkinson (1985) sees Bernstein as more interested in the theoretical architecture that he is developing than, we might argue, its contribution to a sociology of education interested in redemption:

> Bernstein, then, is continually working the same themes into intricate patterns and motifs. Unfortunately for the general reader this work rarely – if ever – quite takes on the appearance of completion. Often the fabric turns out to be the labour of a Penelope: the threads are undone only to be re-worked into ever more intricate designs. Sometimes the patterns that Bernstein weaves become so intricate that the original figures are all but lost to view like an ornate Saxon design, the elements are elaborated and turned back on themselves. It is as if the formal design takes over, and becomes almost as valued as the original representation.
>
> (p. 8)

What Atkinson is describing here is almost a form of gnosticism, albeit one that has proved as suggestive as it has been hard to interpret. But Bernstein's rather inward focus on theoretical elaboration cannot be seen as the only alternative to the sentiment of redemption. In what follows we consider more recent developments in relation to the sociology of educational policy because as this branch of sociology of education has developed it has, in some cases, departed from the question of redemption, although these may be considered a minority.

The new policy turn in sociology of education

The 1990s can be seen as a period where the policies of both major parties progressively sought to 'teacher-proof' pedagogy, curriculum and assessment, while assuming that most research in the sociology of education was of little relevance. Indeed, policy-makers turned to the school effectiveness and improvement tradition for support, largely because its explanations, based on theories of management, were consistent with their own assumptions. One critical response to this renewed interest in education policy was the launching of the *Journal of Education Policy* by Ball and his collaborators. The journal has provided a forum for the critique of current policies and has encompassed two traditions with respect to educational policy which have extended the original substantive and methodological concerns of the political arithmetic tradition; in both, Stephen Ball and his collaborators have made a significant contribution. In the first, Ball's primary focus is on the processes of social and policy change and how they impact on various actors. The method offers theoretically informed qualitative analysis which seeks to capture the meaning of change for different actors at a time of national economic and social transformation. At times, Ball in particular seems to rest content with a more descriptive account of shifting terrains, such as in his recent book (Ball, 2007) on the privatisation of educational services in the UK. At other times, it seems that Ball and his co-researchers are still influenced by the question of agency and redemption, even if the space for agency is rather circumscribed. For example, in a recent study (Vincent, Ball and Braun, 2008) on the working class in relation to childcare, the authors are not interested in a taxonomy of class that might be used in quantitative study but rather in terms of the agency that their respondents are able to exert. The point here is that Ball and his colleagues are concerned with understanding, nuance and insight on the basis of a shifting social terrain, thereby challenging the fixed categories and forms of classification that are used by both policy-makers and indeed quantitative researchers who focus, for example, on social class. It is as if the quest for agency needs to be addressed at the level of the lived reality of working-class mothers rather than in terms of the disciplines, such as quantitative sociology, which may interpret and rather too neatly classify their experience, thereby stripping out the question of agency.

However, the quantitative tradition in sociology of education which began with political arithmetic has continued to thrive, providing a broader canvass for understanding inequalities in educational outcomes.

The extension of the political arithmetic tradition: theoretically informed quantitative analyses

The second tradition can be seen as an extension of the political arithmetic movement in the 1950s through to the 1970s. However, it is has been methodologically updated to develop theoretically informed mixed-method strategies (Lauder *et al.*, 2004). Here the work of Goldthorpe and his colleagues (see, for example, Goldthorpe, 2007 and Goldthorpe and Jackson, 2007) on the continuing inequalities in social class has been prominent, as has the work of Power *et al.* (2003), on the professional middle class, and Nash (2010), who has developed Bourdieu's account of inequality and applied it to quantitative data. What is significant about these studies is that they have the theoretical and empirical resources to develop explanations for the patterns they identify. Feminist scholarship has also sought to apply quantitative analyses (Arnot, David and Weiner, 1999) which has tied issues of gender to those of class. While a similar mapping of inequalities with respect to race and ethnicity has also been undertaken (Gilborn and Mirza, 2000).

Quantitative origins and destination studies also have a rather narrow view of redemption. If qualitative research has focused on the spaces for resistance and agency, which, informed by quantitative studies, often appear rather limited, redemption for quantitative researchers is calculated in odds ratios with respect to the life chances of children of different social-class origins.

However, behind these calculations there is a wealth of theoretical and qualitative studies that can be enlisted in developing plausible explanations for their data patterns. Brown's (1997, 2000, 2003) theoretical contribution to national and global theories of positional competition and the relationship of education to the labour market, Ball's (2003) account of the way middle-class parents develop strategies to deny working-class parents access to good state schools and his analysis with Bowe and Gewirtz (1997) on choice for working-class parents in the educational market serve as plausible explanations for market-based educational inequalities, which could be used as the basis for quantitative analyses in education. With respect to the factors that explain school outcomes, Thrupp, Lauder and Robinson (2002) and Lupton (2005) have examined the relationship between social class and education, the former by looking at the impact of school social-class composition on school performance and the latter by showing how the differential performance of schools in deprived areas is context-based. These studies challenge the managerialist explanations for school outcomes advanced by the school effectiveness tradition.

Equally Diane Reay's (see, for example, Reay, 1998, 2006) exploration of issues of gender and class has made a major contribution to providing explanations for the structural inequalities related to social class and gender. Her work has been extended, for example by Rothon (2007) and Archer and

Francis (2007), in seeking to understand minority ethnic achievement within the context of theories of social class, gender and racism. The latter is an ambitious and understandably complex piece of research which has implications for teachers and policy-makers that they clearly spell out. However, the policy turn has not brought sociologists of education closer to policy-makers for reasons we give below.

These qualitative studies illuminate many of the puzzles raised by quantitative sociology of education and do so in ways that give a rich texture to the social and educational inequalities that have been identified in the quantitative tradition. Nevertheless, it can be argued that the inspiration for all these analyses is an assumption that inequality bears down on agency and autonomy and creates what Richard Sennett and John Cobb (1977) have called 'the hidden injuries of class'.

In turn, Sennett and Cobb's account raises more profound questions about the role of education and the underlying sentiment of redemption. The history of education in the twentieth century and more recent developments relating to the financial crash raise questions about whether a focus on questions of inequality are sufficient in the quest for redemption.

The discipline's dominant sentiment and domain assumptions: a reflection

We should begin by noting that not all traditions in the sociology of education have presupposed the sentiment of redemption. For example, a Parsonian account of education and society was fundamentally concerned with social order and how it could be maintained (Gouldner, 1971), and we have seen that neither Bernstein nor indeed Ball in some of his work see redemption as an underlying factor in their work. Why then has it assumed such dominance among many sociologists of education?

One answer may be to do with the way education itself has been understood. Here we return to an earlier point that, since the Enlightenment, education has been seen as potentially liberating, hence freedom and autonomy have been closely associated with it. In other words, it could be argued that there is an intimate connection between education and a sociology which is guided by the heuristic of redemption. In other words, it could be argued that there is an intimate connection between education and a sociology which is guided by the heuristic of redemption: a relationship which suggests that redemption is at the heart of the enterprise and will not easily be replaced. Here, the turn towards a conflict approach in the domain assumptions of the discipline has meant that educational systems can be seen as requiring liberation from oppressive structures and discourses. Hence, the history of the discipline we have outlined has provided a critique of current educational institutions and practices but it has taken critique in the Marxian sense: it is about a critical analysis of the underlying structures of theories, ideologies or propositions as a means of changing the world. That may be so but it suggests that education can be genuinely liberating if only the proper forms of access, pedagogy and curricula can be found.

However, against this dominant view it can be argued that the focus on inequalities and the structures that maintain them may be a necessary, but not sufficient a condition for a more inclusive and enlightened form of education. There are two points here that we want to make. The first is that we need to see how educational systems are situated within the wider social formation; the second concerns the issue of social mobility.

The history of the twentieth and early twenty-first centuries suggests that we should examine where education seems to have played a peripheral role or worse in restraining the brutality that humans have exerted on one another. In both the cases we will refer to there is an issue not only about inequality and the damage it can inflict on individuals but about the nature and content of education itself.

Steiner (1971) posed the brutal paradox of German high culture during the Nazi era. He notes that Hitler's Death's Head Division, which had responsibility for running the concentration camps, was led by an officer corps of whom 22.3 per cent were graduates and 18.9 per cent held PhDs, at a time when only 2–3 per cent of the German population had completed a university education.

At best these shocking figures raise the question 'How was it possible for Hitler's SS troops to carry copies of Goethe's poems in their back pockets as they went about their daily dark deeds?' (Karier, 1990, pp. 49–50). In turn, it prompts enquiry into the social conditions under which education can be involved in such a brutal paradox.

It is a question, in a more moderate light, we may ask of education today. At root is the point that education's rationale is now seen to be to service the economy by providing appropriate forms of human capital. The elite universities of the UK and USA enabled their graduates who enter the City of London and Wall Street to make multiples of the average graduate wage (Brown and Lauder, 2009) with seemingly no responsibility attached to them for the economic crisis they and the system, of which they are a part, engineered. Greed, it seems, until the crash of 2008 remained good!

These examples raise questions not only about the nature and content of higher education but also the focus on social mobility and equality of opportunity as distinctive concerns for sociologists. We may wish to focus on issues of mobility because they relate to fairness or justice and, indeed, social cohesion, but it is quite possible to consider authoritarian societies in which there is a high degree of social mobility. In other words, it is not only social mobility that is important but the particular nature of the relationship of education to society, such that it can make a moral difference with respect to freedom and autonomy. If so, what is the nature and content of such an education? Such a possibility has been considered by us in different ways: through ethical socialism in the case of Halsey (2007), and in Brown and Lauder's notion of 'reflexive solidarity' (Brown and Lauder, 2001). It is arguable in a liberal society if and whether education should be seen to develop a moral concern for the lives of others, but both the examples we have referred to suggest it might. And, more provocatively, part of the notion of redemption embraced by many current sociologists of education may well assume that education should at heart embrace such a moral concern.

We make these points because in the critiques of current educational institutions and practices by the core oeuvre in the sociology of education the alternative always remains silent. Some sociologists have argued there are good reasons for such a silence (Whitty, 2002), but in our view it is now time that this 'silence' was examined more rigorously.

What we are arguing for at this historical moment is a much wider vision of what is possible within the sociology of education and beyond its current disciplinary framework that may gain the attention and respect of its various audiences. Such a vision may encompass child poverty or it may ask the kinds of questions about the relationship between education and society prompted by Steiner's brutal paradox. It would mean recasting the fundamental questions that we listed at the start of this chapter and rather than a focus on the spaces for agency, we need now to reconsider the global and national economic and cultural structures into which education is being restructured. For example, it seems most likely that there will be significant retrenchment in higher education and, given that it is now part of a global market, there is the distinct possibility that the British and American strategies for funding the sector through foreign students may be eclipsed. When we are clearer about how these various structures that frame education are being recast we may then return to questions of agency. But if the focus is on a wider vision of the kind just sketched then it requires a form of critical realism (e.g. Bhaskar, 1977; Young, 2008), rather than relativism, that can comprehend both underlying structures and agency as well as a wider range of methods than just the qualitative.

Conclusion: whither redemption?

Redemption is presupposed by what we have identified as the core tradition within the discipline: it does not logically entail a particular theoretical or methodological approach. It is a heuristic and can be a moral inspiration providing a purpose for researchers. Given the comments made above about how the combination of sentiment, institutional structures, audience, theories and methods have conspired to focus on the spaces for agency and resistance, our guiding sentiment may seem more akin to Weber's pessimism in describing the iron cage of bureaucracy. However, we need only consider the moral outrage that lies beneath Bourdieu *et al.*'s (1999)

The Weight of the World to see that sociology can be placed in the service of promoting, at least, the hope of redemption.

The political consequences of the suggestions for the future of the discipline we have made should, in our view, be an aspect of the wider democratic debate; such a debate will not necessarily have direct policy consequences because of what we have called an asymmetry between the interests of policy-makers and those of social scientists (Lauder *et al.*, 2004). While sociologists of education seek explanations for phenomena such as inequality, policy-makers may well prefer their own accounts for the same set of inequalities because they fit their political agendas. In contrast, sociological explanations may challenge those agendas. In essence, sociologists of education may constitute a disruptive but necessary voice in democratic debate at a time of economic and social crisis.

However, in the light of Steiner's brutal paradox and the example of the 'greed is good' philosophy of the alumni of elite American and British universities, we have argued that we need to look at the 'silence' which lies on the other side of redemption: about the social relations underlying the moral purpose of education and indeed how we might best understand that moral purpose. This project points towards an interdisciplinary approach which may challenge much more profoundly the current utilitarian policy approaches to education.

Acknowledgements

Our thanks to John Furlong, Martin Lawn, Michael Young, Geoff Whitty, Roger Dale and Maria Balarin for insights and comments on this chapter.

Notes

1 This history begins in the 1950s and therefore excludes developments prior to this (Floud and Halsey, 1958). It can be argued that it was in this period that the main currents in the sociology of education which have brought us to the current situation began. Perhaps our most notable omission is the work of Mannheim. See, however, the criticisms of Mannheim by Floud and Halsey (2008) in their historical review of the discipline.

2 There were others, such as Basil Bernstein, who was also at LSE at the time and whose research took them in a different direction, a thread we shall pick up later in the chapter.

3 A.H. Halsey (2004) found a strong interest in qualitative research reflected in leading sociology journals during the period 1995–2000, which raises the question of the degree to which developments in the sociology of education mirrored those in mainstream sociology.

References

Althusser, L. (1972) Ideology and Ideological State Apparatuses, in Cosin, B. (ed.) *Education, Structure and Society*, Milton Keynes: Open University Press.

Archer, L. and Francis, B. (2007) *Understanding Minority Ethnic Achievement: Race, Gender, Class and Success*, London: Routledge.

Arnot, M., David., M and Weiner, G. (1999) *Closing the Gender Gap: Postwar Education and Social Change*, Cambridge: Polity Press.

Atkinson, P. (1985) *Language, Structure and Reproduction: An Introduction to the Sociology of Basil Bernstein*, London: Methuen.

Ball, S. (1981) *Beachside Comprehensive*, Cambridge: Cambridge University Press.

Ball, S. (2003) *Class Strategies and the Education Market: The Middle Classes and Social Advantage*, London: Routledge.

Ball, S. (2007) *Education Plc: Private Sector Participation in Public Sector Education*, London: Routledge.

Ball, S. (2008) Some Sociologies of Education: A History of Problems and Places, and Segments and Gazes, *The Sociological Review*, 56, 4: 650

Ball, S., Bowe, R. and Gewirtz, S. (1997) Circuits of Schooling: A Sociological Exploration of Parental Choice of School in Social Class Contexts, in Halsey, A.H., Brown, P. and Stuart Wells, A. (eds) *Education, Culture, Economy and Society*, Oxford: Oxford University Press.

Beck, J. (1999) Makeover or Takeover? The Strange Death of Educational Autonomy in Neo-Liberal England, *British Journal of Sociology of Education*, 20, 2: 223–237.

Bernstein, B. (1971) On the Classification and Framing of Educational Knowledge, in Young, M. (ed.) *Knowledge and Control: New Directions for the Sociology of Education*, London: Collier-Macmillan.

Bernstein, B. (2000) *Pedagogy, Symbolic Control and Identity*, Lanham, MD: Rowman & Littlefield.

Bhaskar, R. (1977) *The Possibility of Naturalism*, Brighton: Harvester Press.

Bourdieu, P. (1971) Systems of Education and Systems of Thought, in Young, M. (ed.) *Knowledge and Control: New Directions for the Sociology of Education*, London: Collier-Macmillan.

Bourdieu, P. *et al.* (1999) *The Weight of the World: Social Suffering in Contemporary Society*, Cambridge: Polity Press.

Bowles, S. and Gintis, H. (1976) *Schooling in Capitalist America*, London: Routledge.

Brown, P. (1997) The 'Third Wave': Education and the Ideology of Parentocracy, in Halsey, A.H., Lauder, H., Brown, P. and Stuart Wells, A. (eds) *Education, Culture, Economy and Society*, Oxford: Oxford University Press.

Brown, P. (2000) The Globalization of Positional Competition, *Sociology*, 34, 4: 633–653.

Brown, P. (2003) The Opportunity Trap: Education and Employment in a Global Economy and Employment in a Global Economy, *European Education Research Journal*, 2, 1: 142–180.

Brown, P. and Lauder, H. (2001) *Capitalism and Social Progress*, Basingstoke: Palgrave.

Brown, P. and Lauder, H. (2009) Economic Globalisation, Skill Formation and the Consequences for Higher Education, in Ball, S. and Apple, M. (eds) *The International Handbook of the Sociology of Education*, London: Routledge.

Centre for Contemporary Cultural Studies (1982) *The Empire Strikes Back: Race and Racism in 1970s Britain*, London: Hutchinson.

Dale, R. (2001a) The Sociology of Education over 50 Years, in Demaine, J. (ed.) *Sociology of Education Today*, London: Palgrave.

Dale, R. (2001b) Recovering from a Pyrrhic Victory? Quality, Relevance and Impact in the Sociology of Education, in Arnot, M. and Barton, L. (eds) *Voicing Concerns: Sociological Perspectives on Contemporary Education Reforms*, Wallingford: Triangle Books.

Daniels, H. (1995) Pedagogic Practices, Tacit Knowledge and Discursive Discrimination: Bernstein and Post-Vygotṣkian Research, *British Journal of Sociology of Education*, 16, 4: 517–532

Edwards, A.D. and Furlong, V.J. (1978) *The Language of Teaching: Meaning in Classroom Interaction*, London: Heineman.

Eysenck, H. (1971) *Race, Intelligence and Education*, London: Temple Smith.

Feinstein, F. (2003) Inequality in the Early Cognitive Development of British Children in the 1970 Cohort, *Economica*, 70: 73–97.

Floud, J. and Halsey, A.H. (1958) The Sociology of Education (with Special Reference to the Development of Research in Western Europe and the United States of America), *Current Sociology*, 7, 3: 165–194.

Floud, J. and Halsey, A.H. (1961) Social Class, Intelligence Tests and Selection for Secondary Schools, in Halsey, A.H., Floud, J. and Anderson, C.A. (eds) *Education, Economy and Society*, New York: The Free Press.

Ford, J. (1969) *Social Class and the Comprehensive School*, London: Routledge & Kegan Paul.

Gilborn, D. and Mirza, H. (2000) *Educational Inequality: Mapping Race, Class and Gender*, London: OfSTED.

Goldthorpe, J. and Jackson, M. (2007a) Education-Based Meritocracy: The Barriers to its Realisation, in Lareau, A. and Conley, D. (eds) *Social Class: How Does It Work?*, New York: Russell Sage Foundation.

Goldthorpe, J. and Jackson, M. (2007b) Intergenerational Class Mobility in Contemporary Britain: Political Concerns and Emprical Findings, *The British Journal of Sociology 200*, 58: 525–546.

Goldthorpe, J., with Llewellyn, C. and Payne, C. (1980) *Social Mobility and Class Structure in Modern Britain*, Oxford: Clarendon Press.

Goldthorpe, J. and McKnight, A. (2006) The Economic Basis of Social Class, in Morgan, S., Grusky, D. and Field, D. (eds) *Mobility and Inequality: The Frontiers of Research in Sociology and Economics*, Stanford: Stanford University Press.

Gorard, S. (2008a) A Reconsideration of Rates of Social Mobility in Britain: Or Why Research Impact Is Not Always a Good Thing, *British Journal of Sociology of Education*, 29, 3: 317–324.

Gouldner, A. (1971) *The Coming Crisis of Western Sociology*, New York: Avon Books.

Grubb, N. and Lazerson, M. (2006) The Globalization of Rhetoric and Practice: The Education Gospel and Vocationalism, in Lauder, H., Brown, P., Dillabough, J.-A. and Halsey, A.H. (eds) *Education, Globalization and Social Change*, Oxford: Oxford University Press.

Halsey, A.H. (2004) *A History of Sociology in Britain: Science, Literature and Society*, Oxford: Oxford University Press.

Halsey, A.H. (ed.) (2007) *Democracy in Crisis? Ethical Socialism for a Prosperous Country*, London: Politico's.

Halsey, A.H., Heath, A. and Ridge, J. (1980) *Origins and Destinations*, Oxford: Clarendon Press.

Hammersley, M. (1976) The Mobilisation of Pupil Attention, in Hammersley, M. and Woods, P. (eds) *The Process of Schooling: A Sociological Reader*, London: Routledge & Kegan Paul, in association with the Open University.

Hargreaves, D. (1967) *Social Relations in a Secondary School*, London: Routledge & Kegan Paul.

Jencks, C. (1972) *Inequality: A Reassessment of the Effect of Family and Schooling in America*, New York: Basic Books.

Jensen, A. (1969) How Much Can We Boost IQ and Scholastic Achievement? *Harvard Educational Review*, 39, Winter: 1–23.

Karabel, J. and Halsey, A.H. (1977) *Power and Ideology in Education*, New York: Oxford University Press.

Karier, C. (1990) Humanzing the Humanities: Some Reflections on George Steiner's 'Brutal Paradox', *Journal of Aesthetic Education*, 24, 2: 49–63.

Kuhn, T. (1962) *The Structure of Scientific Revolutions*, Chicago: Chicago University Press.

Lacey, C. (1970) *Hightown Grammar: The School as a Social System*, Manchester: Manchester University Press.

Lakatos, I. (1970) The Methodology of Scientific Research Programmes, in Lakatos, I. and Musgrave, A. (eds) *Criticism and the Growth of Knowledge*, Cambridge: Cambridge University Press.

Lauder, H., Brown, P. and Halsey, A.H. (2004) Sociology and Political Arithmetic: Some Principles of a New Policy Science, *British Journal of Sociology*, 55, 1: 1–22.

Lupton, R. (2005) Social Justice and School Improvement, *British Educational Research Journal*, 31, 5: 589-604.

Mac an Ghaill, M. (1994) *The Making of Men: Masculinities, Sexualities and Schooling*, Buckingham: Open University Press.

Mirza, H. (2005) The More Things Change the More They Stay the Same: Assessing Black Underachievement 35 Years On, in Richardson, B. (ed.) *Tell it Like it Is: How Our Schools Fail Black Children*, London and Stoke on Trent: Bookmarks and Trentham Books.

Moore, R. (2009) *Towards the Sociology of Truth*, London: Continuum.

Nash, R. (2010) *Explaining Inequalities in Education*, Aldershot: Ashgate Publishing.

Pollard, A. (1987) Goodies, Jokers and Gangs, in Pollard, A. (ed.) *Children and Their Primary Schools*, London: Falmer Press.

Power, S. and Rees, G. (2006) Making Sense of Changing Times and Changing Places: The Challenges of the New Political Arithmetic of Education, paper presented at the BERA Symposium on the Future of Sociology of Education, Warwick, September.

Power, S., Edwards, T., Whitty, G. and Wigfall, V. (2003) *Education and the Middle Class*, Buckingham: Open University Press.

Reay, D. (1998) Engendering Social Reproduction: Mothers in the Educational Marketplace, *British Journal of Sociology of Education*, 19: 195–209.

Reay, D. (2006) The Zombie Stalking English Schools: Social Class and Educational Inequality, *British Journal of Sociology of Education*, 54, 3: 288–307.

Ridge, T. (2002) *Childhood Poverty and Social Exclusion from a Child's Perspective*, Bristol: Policy Press.

Ridge, T. and Millar, J. (2000) Excluding Children: Autonomy, Friendship and the Experience of the Care System, *Social Policy and Administration*, 34, 2: 160–175.

Rothon, C. (2007) Can Achievement Differentials be Explained By Social Class Alone? *Ethnicities*, 7, 3: 306–322.

Sennett, R. and Cobb, J. (1977) *The Hidden Injuries of Class*, Cambridge: Cambridge University Press.

Shain, F. and Ozga, J. (2001) Identity Crisis? Problems and Issues in the Sociology of Education, *British Journal of Sociology of Education*, 22, 1: 109–120.

Steiner, G. (1971) *In Bluebeard's Castle: Some Notes towards the Redefinition of Culture*, New Haven: Yale University Press.

Thrupp, M., Lauder, H. and Robinson, T. (2002) School Composition and Peer Effects, *International Journal of Educational Research*, 37: 483–504.

Vincent, C., Ball, S. and Braun, A. (2008) It's Like Saying 'Coloured': Understanding and Analysing the Urban Working Classes, *The Sociological Review*, 56, 1: 61–77.

Whitty, G. (2002) *Making Sense of Educational Policy*, London: Paul Chapman.

Whitty, G. (2008) Knowledge/Policy/Knowledge: Revisiting the Sociology and Politics of School Knowledge, paper presented to the Master's degree programme in the Sociology and Politics of Education, Turku, Finland.

Willis, P. (1977) *Learning to Labour*, Farnborough: Saxon House.

Woods, P. (1979) *The Divided School*, London: Routledge & Kegan Paul.

Young, M. (ed.) (1971) *Knowledge and Control: New Directions for the Sociology of Education*, London: Collier-Macmillan.

Young, M. (2008) *Bringing Knowledge Back In: From Social Constructivism to Social Realism in the Sociology of Education*, London: Routledge.

3   The psychology of education
Achievements, challenges and opportunities

W. Ray Crozier

Introduction

Psychology is a broad discipline, and its constituent areas – which might be identified as social psychology, developmental psychology, biological psychology, cognitive psychology and individual differences – are applied to the study of education and to educational policy and practice. How could they not, one might think, given psychologists' extensive studies of processes of learning and memory and of children's development, their acquisition of skills such as reading and writing, their understanding of number, science or moral principles? Psychology also studies children of exceptional abilities, problems of adjustment, parent–child relations, social interactions and relationships, friendships, peer influences, inter- and intra-group processes, bullying, attitudes, motivation and emotion and so on. Nevertheless, despite these endeavours the relation of psychology to education is problematic. There are debates within psychology as to how these topics should be conceptualised and studied and there are sustained criticisms of the nature of the discipline from within and outside psychology.

The concerns of this volume are the relations between education and its disciplines in the context of the 'demographic crisis' in education research (Mills *et al.*, 2006). I address these concerns in relation to psychology by offering a brief overview of psychology's major contributions to education in the past, a description of the organisational framework of psychology and its relation to education, consideration of the state of research in the psychology of education and reflections on selected current applications. One theme relates to the implications of the distinction between research in the psychology of education that is undertaken in university psychology departments and research that is located in departments and schools of education. The distinction is relevant for a number of reasons. First, the demographic profiles of psychology and education are quite distinct when these are defined in terms of Research Assessment Exercise (RAE) units of assessment (Mills *et al.*, 2006). Second, the division between departments may contribute to the fragmentation of research in the psychology of education. On the one hand, the psychology of education plays only a small part in the research activities of psychology departments, where theoretical developments and methodo-logical originality and refinement tend to be valued more highly than appli-cations. On the other hand, psychological research is scattered across many education departments, few of which have a significant presence of psychologists (Crozier, 2007). The demographic crisis ought to be considered in this context.

Psychology's major contributions in the past

Psychology has been closely involved with educational research, policy and practice since its emergence as a scientific discipline in the final years of the nineteenth century. The first professors of education in British day training colleges and universities drew upon psychological principles in their teach-ing and textbooks, and their work in education departments preceded, and in a number of cases led directly to, the establishment of departments of psy-chology in the universities (Thomas, 1996). The research conducted in edu-cation departments contributed to the development of psychology as a research-based discipline; theoretical and methodological advances in psy-chology were located in both education and psychology departments. A similar picture emerges if we focus on the application of psychology to the education of children with special educational needs; the seminal contribu-tions of Ann and Alan Clarke, Neil O'Connor and Jack and Barbara Tizard in the 1950s were made in psychology and education departments (Hall, 2008); psychologists would move from one to the other without detriment to their research.

Thus, psychology played a key role as 'a foundation discipline' in the emergence of educational studies. Psychological theory and research were applied to a range of educational matters, from the study of learning pro-cesses in individuals, including students with learning difficulties, to peda-gogy. Psychologists were confident in the benefits of the application of theory to matters of policy and practice. Theory and practice were regarded as closely allied; the relation was reciprocal, each enriching the other. Psy-chology was widely taught on teacher-training courses. In addition, unlike other disciplines contributing to educational research, professional psycholo-gists established a statutory role within the educational system. By the 1920s the role of the educational psychologist was established in the British educational system, particularly in the field of special educational needs. Educational psychologists continue to have a statutory role in assessment and the provision of services for children; they also consider research to be an important part of their role.

Yet recent commentators on psychology, both within and beyond the dis-cipline and profession, see its influence as having waned and the value of its contributions as less certain. These concerns are not new; Thomas (1996, p. 240) points out that doubts about the application of general psychological principles to teaching individuals were expressed as early as 1904. Francis

(2004) suggests that the position of psychology in teacher training had declined markedly by the 1980s. In part, this was influenced by changes to teacher training introduced by government; more generally, psychology shares with other disciplines the 'fall from grace' discussed by Lawn and Furlong (this volume). Popularisation of psychology, particularly the dissemination of claims about genetic determination of ability, elicited negative public reactions, as these assertions did not fit a Zeitgeist characterised by an increasingly socially mobile and pluralistic society. Norwich (2000) analyses psychology's difficulties in terms of uncertainties within psychology, uncertainties within education and uncertainties in the relations between the two. Anxieties about the psychology of education pre-date the concerns about the demographic crisis in educational research and scholarship that are the focus of this volume, yet will no doubt contribute to the crisis and the form of its resolution.

The mechanisms and sites of production

A useful starting point is to consider the role of the British Psychological Society (BPS). It was founded as a scientific learned society in 1901. By 1919 it had recognised the need to support applied psychology and Sections were set up in the fields of Education, Medicine and Industry. The Society has grown enormously in size since then, with over 33,000 members, and still aims to be 'the Learned Society and Professional Body for the discipline' (British Psychological Society, 2009). It accredits undergraduate degree courses, setting out a curriculum to be followed and minimum standards of resources. It currently approves nearly 400 degree courses at over 100 institutions, approximately 11,000 students graduating each year with an accredited degree. The BPS also accredits postgraduate professional training courses including courses leading to the qualification for educational psychologists (most recently the Doctorate in Educational and Child Psychology, which admitted its first cohort in 2006). The Society's structure includes Sections, which bring together researchers in areas of psychology (for example, the Education Section), and Divisions, which are organisations of professional psychologists, including a division for educational psychologists. This structure effectively maintains the distinction between a learned society (Sections) and a professional body (Divisions), a separation that is not necessarily helpful for the development of research in the psychology of education.

The introduction in July 2009 of statutory regulation of psychologists, with the setting up of the Health Professions Council Register of practitioner psychologists and restriction of use of titles such as 'Educational Psychologist' to those who are registered, may have implications for the BPS and the position of psychology within universities in the longer term. Until July 2009 entry to professional training courses in educational psychology required that a candidate had a degree accredited by the BPS. It is conceivable that the

Health Professions Council might in the future specify alternative routes to registration, which could have implications for the accreditation process, which in turn could impact on the psychology curriculum and psychology staffing levels on undergraduate psychology courses.

The BPS organises and facilitates conferences and symposia and publishes major research journals including the *British Journal of Educational Psychology*, first published in 1930. In summary, research in psychology, including the psychology of education, is supported directly and indirectly by a national organisation which is outside the university and research centre systems but is closely linked to them. There are inevitably tensions within an organisation that is the representative body for British psychologists and which has to accommodate diverse positions within a discipline with conflicting theoretical and methodological approaches. Notwithstanding these tensions, it has helped to provide coherence to psychology. There is a degree of consensus on what constitutes the mainstream and the BPS plays a significant role in this.

The good health of psychology as a discipline is evident in the numbers studying it at university (Higher Education Statistics Agency data for 2006–2007 show that it is among the most popular subjects in higher education, with 72,475 students, including 6,415 full-time postgraduate students) and in the rapidly growing numbers at GCSE, A-level and foundation levels (52,827 students sat Psychology A-levels in 2009, the fourth most popular subject; only English, Maths and Biology were taken by more candidates). This helps sustain a sizeable academic community of lecturers and, indirectly, researchers. A survey conducted in 2003 showed that psychology departments had an average of 5.6 postdoctoral researchers and 8.3 final-year PhD students (Norgate and Ginsborg, 2006), suggesting that future generations of researchers are being nurtured.

Nationally, student numbers on education degree courses are comparable to psychology numbers. However, psychology plays only a small part in the education degree curriculum and this part has been shrinking since the 1980s following government-led changes to teacher training which introduced a greater emphasis on students' experience in schools and, within the shorter time spent in university, increased focus on curriculum subjects. Consequently, education students spend much less time on psychology, which tends to form part of a general professional studies component of the university course (Norwich, 2000, p. 165). This trend augments the problems faced by research in the psychology of education that are associated with the demographic trends identified by Mills *et al.* (2006); education departments might not regard it as a priority to replace a vacant psychology post with a psychologist.

In summary, the discipline of psychology is currently in a strong position, attracting substantial numbers of undergraduate and postgraduate students and supported by an organisation that has close links with university departments and professional practitioners and which, through its accreditation of undergraduate degrees and postgraduate professional courses, has considerable influence on the university curriculum. The position of psychology within education departments is less secure. How might this impact upon research in the psychology of education? It is relevant to note that research in the psychology of education is located in university psychology departments as well as in education departments. As an illustration, a snapshot of the 83 articles published in two recent volumes of the *British Journal of Educational Psychology* shows that 50 per cent of the articles had first authors whose affiliation was in psychology, compared to 32 per cent in education and 5 per cent in educational psychology (the remainder had other affiliations in health, communication and so on). The proportions are similar for UK and international authors (68 per cent of authors were based outside the UK). A different picture emerges if comparable issues of the *British Educational Research Journal* are analysed: 4 per cent of affiliations were from the Psychology and Human Development Department at the Institute of Education, London (no other psychology departments were represented); 8 per cent of articles had international authors.

One picture of the capacity of research in the psychology of education can be obtained from analysis of RAE information on British university research publications. Crozier (2007) reported an analysis of the outputs submitted by university institutions to the RAE 2001 Education Unit of Assessment (UoA) (HERO, 2002). A systematic search for authors of publications in psychology journals identified 235 individuals who were located in 56 of the 82 institutions making submissions; this constitutes some 10 per cent of the 2,330 individuals whose work was submitted to the Education UoA. The psychologists (defined in this way) were dispersed across institutions. The mean number of psychologists per institution where they were located was 4.2; 17 institutions were represented by a single psychologist while only five submitted 12 or more. The psychological research submitted to the Education UoA was also dispersed, and psychologists' outputs were published in a large number of different journals (351 articles published in 106 journals). The journals could be classified into four groups: general psychology (22 per cent of journal submissions); psychology of education (32 per cent); special educational needs (36 per cent); counselling, psychotherapy and psychiatry (9 per cent). Few of the journals were international and not many are rated as having 'high impact' in the social sciences.

These data omit research in education that was submitted to the Psychology UoA and thus this representation of psychology of education research underestimates its capacity. Nevertheless, when considering the impact of demographic changes on research in education it is important to have some sense of the capacity of its constituent disciplines. This analysis shows that psychology was dispersed across university education departments, few of which had a concentration of psychologists. This may diminish the capacity to undertake sustained, large-scale psychological research. If research were published in a smaller number of 'high-impact' journals this could encourage more stringent criteria for publication, potentially requiring authors to produce more convincing evidence. It would facilitate the cumulative development of a knowledge base as advocated, among others, by the National Education Research Forum (2000). It would be valuable to conduct a comparable study of the outputs of the 2008 RAE (the exercise that followed the 2001 RAE) to see if capacity has changed and what the implications of findings might be for the future of psychology applied to education. The 2008 data show that Education remains a large research field, comparable in numbers of full-time equivalent research active staff to psychology (1,696 compared with 1,659). Whether the numbers and distribution of psychologists submitting to the Education UoA have changed requires closer analysis of the data since identification of psychologists' submissions is not straightforward.

In summary, psychology faces difficulties in its position in education degree and teacher-education courses and, as this analysis of 2001 RAE data implies, in educational research. Nevertheless, high-quality applied research is being conducted and I now consider issues in the application of psychology to education before reviewing examples of such research.

Selected contributions to the psychology of education

Applications of psychology

As indicated at the beginning of this chapter, psychology is a broad discipline. It eschews overarching theory and its explanatory models tend to have specific areas of focus. Cognitive psychology is the dominant paradigm within the mainstream. The cognitive process models that have been constructed are increasingly augmented by cognitive neuroscience models that aim to relate these processes to brain structures and functions. The influence of European-led contributions to cognitive psychology – the theories and research of Piaget and Vygotsky, for example – has grown and has provided a framework for the development of theories and research that aim to embed cognitive processes within their cultural and social context. This trend is evident in both psychology and the psychology of education.

Theoretical and methodological developments have gone hand in hand with technological innovations. The computer metaphor of mind led to the development of cognitive psychology and, more recently, to connectionist models that aim to model the neural networks that underpin learning. Innovations in information technology have facilitated increasingly sophisticated studies of perception and memory. Developments in brain imaging have encouraged the rapid growth of cognitive neuropsychology. Much cognitive research is laboratory-based, although these laboratories can be located in or are associated with applied settings, in medicine, for example. Computing power has facilitated developments in multivariate statistical methods, which enable researchers to analyse large data sets, including the data from longitudinal studies. Techniques of meta-analysis and systematic review enable researchers to integrate findings across studies. How is this research applied to education? To begin to answer this, it is useful to consider the nature of applied psychology. Smith (2005) proposed a typology of relations between developmental psychology and education.

1   *Independence*. Each field pursues its research agenda without reference to the other. Much psychological research is of this nature and much educational research does not draw upon psychology, explicitly rejects it or seeks a different kind of psychology to the one that is currently dominant. Nevertheless, the education of children must draw upon some kind of theory of child development, if only to select age-appropriate materials and teaching strategies. This theory can be built up through teachers' classroom experience to exert a powerful influence on practice and in socialising new teachers into 'what works'. Policies and guidelines produced by the government and agencies also exert an influence on practice; these do not necessarily draw upon educational psychology and may or may not be consistent with teachers' understanding of what works. Theories of practice are systematised and promoted through instruction and textbooks in pedagogy, again without necessarily drawing upon social science theory. It can be bolstered by empirical research that uses social science methodology. For example, research investigates the influence of ability grouping on attainment (reviewed by Hallam, 2002), using established research methodology without necessarily making reference to psychological theorising on learning, the role of social groups in learning or the nature or measurement of ability. Advocates for evidence-based policy reform argue that educational practice – 'what works' – needs to have a sound research basis. They stress the necessity of government-funded systematic, replicable empirical research studies to test programmes before they are widely implemented. Studies are submitted to systematic review and the outcomes of these are available to educational policy-makers. For example, Slavin (2009) draws attention to systematic reviews in the USA and UK, including the *Evidence for Policy and Practice Information and Co-ordinating Centre* (EPPI-Centre, 2009) at the Institute of Education, University of London since 1993 and the *Best Evidence Encyclopaedia* (2009), which was set up in 2005 in Johns Hopkins University in the USA and now has a UK base in the University of York. Psychologists working within the mainstream paradigm with interests in empirical methods and systematic review will be sympathetic to research that can be used to promote evidence-based policy (as noted below, Goswami and Bryant, 2007, provided a review of research on cognitive development as an interim report of the Cambridge Primary Review). Nevertheless, psychologists working within multi-disciplinary education departments will be aware that other educational researchers are sceptical of this approach, for various

reasons. There is not necessarily consensus on the nature of the questions to be put to test or agreement that quantitative empirical research is the appropriate basis for evidence. Psychologists will be conscious of the frustration that can be experienced when recommendations based on integration of research findings and evidence of good practice are rejected almost immediately by government because they are not consistent with existing policies or priorities. One illustration is the negative reaction of the Department for Children, Schools and Families (Cambridge Primary Review, 2009) to the publication of the Cambridge Primary Review (Alexander, 2009). A dispassionate appraisal of research findings is not necessarily the response of policy-makers to evidence-based proposals.

2   *Relevance.* Smith discusses this in terms of speculation that developments in one field might be useful to the other: relevance is asserted but not pursued. Psychologists frequently allude to possible educational benefits of their work without spelling these out. Also, there are many claims, often made by commercial organisations, about the effectiveness of particular forms of instruction being based on findings about brain function or learning styles, and psychologists have a valuable critical role here, helping education professionals to understand what claims can be supported by current psychological and neuropsychological evidence (Goswami, 2008b).

3   *Implication.* This goes beyond relevance in that development in one field leads to greater understanding in the other, and can lead to change in practice. Implication can be at a very general level, for example, the change in understanding the nature of learning from reliance on drill, repetition and 'mental exercise' to emphasis on children's thinking, imagination, play and the social nature of learning, that followed changes in views on the nature of childhood influenced by educational thinkers such as Rousseau and Pestalozzi, as well as by psychologists such as Piaget, Vygotsky and Bruner. Implication can also be more specific, for example, the emphasis on whole-word reading and learning to read as a 'guessing game' that was influenced by reading research in the 1970s.

4   *Application.* This tests whether an implication works in practice and whether it is conducive to good educational practice. I consider this in the next section.

5   *Inter-dependence.* Rather than application from one field to the other, this involves both fields working together at their intersection. Smith considers this to be rare in the case of developmental psychology and education. A similar point is made by Norwich (2000, p. 169), who argues for a psychology grounded in educational practice rather than a field of knowledge to be applied to education from general psychology.

The next section offers a selective review of recent research that has aimed to apply psychology to education and that offers more than 'relevance' in

Smith's terms. It has to be selective because theories and research in all areas of psychology have been applied to education; I emphasise cognitive psychology, focusing on applied research carried out in the UK even though the theoretical underpinnings may have been developed elsewhere. A more detailed review of research into cognitive development together with an indication of some of its implications for learning is provided by Goswami and Bryant (2007).

Working memory

The model of working memory developed by Baddeley and Hitch (1974) is distinctive in that it occupies a central place in contemporary cognitive psychology and is one of the few theoretical developments to do so that originated in the UK. Rather than conceptualise memory as a series of passive stores, the model analyses it as a structured process that we use to carry out a wide range of mental tasks. Baddeley and Hitch derived a number of predictions about performance, many flowing from the proposition that working memory has limited capacity in its executive processes and in the phonological or visuo-spatial coding that keeps material temporarily active. The educational application of the model has been investigated in a number of studies, for example, of children's mental arithmetic (Adams and Hitch, 1997) and specific learning difficulties of children with Down's syndrome (Hulme and Mackenzie, 1992). Research conducted by Gathercole and her associates (Gathercole *et al.*, 2006, provide a review) has shown that individual differences in children's performance on working-memory-dependent tasks predict their subsequent reading, vocabulary and mathematical attainments even when other sources of variation, for example in ability test scores, are statistically controlled. The research shows that the precise relations between working memory and school attainment depend on the child's age and the curriculum – what is being learnt at any one time. It found that teachers were frequently unaware of their students' difficulties on memory tasks. Working closely with teachers, the team has developed materials for assessing students' memory-task performance and supporting their learning in the classroom (Gathercole and Alloway, 2008). Current projects include classroom-based studies, the construction of screening techniques, intervention studies and work with children with learning difficulties.

Learning to read

Our second example concerns issues that would be important for education whether or not there was any relevant psychological evidence, namely how children in a literate society learn to read. Huey (1908, p. 6) wrote that 'to completely analyse what we do when we read would almost be the acme of a psychologist's achievements, for it would be to describe very many of the most intricate workings of the human mind'. Considerable progress has been made in this analysis. For example, Gough (1972) drew upon eye-movement studies to construct a model that had the bold aim of specifying what takes place during one second of reading, from the eye alighting on the text to speech. Recent research based on brain-imaging techniques has begun to specify the activity in the brain that takes place during this process. Wolf (2008, pp. 145–155) extends Gough's work to offer a neuroscientific account of the processes that take place in the first half-second of reading. Research has also made significant progress in investigating the neural structures involved in learning to read (Goswami, 2008a). Huey would surely have been impressed with the progress made in analysing the intricate processes involved in reading and learning to read. Research also investigates children's phonological awareness (Bradley and Bryant, 1983; Goswami and Bryant, 2007, pp. 16–17) and comprehension, including the study of children who have adequate decoding skills but demonstrate reading comprehension difficulties (Nation, 2005).

The teaching of reading has been central to debates about standards in education and policies designed to raise standards. Psychological research has the potential to inform best practice in teaching reading in various ways. First, its evidence contributes to reports that influence national policies, for example, the Rose Review (Rose, 2006), which was commissioned by the government to review the teaching of early reading in England.

Second, psychologists engage in debate with educational researchers and other experts on literacy and the teaching of reading, writing and spelling, for example, a series of articles on the 'simple model' of reading in *Literacy*, the journal of the United Kingdom Literacy Association (Goswami, 2008a; Kirby and Savage, 2008; Stuart *et al.*, 2008). Psychologists also offer critiques of approaches to teaching reading and related skills, on the basis of theoretical understanding of the processes involved and the quality of the research evidence that is presented in reports and policy documents, for example, the insufficient weight given to randomised control trials (Wyse and Goswami, 2008).

Third, psychologists are involved in large-scale intervention studies of approaches to teaching reading. One example is the ambitious project in West Dunbartonshire led by educational psychologist MacKay, which aims for 'the total eradication of illiteracy' in one local authority. The multiple-component study had a cross-lagged design comparing pre- and post-intervention cohorts, lasted ten years and involved all pupils in the pre-school year in the authority, 35 primary schools and 23 nurseries, resulting in a total intervention sample of 27,244 children and control sample of 3,659, all tested individually (MacKay, 2007). Large-scale studies have also researched the social factors that influence reading development. An example is the Effective Provision of Pre-School Education (EPPE) project, a government-funded longitudinal study of the effects of different kinds of pre-school experience upon children's cognitive and social/behavioural development (Sammons *et al.*, 2004).

Teaching thinking skills

Vygotsky's theorising has a growing influence on psychology of learning, particularly his emphasis on the social context of learning and thinking. His influence has taken various forms, for example, the increased attention given to social interaction processes in learning (examples are Howe *et al.*'s (2007) studies of group activities in science education and Mercer's (2008) research on classroom discourse). It has provided researchers and teachers with concepts such as zone of proximal development, scaffolding and guided participation (Slee and Shuter, 2003) that have heuristic value. The influence is evident in educational programmes designed to teach children thinking skills explicitly, motivated by the belief that these skills are not adequately developed through the standard curriculum. CASE (Cognitive Acceleration for Science Education) has been developed by Adey and his associates at King's College, London since 1982 (Adey *et al.*, 2001). Adey's background is in chemistry and science education but the conceptual framework for the project draws explicitly upon Piaget and Vygotsky. The programme, which is delivered by science teachers in science lessons set aside for the purpose, is based upon the careful arrangement of management of cognitive conflict and attaches considerable importance to social interaction in the development of cognition and metacognition. CASE has been systematically evaluated over several years through quasi-experimental designs with a longitudinal dimension (see, for example, Adey *et al.*, 2002; Adey, 2004). The success of the programme and the teaching materials designed to support it (Adey, 2008) has led to its widespread implementation and to its extension to additional curriculum subjects. Other thinking-skills programmes are being researched, for example, ACTS (Activating Children's Thinking Skills), currently being developed in Northern Ireland by McGuinness *et al.* (2007).

Our selection of case studies has focused on areas that are at the heart of the cognitive psychology agenda – memorising, thinking and the processes involved in reading and learning to read. It is important to note that the cognitive paradigm has penetrated many areas of psychology including social psychology, personality psychology and clinical psychology. It has been applied *inter alia* to the study of motivation for learning (Pintrich and Schunk, 2002), the self-concept (Dweck, 2003) and specific disorders, for example, autism, where teaching aids are being developed for parents and teachers of young children diagnosed with autism and Asperger's syndrome (Baron-Cohen *et al.*, 2007).

Discussion

My examples are taken largely from one area of psychological research that has been applied to education. The emphasis has been on studies of learning and thinking from a cognitive perspective, to the neglect of important topics such as social relationships, children's emotions and classroom behaviour.

Other authors would make a different selection and no doubt would interpret differently the research I have presented. I have been biased towards intervention studies but I do not intend to imply that other kinds of research are not valuable. Much teaching and learning takes place within groups and social interactions, as illustrated in the CASE programme, and this is a key dimension that warrants consideration at greater length.

I have aimed to show that vigorous lines of research are being pursued by psychologists working closely with schools. They collect fresh data in classrooms. Not all educational research is of this kind. Much is theoretical while some draws upon analysis of secondary data or upon interviews with teachers or pupils outside the classroom. Of course, psychologists are not the only researchers active within classrooms but their work represents a rich source of data that is not necessarily collected by anyone else. Researchers are welcome in busy schools only as long as schools value their contribution or see the potential for application. There is evidence that this does occur, for example, in the implementation of CASE in primary and secondary schools, the expansion of thinking-skills programmes and psychologists' contributions to teaching reading. There is increasing recognition among researchers of the importance of longitudinal designs and randomised control trials in educational research and these necessitate long-term commitment from both participating schools and researchers. They demand the formulation of worthwhile research questions, skills in research design and analysis and serious attention to ethical issues.

My examples come from both psychology and education departments. If trends identified by Mills et al. (2006) are maintained, what would be the consequences for psychological research if the capacity of research undertaken within education departments were reduced? Psychologists within education departments have a key role to play. They work alongside colleagues from other disciplines involved in educational research; awareness of how problems and issues are approached by other disciplines enriches psychological research and increases psychologists' sensitivity to criticisms of their research and the assumptions it makes. They are also close to educational practice; they frequently have teaching qualifications and experience and their contributions to teacher training and teachers' higher qualifications and professional development bring them into close contact with practitioners. This helps generate and refine research questions. It also has practical value in forging links with schools that are interested in involvement in research. Not least, psychologists within schools of education are primarily interested in education. Psychologists located within psychology departments have other obligations. In a climate that places increasing emphasis on competition for external sources of research funding and where departments' research income is related to performance in national research assessment exercises, whether these are based on peer evaluation, citation metrics or evidence of success in attracting funding, the pressure is on psychologists to pursue research that is valued by their peers and, to be maximally effective, has to meet the criterion of being regarded as 'world-leading'. The research that gains these plaudits and funding is not necessarily applied research or targeted at education.

Education raises many moral, economic and political questions – the attention that is paid to 'educational standards' by politicians and the significance of education for economic development are but two indications of this. The study of a complex educational system, where children are taught mostly in large classes in schools that can have thousands of pupils, is necessarily difficult, with very many variables at different levels of analysis in interaction with one another. It is unlikely that a single discipline, particularly one that emphasises the individual learner, albeit within a social context, can answer educational questions on its own. Even when research seems to have potential for application there are problems of sustaining the features that have been identified as crucial for success and of disseminating the research and embedding it in practice across an education system that has competing interest groups and many 'stakeholders'. A challenge for even the best research is to avoid programmes losing their impetus or receiving merely lip service, giving rise, perhaps, to a sense that 'it's Thursday at 3 p.m., it must be CASE'.

While psychology is only one discipline that can be brought to bear on the complexities of education, its emphasis on the study of the individual learner will, I believe, continue to have an important place in educational research. Individuals are different, and their differences cannot be reduced to variables such as social class or socio-economic factors, important as these undoubtedly are. Children within the same family are different from one another, and differences detected in the first weeks of life presage later development (Rubin *et al.*, 2009). Research into child development is neither static nor a simple accumulation of facts. It is rich in the generation of theory, but theory that is submitted to empirical test. Psychology is regularly criticised for its individualistic bias, positivism and reductionism, but I think these criticisms do not pay sufficient attention to the role of theory in psychology, to its capacity for self-criticism or to the range of quantitative and qualitative methods that characterise it (Crozier, 2007, found that psychology submissions to the 2001 Education UoA were characterised by a range of conceptual, quantitative and qualitative approaches). They fail to acknowledge the value of testing hypotheses, not in the pursuit of some 'objective truth', but to test our understanding: 'If I really understand X, then I expect to find A to happen in particular circumstances, or not to find B, or to find A but not B', and so on. If we are not putting hypotheses to the test then our claims to understanding join all the other claims about X and add little to them. Of course, what a particular hypothesis is and what counts as a test are complex matters, but dealing with that complexity is the nature of social science.

What substantive contributions can psychology make in the future? Within my area of focus – cognitive psychology of education – one can expect that significant advances in cognitive development, in neuropsychology and in understanding the influence of the social and cultural context on development will continue. The 2008 RAE Education Subject Panel Report reported an expansion in psychological activity since the 2001 RAE, noting examples of collaboration with neuroscientists (RAE 2008 UO45, 2009), and these endeavours are likely to continue. As argued above, Vygotsky's influence upon the psychology of education has been extensive, leading to developments in socio-cultural theory, which has generated research into social interaction processes in teaching and learning in school and which has encouraged psychologists to take the social and cultural context of learning into account in their theorising (Daniels, 2001). This research addresses one of the criticisms made of the psychology of learning, its neglect of the cultural and institutional context in which learning takes place, and hence the meanings that learning has. What is to be learned and where learning takes place have too readily been regarded as unproblematic.

Psychology is characterised by competing paradigms, encompassing biological and social influences on behaviour, qualitative and qualitative analyses, and ranging from evolutionary psychology to critical psychology. Research is pursued on many fronts and since it is aimed at understanding mind and behaviour it inevitably has some relevance for education. Many programmes would fall within the 'relevance' and 'implication' categories of Smith's scheme. These studies have value, even though they are not direct applications. They yield insight into concepts such as 'ability' that are common in educational discourse. Current approaches to ability place greater emphasis on a broader conception of intelligence, for example, Gardner's (1999) theory of multiple intelligences that has been valued by educationalists, if not by psychometric psychologists. Research into behavioural genetics draws attention to sources of variation within families and between families and identifies complex interactions between genetic and environmental influences (Rutter, 2006). In conjunction with findings from longitudinal studies this should refine the analysis of 'environmental influences' and aid understanding of differences in the personal characteristics that children bring to school.

The self-concept has attracted considerable attention in recent years. Studies of self-esteem reveal that the relationship between self-concept and academic achievement is moderated by contextual factors, for example, the 'big-fish-little-pond effect' (Marsh *et al.*, 2008) which proposes that the relationship between achievement and academic self-concept depends on the average achievements of the class or school: an able child might not have a positive view of him or herself if they attend a school where average ability is high. Research programmes are investigating links among self-beliefs, self-regulation and motivation (see Pintrich and Schunk, 2002, and Smith *et al.*, 2003, for reviews) and have elaborated constructs such as self-worth protection strategies, self-handicapping and learned helplessness, which have been explored in relation to, among other topics, disengagement from school (Chaplain, 1995) and 'laddishness' (Jackson, 2002). The outcomes of these studies will have heuristic value for practitioners, providing concepts that aid understanding of learning and development. However, this research has not yet fulfilled its potential for developing programmes and materials for practitioners, and achieving this is the type of role that psychologists in education departments are well qualified to play, working with colleagues, schools and colleges.

The potential for such developments is also evident in research into bullying, which has investigated the extent and nature of bullying, constructed and evaluated interventions and made recommendations for whole-school policies that have been widely implemented (Olweus, 2004). This is research that has made a difference. Nevertheless, bullying has not been eradicated and prevention programmes vary in their effectiveness, and continuing research and development of programmes are necessary.

I have argued that schools can benefit from high-quality interventions that draw upon psychological theory and research, and this promises much for the future. Yet there are reasons not to be complacent. This research is effective only when it is sustained and involves close collaboration between researchers and practitioners; these factors are vulnerable to demographic changes. Over-reliance on research produced within psychology departments may be a problem for the reasons discussed above, and there is no guarantee that the strength of psychology departments will persist in the future. There is a risk of a downward spiral in educational research where smaller capacity generates less influential research, which feeds back into further reductions in capacity. Promising developments in memory research, large-scale reading interventions and teaching thinking programmes have to be analysed (which elements of a multi-component intervention are key and which need to be strengthened?), improved, evaluated and disseminated, all of which are demanding of resources.

Finally, there is a need, as Norwich (2000) and Smith (2005) have argued, to develop a psychology of education that works closely with other disciplines to generate original education-based research. Psychologists who have training and experience of education can play an important mediating role in such developments. What are the obstacles to the interdependence of education and psychology advocated by Smith (2005)? One is the unidirectional nature of influence where there is absence of feedback into psychology from educational research. For example, research into working memory can enrich teaching but there is as yet little evidence for the application enriching psychological theory. This is surely desirable, as the learning that is required in school and in various forms of apprenticeship makes significant demands on cognitive, motivational and emotional processes and its study ought to contribute to the refinement of theory. Research into CASE offers a promising example of this advancement of theory. There are methodological hurdles too. Psychology relies on statistical evidence, which may identify meaningful trends and offer support for specific theories but which may not be useful to the practitioner, who works with individual students and groups of students, not with 'samples'. A similar issue is faced in clinical research. Cognitive psychology has provided an analysis of, for example, anxiety, which clinical researchers have drawn upon to develop therapy, testing its effectiveness by means of randomised control trials, statistical analysis and systematic review (for example, a review by Cartwright-Hatton *et al.*, 2004, of cognitive behaviour therapies applied to children's anxiety). Nevertheless, the effectiveness of the therapy depends on the clinical skills and sensitivities of the individual therapist and on the quality of the relationship between therapist and client. There is a burgeoning research literature on this application that contributes to the effectiveness of the practice and the refinement of the cognitive theory of anxiety, and which accommodates critical analyses of practice and theory from within and outside psychology.

I have aimed to show through selected examples from one area of the discipline the contribution that psychology is making and can make to education. The changes advocated by Norwich (2000) and Smith (2005) require a robust psychology of education working closely with other disciplines and with practitioners. This is less likely to come about if crises of confidence, inadequate communication between disciplines or demographic trends reduce the capacity for such endeavours.

References

Adams, J.W. and Hitch, G.J. (1997) Working memory and children's mental addition, *Journal of Experimental Child Psychology*, 67, 21–38.

Adey, P. (2004) Evidence for long-term effects: promises and pitfalls, *Evaluation and Research in Education*, 18, 83–101.

Adey, P. (ed.) (2008) *Let's Think handbook: cognitive acceleration in the primary school* (London, nfer-Nelson).

Adey, P., Robertson, A. and Venville, G. (2002) Effects of a cognitive acceleration programme on Year 1 pupils, *British Journal of Educational Psychology*, 72, 1–25.

Adey, P., Shayer, M. and Yates, C. (2001) *Thinking science*, 3rd edn (London, Nelson Thornes).

Alexander, R. (ed.) (2009) *Children, their world, their education. Final report and recommendations of the Cambridge Primary Review* (London, Routledge).

Baddeley, A.D. and Hitch, G.J. (1974) Working memory, in G. Bower (ed.) *The psychology of learning and motivation* (New York, Academic Press).

Baron-Cohen, S., Golan, O., Chapman, E. and Granader, Y. (2007) Transported to a world of emotion, *The Psychologist*, 20 (2), 76–77.

Best Evidence Encyclopaedia (2009) *Best evidence encyclopaedia*. Available online at www.bestevidence.org (accessed 27 October 2009).

Bradley, L. and Bryant, P.E. (1983) Categorizing sounds and learning to read: a causal connection, *Nature*, 301, 419–421.

British Psychological Society (2009) *Strategic plan 2010–2015*. Available online at www.bps.org.uk/the-society/aims-and-objectives/bps_strategic_plan/bps_strategic_plan_home.cfm (accessed 27 October 2009).

Cambridge Primary Review (2009) *Full text of the government's response to the final report of the Cambridge Primary Review*. Available online at www.primaryreview.org.uk/Downloads/Finalreport/DCSF_PR_091016.pdf (accessed 2 November 2009).

Cartwright-Hatton, S., Roberts, C., Chitsabesan, P., Fothergill, C. and Harrington, R. (2004) Systematic review of the efficacy of cognitive behaviour therapies for childhood and adolescent anxiety disorders, *British Journal of Clinical Psychology*, 43, 421–436.

Chaplain, R. (1995) Making a strategic withdrawal: disengagement and self-worth protection in male pupils, in J. Rudduck, R. Chaplain and G. Wallace (eds) *School improvement: what can pupils tell us?* (London, David Fulton), 101–115.

Crozier, W.R. (2007) Capacity and methodology in university educational research: psychology of education as a case study, *Higher Education Review*, 39, 25–41.

Daniels, H. (2001) *Vygotsky and pedagogy* (London, Routledge).

Dweck, C.S. (2003) Ability conceptions, motivation and development, in L. Smith, C. Rogers and P. Tomlinson (eds) *Development and motivation: joint perspectives, British Journal of Educational Psychology*, Monograph Series II, 2, 13–27.

EPPI-Centre (2009) *EPPI-Centre*. Available online at http://eppi.ioe.ac.uk/cms (accessed 27 October 2009).

Francis, H. (2004) A personal perspective on the Section's history. From growth to struggle – where next? *The Psychology of Education Review*, 28 (2), 4–8.

Gardner, H. (1999) *Intelligence reframed: multiple intelligences for the 21st century* (New York, Basic Books).

Gathercole, S.E. and Alloway, T.P. (2008) *Working memory and learning: a practical guide* (London, Sage).

Gathercole, S.E., Lamont, E. and Alloway, T.P. (2006) Working memory in the classroom, in S. Pickering (ed.) *Working memory and education* (London, Academic Press), 219–240.

Goswami, U. (2008a) Reading, complexity and the brain, *Literacy*, 42, 67–74.

Goswami, U. (2008b) Neuroscience and education: from research to practice, *Nature Reviews Neuroscience*, 7, 406–413.

Goswami, U. and Bryant, P. (2007) *Children's cognitive development and learning: Primary Review Research Survey 2/1a* (Cambridge, University of Cambridge Faculty of Education).

Gough, P.B. (1972) One second of reading, in J. Kavanaugh and I. Mattingley (eds) *Language by ear and by eye* (Cambridge, MA, MIT Press), 331–358.

Hall, J. (2008) Mental deficiency: changing the outlook, *The Psychologist*, 21 (11), 1006–1007.

Hallam, S. (2002) *Ability grouping in schools* (London, Institute of Education, University of London).

HERO (2002) *RAE 2001*. Available online at http://www.hero.ac.uk/rae/index.htm (accessed 4 February 2009).

Howe, C., Tolmie, A., Thurston, A., Topping, K., Christie, D., Livingston, K., Jessiman, E. and Donaldson, S. (2007) Group work in elementary science: towards organisational principles for supporting pupil learning, *Learning and Instruction*, 17, 549–563.

Huey, E. (1908) *The psychology and pedagogy of reading* (1968 edn, Cambridge, MA, MIT Press).

Hulme, C. and Mackenzie, S. (1992) *Working memory and severe learning difficulties* (Hove, Lawrence Erlbaum Associates).

Jackson, C. (2002) 'Laddishness' as a self-worth protection strategy, *Gender and Education*, 14, 37–51.

Kirby, J.R. and Savage, R.S. (2008) Can the simple view deal with the complexities of reading? *Literacy*, 42, 75–82.

McGuinness, C., Eakin, A., Curry, C., Sheehy, N. and Bunting, B. (2007) *Building thinking skills in thinking classrooms: ACTS in Northern Ireland*. Paper presented at the 13th International Conference on Thinking, Norrköping, Sweden. Available online at www.ep.liu.se/eco/021/vol1 (accessed 1 December 2008).

Mackay, T. (2007) *Achieving the vision. The final research report of the West Dunbartonshire Literacy Initiative* (Dumbarton, West Dunbartonshire Council).

Marsh, H.W., Seaton, M., Trautwein, U., Lüdtke, O., Hau, K.T., O'Mara, A.J. and Craven, R.G. (2008) The big-fish-little-pond-effect stands up to critical scrutiny: implications for theory, methodology, and future research, *Educational Psychology Review*, 20, 319–350.

Mercer, N. (2008) Talk and the development of reasoning and understanding, *Human Development*, 51, 90–100.

Mills, D., Jepson, A., Coxon, T., Easterby-Smith, M., Hawkins, P. and Spencer, J. (2006) *Demographic review of the UK social sciences* (Swindon, ESRC). Available online at www.esrcsocietytoday.ac.uk/ESRCInfoCentre/Images/Demographic_Review_tcm6-13872.pdf (accessed 1 December, 2008).

Nation, K. (2005) The connections between language and reading in children with poor reading comprehension, in H.W. Catts and A. Kahmi (eds) *The connections between language and reading disabilities* (Mahwah, NJ, Lawrence Erlbaum), 41–53.

National Educational Research Forum (2000) *Building research capacity: sub-group report* (London, National Educational Research Forum).

Norgate, S. and Ginsborg, J. (2006) *A survey of postdoctoral researchers and final-year PhD students in psychology: research funding, career needs and working conditions* (Leicester: British Psychological Society).

Norwich, B. (2000) *Education and psychology in interaction: working with uncertainty in interconnecting systems* (London, Routledge).

Olweus, D. (2004) The Olweus Bullying Prevention Programme: design and implementation issues and a new national initiative in Norway, in P.K. Smith, D. Pepler and K. Rigby (eds) *Bullying in schools: how successful can interventions be?* (Cambridge, Cambridge University Press), 13–36.

Pintrich, P.R. and Schunk, D.H. (2002) *Motivation in education: theory, research and applications* (Upper Saddle River, NJ, Merrill Prentice Hall).

RAE 2008 UO45 (2009) *Sub Panel 45 Education: subject overview report*. Available online at www.sfre.ac.uk/wp-content/uploads/2009/01/uoa45-education.pdf (accessed 1 November 2009).

Rose, J. (2006) *Independent review of the teaching of early reading* (Nottingham, DfES Publications).

Rubin, K.H., Coplan, R.J. and Bowker, J.C. (2009) Social withdrawal in childhood, *Annual Review of Psychology*, 60, 141–171.

Rutter, M. (2006) *Genes and behaviour: nature–nurture interplay explained* (Oxford, Blackwell).

Sammons, P., Sylva, K., Melhuish, E., Siraj-Blatchford, I., Taggart, B., Elliot, K. and Marsh, A. (2004) *The continuing effects of pre-school education at age 7 years. Technical Paper 11* (London, Institute of Education, University of London).

Slavin, R.E. (2009) *Evidence-based policies for education in the United Kingdom: the Education Section of the British Psychological Society 28th Vernon-Wall Lecture* (Leicester, The British Psychological Society).

Slee, P. and Shuter, R. (2003) *Child development: thinking about theories* (London, Arnold).

Smith, L. (2005) Education, in B. Hopkins, R.G. Barr, G.F. Michel and P. Rochat (eds) *The Cambridge encyclopedia of child development* (Cambridge, Cambridge University Press), 487–490.

Smith, L., Rogers, C. and Tomlinson, P. (eds) *Development and motivation: joint perspectives, British Journal of Educational Psychology*, Monograph Series II.

Stuart, M., Stainthorp, R. and Snowling, M. (2008) Literacy as a complex activity: deconstructing the simple view of reading, *Literacy*, 42, 59–66.

Thomas, J.B. (1996) The beginnings of educational psychology in the universities of England and Wales, *Educational Psychology*, 16, 229–244.

Wolf, M. (2008) *Proust and the squid: the story and science of the reading brain* (Cambridge, Icon Books).

Wyse, D. and Goswami, U. (2008) Synthetic phonics and the teaching of reading, *British Educational Research Journal*, 34, 691–710.

4 Philosophy of education

The historical and contemporary tradition

Alis Oancea and David Bridges

Introduction

The roots of even the most contemporary philosophy and philosophy of education run deep. Philosophers return to the ideas of Habermas and Heidegger, of Wittgenstein and Dewey, of Mill and Kant, of Hume and Locke and, to leap a few centuries, of Plato and Aristotle, not just out of historical curiosity but because of their continuing power to illuminate and reinterpret contemporary experience. This is partly because the substantive preoccupations of philosophy, past, present and (we might expect) future, change in their specific expression, but not in terms of their fundamental concerns. Questions to do with the principles that should govern human conduct, the requirements for human flourishing, the nature of a just society, the meaning and conditions of liberty, the nature of human being and the possibilities for and limits upon human understanding of the natural and social worlds are ones with which successive generations have grappled and ones which continue to occupy us in the contemporary world.

These and similar questions of a philosophical nature are also central to every significant debate in the field of educational theory, policy, practice and research. National and international debates about the aims of education and the principles which should govern educational practice, the scope of the curriculum, education for citizenship, faith schools, parents' and children's rights, education in a multi-racial/culturally diverse society, the role of the university in a mass higher-education system all rest on essentially philosophical considerations, as well as empirical data. More specifically, in the educational *research* environment, contest about what forms of enquiry can illuminate and inform educational experience and practice and what kind of evidence can provide a reliable basis for policy, and about the kind of 'competently produced web of argument' (Phillips, 2007, p. 328) or practical judgement which can enable one to combine evidence, experience, political understanding and normativity into a sensible decision − all of these, too, rest on philosophical understanding, in this case rooted in theory of knowledge and logic.

And again, as in other branches of philosophy, philosophers of education turn not just to contemporary sources but to the philosophical tradition for insights and arguments. Contemporary work in philosophy of education helps to illustrate this historical connectedness. There has, for example, been something of a revival of interest in contemporary philosophy in 'virtue ethics', i.e. that thread of ethical theory which relates to human qualities and dispositions, the qualities of character which ought to be cultivated, in general or, for example in the case of 'intellectual virtue', in the service of particular spheres of human endeavour. The classical source for any discussion of virtue is in Aristotle, notably in the *Nicomachean Ethics*, but it has been taken up in more contemporary writing in all sorts of interesting ways by, for example, MacIntyre (1985) and Zagzebski (1996). Equally it has attracted the attention of contemporary UK-based philosophers of education, in relation to moral education (D. Carr, 2007; but see also McLaughlin and Halstead, 1999), education for citizenship (D. Carr, 2006) and the ethics of educational research (Pring, 2000, 2001).

Of course, it has not just been Aristotle's writing on ethics which has inspired contemporary writing about education. His subtle characterisation of different kinds of knowledge has informed, among others, conceptions of action research as 'practical philosophy' (Elliott 1987, 2000; W. Carr 2006), of vocational education (Winch, 2000) and of excellence in applied and practice-based research (Oancea and Furlong, 2007).

To take a second example, perhaps one of the major inspirations for contemporary writing in philosophy of education has been the writing of Ludwig Wittgenstein, notably in *Philosophical Investigations* (1958). Peter Winch's *The Idea of a Social Science* (1958), one of the most influential contributions to the philosophy of social science, drew directly from Wittgenstein's thought and was in turn linked to educational philosophy by Smeyers (2006). The notion of a social practice, which had its roots in Wittgenstein, was fruitfully developed by Alasdair MacIntyre (1985) – and this, as well as Wittgenstein's original work, has provided an important starting point for a number of recent contributions to philosophy of education (McLaughlin, 1995; McLaughlin and Halstead, 1999; Dunne, 2002; Blake *et al.*, 2000; Smeyers *et al.*, 2007; Smeyers and Burbules, 2008). A further routing of Wittgensteinian thought into philosophy of education was via the American philosopher, Stanley Cavell (see, for example, Cavell, 1979, 2004), who is also a link to the Deweyite tradition and is cited in all of the above. Standish (for example, 2006) in particular has taken up the work of Cavell and also found interesting resonance for this enthusiasm among Japanese philosophers of education, especially Naoko Saito (2006).

These examples – and we might have extended these and provided many more, from within and beyond anglophone contexts – help to illustrate the embeddedness of contemporary philosophy of education in both the historical tradition of philosophical writing and the contemporary expression of that tradition. We get glimpses too (which might have been greatly expanded with a wider international perspective) of the conversational communities which develop around particular sources and themes. They also illustrate the contribution which philosophers of education are making to educational enquiry by drawing on the powerful intellectual resources of that tradition to reinterpret, critique and expand contemporary educational thought and supporting 'the more wide-ranging reflection and the development of practical reason (*phronesis*) that philosophy can encourage' (Standish, 2007b, p. 169).

When the Oxford philosopher A.J. Ayer was asked 'what is philosophy?' he reputedly answered by waving his arm in the direction of his capacious bookshelves, heaving with texts from across the ages, and said 'it's all that'. Our first point is, then, that philosophy of education is rooted and will continue to be rooted in 'all that'. In one sense, its aspiration is to ensure that 'all that' continues to be part of the conversation of the educational community and informs its argument, debate and development.

Philosophy of education: analysis and argumentation

We have emphasised so far the historical sources which continue to inform philosophical and educational understanding – historical sources which are rooted in Graeco-Roman civilisation and in its more modern expression in both the English and what is sometimes referred to as the continental tradition, but with increasing reference too to different cultural sources such as the writing of Confucius. A special issue of *Comparative Education* (Halstead and McLaughlin, 2004) illustrates the wide sources of international and multi-cultural reference on which contemporary philosophers of education are drawing. There is an important sense in which philosophy, even more than other disciplines, needs to be international, universal perhaps, in its sources of reference and in what it identifies as the really important issues – ones which might transcend, in some cases, the immediate and local preoccupations of policy-makers and practitioners in any particular country. This is an increasingly common feature of a discipline which is global in its questions and conversations and international in its settings and modes of knowledge production. In this chapter, however, we focus on developments in the UK, seen through a mainly UK perspective, not least because reviewing these developments is a task already large and challenging enough in the space available.

A generation of students, including many from overseas, trained in philosophy of education in the UK in the late 1960s and early 1970s encountered the subject at a time when the 'Oxford' school of analytic philosophy was especially influential. At that time the focus was very strongly on the analysis of the language of education or the concepts which constructed and also commonly confused educational discussion. This approach was subject to debate in more recent years in terms of the contribution of philosophy to educational research (e.g. Bridges, 1997; Wilson,

1998), but for a long time it was the central focus of a good deal of literature (e.g. Peters, 1967; Wilson, 1965). Contrary to some views (Standish, 2007b), however, this literature was never really detached from the historical tradition of philosophical writing, though it may have drawn rather selectively from it. For example, Richard Peters, a major force in bringing the analytic rigour of the Oxford school into philosophy of education, described philosophers as 'the inheritors of a tradition which had achieved an autonomous status in relation to the particular presuppositions of evolving societies' (Peters, 1966, p. 61).

There remains in twenty-first-century writing in philosophy of education an important contribution that draws on the analytic tradition, though this tradition has nothing like the dominance it achieved in that earlier period. The quality of educational debate and argumentation would be improved, we suggest, if greater attention was paid to, for example, understanding the rhetorical and logical functions of the language used in particular debates; observing, rather than blurring, significant distinctions; observing tautology or circularity in the use of language; observing the normativity which creeps into apparently innocuously descriptive terms; recognising 'category mistakes' (including, for example, the complex and contested relationship between 'is' and 'ought' statements); observing the gap between evidence of correlations and causal relations; routinely considering counter-arguments and the possibility of their refutation alongside the presentation of a thesis – in short, giving attention to rigour and precision in the argument which underpins the presentation of educational ideas and research. Such concern for clear thinking and logical argument in educational thought long predates the application of analytic philosophy to the field. It is to be found, for example, in such landmark contributions to the development of disciplined educational enquiry as Bain (1897) and Hardie (1942).

Clearly, philosophy is not and should not be the only discipline in which these principles are honoured. One should expect exactly this rigour in psychology or sociology or history. Some of the practices that have recently joined the repertoire of educational enquiry, such as work, including discourse analysis and deconstruction, which spans the boundaries between literary theory, philosophy and social theory, themselves offer specialist attention to some of these features of argumentation. However, it is philosophy, including both the technical and the more general ends of logic, in which these features of *analysis*, *argumentation* and *critique* are given most central, systematic and comprehensive attention, and this is a legacy which the tradition of conceptual analysis enriched. In the UK, this tradition, well established by leading figures like Richard Peters, Paul Hirst and Robert Dearden in the 1970s, was maintained from that period by, among others, John and Patricia White and Terence McLaughlin (see Carr *et al.*, 2008), but is also admirably illustrated in the contemporary work of, for example, Haydon (e.g. 2004), Davis (e.g. 2005) and Hand (e.g. 2003), among others.

Philosophy of education, democratic conversation and practical deliberation

Philosophy and philosophical thinking may permeate research and practice (including policy) in education not only by developing critique, analysis and argument, as described above, but also in ways that are possibly even more organically connected to the worlds of practice and practitioners (be they educators, researchers or policy-makers) (Pring, 2007; Standish, 2007b).

First, these connections between philosophy, policy and practice can spring from nurturing *democratic conversation* about education – including responsible critique, public dialogue (or, rather, successful many-voiced communication), multiple forms of evidence and humanity-enhancing relations. One recent example of the role of philosophy in these conversations was that offered by the Nuffield Review of 14–19 Education and Training in England and Wales (2003–2009), which was a review of the evidence available about all aspects of 14–19 education and training, structured around a philosophical question: 'what counts as an educated 19 year-old in this day and age?' (Pring *et al.*, 2009). Philosophy, the Review argues, contributes to addressing major issues facing education and education research, currently and in the future, including revived debates about aims, values and the curriculum in the current policy and international context; the role of the state, private sector and parents; or the educational implications of, and responses to, the wider challenges of the contemporary world (e.g. globalisation, environment, technological change, multi-culturalism and social cohesion, spirituality). But for this to happen, the 'impoverished metaphors' (Pring, 2007) of much recent public discourses (e.g. about 'raising standards', 'attaining targets', or 'effective curriculum delivery') would need to be replaced with ones that are more democratic, as well as more human – such as Oakeshott's (1962) 'conversation' or Dewey's (1916) 'organic growth'.

A second example of how philosophy and educational practice can be linked organically is that of philosophy *supporting practical deliberation* at all levels and on all aspects of educational practice. For some, this role is reserved to 'practical' rather than 'theoretical' philosophy; it is a phronetic, rather than technical, role. Although we would argue for a synergy, rather than opposition, of 'practical' (praxis *and* poiesis) and 'theoretical', we agree that the way forward for philosophy of education is likely to include support for practitioners in their efforts to 'expose and examine the taken-for-granted presuppositions implicit in their practice in order that they may reflectively reconstruct their understanding of their practice and of how its internal good may, in their own practical situation, be more appropriately pursued' (W. Carr, 2004, p. 62).

What has happened to philosophy of education in the UK?

We have indicated something of the kind of contribution that philosophy of education *can* make to educational understanding and enquiry. This case has, of course, been much more extensively developed elsewhere (see, classically, Hirst, 1966, and Peters, 1966). However, the very existence of the current book reflects a wider consciousness that philosophy (along with the other 'foundation' disciplines) does not occupy the place that it once did in universities and colleges in the UK or, specifically, in the education of teachers. What has happened?

When, in the late 1960s, teacher training was upgraded to degree level in the UK, the 'foundation' disciplines of psychology, sociology, philosophy and history of education provided the academic content which degree-level work was deemed to require (see Tibble, 1966). The demands of the undergraduate programmes also created a demand for people equipped to teach on them, so there was a flurry of activity to create and expand Diploma and Master's level courses in, among other things, philosophy of education. For a while this activity expanded as those teaching the discipline wanted to pursue their own studies at doctoral level and also to set up their own Diploma and Master's level programmes locally.

This flourishing depended, however, on the platform of employment which was provided by the BEd degree, in particular, and, later, by in-service programmes for teachers provided by higher education institutions. Two developments in the 1980s brought this platform crashing down. The first was the movement towards more school-based and practice-oriented training, reinforced by a national curriculum for teacher training, from which philosophical work was effectively excluded. The second was the transfer of in-service funding from higher education to schools, where much of it got lost in the competition for expenditure on staff, IT and other resources, and where priorities were focused on much shorter-term and applied forms of staff development. The party, not just for philosophy, but also for the disciplined study of psychology and sociology and history, was over – or, at least, so it seemed.

In certain ways, nevertheless, and from a much reduced base, the discipline has continued to thrive. The Philosophy of Education Society is perhaps more buoyant than ever, as illustrated by its successful annual conferences, its world-leading *Journal of Philosophy of Education* (JOPE), its *Impact* series, its graduate summer school and its local events, organised through its 16 branches. The JOPE has been transformed over this period from an original publication that included about 80 pages of conference papers each year to a prestigious international journal with about 800 pages of high-quality articles each year, as well as a spin-off series of books. Following a succession of successful presentations and symposia at the annual conference of the British Educational Research Association, a BERA Special Interest Group in Philosophy of Education was established in 2007. The European Educational Research Association had already had a thriving network for the previous ten years and this, like the Biennial Conference of the International Network of Philosophers of Education, featured regular and significant contributions from UK philosophers of education. The strength of the international networks of philosophers of education has indeed been one of the sustaining forces for the discipline in the UK. Though there is only one Chair in the UK specifically allocated to philosophy of education (at the London Institute of Education), philosophers of education have nevertheless managed to be elected to chairs of a generic nature, or on personal merit. A new generation of philosophers of education is already making important contributions to the discipline and to educational policy and practice. So, in spite of the systematic exclusion of philosophy of education from initial teacher education and the limited scope for the discipline in Master's level programmes under the current funding regimes, the discipline has maintained and indeed developed considerable vitality – partly because its reputation runs high internationally and programmes continue to attract international students.

The current disciplinary infrastructure of philosophy of education in the UK

The important contributions, current and future, from philosophy of education to education and education research do not, however, always reflect a thriving infrastructure. Rather, overall, UK philosophy of education is becoming an area of work where human resource is scattered, under-funded and often swimming against the currents of postgraduate training programmes. Before reflecting on the future potential of philosophy of education in the UK, we shall comment briefly on several indicators of the current state of its disciplinary infrastructure, including: the size and scale of 'human resource'; their publication outlets; the breadth and nature of their work; their audiences and funding sources; and the education of future contributors to the field. We will use the UK Research Assessment Exercise (RAE) and the JOPE as the best available, albeit partial, sources of data we could find.

Contributors to philosophy of education

Some idea of where 'active' philosophers of education in the UK are located may be gained by analysing the authorship of articles published in the leading journal of the field, the JOPE. Of the 281 articles published from 1 January 2001 to 31 December 2007, 121 had UK-based (co-)authors, of whom 106 were in England, ten in Scotland, three in Wales and two in Northern Ireland. Of these, 89 articles had authors based in university departments of education (rather than, for example, in other HEI departments or other sectors). Most of these authors were in universities established before 1992 – including a 19 per cent share of the total from the London Institute of Education.

Further details of activity in the subject may be pieced together using RAE data, although they enable only a partial picture, for a number of reasons. First, it is possible that some people working in philosophy of education were not included in the submissions. Second, a small number of people working in philosophy of education were entered in the RAE, but under other subject areas. Finally, some philosophers of education who were entered under Education combined philosophical work with empirical work – and some or all of the publications they entered were in the form of empirical writing. We counted them as philosophers of education, provided that at least one of their submitted outputs was clearly in this field. There are other cases where it was difficult to judge quite whether work in the wider field of, for example, social theory was strictly philosophical. There were only a small number of such cases and we have tended to be inclusive when in doubt.

With these reservations, the picture provided by the RAE 2008 shows 63 active contributors to philosophy of education in the whole of the UK, based in 27 (23 in England, four in Scotland) university departments of education. Of these departments, only eight (one of which in Scotland) have three or more writers in philosophy of education (i.e. by a very modest standard, 'critical mass'). A further 59 have none. This picture may have changed since the RAE census date (October 2007, for RAE 2008).

Publication outlets

Again, the RAE 2008 submissions provide fairly recent data on types of output and publication outlets for philosophy of education in the UK. Some 199 outputs that were identifiable as philosophical were submitted to RAE 2008, and about 300 to RAE 2001. The 199 outputs submitted in 2008 which are recognisably philosophical in character included 33 books, four monographs, 15 chapters in books, four reports and 143 journal articles (scattered over 50 journals, among which the JOPE had the largest share, followed by the *British Journal of Educational Studies*). Again, we have to be careful how we interpret this information. For example, some universities are reported to have advised staff to submit work published in international refereed journals wherever possible, so these results may not reflect the wider pattern of publication.

For comparison, over the period of time covered by the RAE 2008, JOPE, the main journal in the field, published 253 articles (excluding reviews, prefaces and brief introductions, translations of mainstream philosophy texts, as well as chapters in monographs published as special issues, which were counted as a single paper). Of these, 83 articles (33 per cent of the total) had authors based in UK HE departments of education, continuing education and professional development, or lifelong learning.

Substantive topics

The submissions to RAE also give an idea of main research interests and substantive contributions of philosophers of education over the past eight years. We coded all papers identifiable as philosophical in the RAE 2008 and RAE 2001 exercises on the basis of their titles and brief descriptions (mostly under 100 words), as included in the submissions; and we did so independently of each other on separate batches of papers, albeit using a common coding frame, so there is space for improvement in the reliability of coding. In both exercises, a large proportion (around 30 per cent) of the papers submitted addressed issues of education and values (moral, aesthetic, religious and spiritual, democracy, multi-culturalism, intellectual, environmental). We also noted a remarkable (more than doubling) increase, from 2001 to 2008, in the proportion of publications on religious and spiritual education and faith schools; on democracy, liberalism, community and citizenship; and on multi-culturalism, diversity, pluralism and identities.

This distribution is strikingly different from what we found by coding in a similar way the 617 papers (excluding most editorials, as well as the review essays) published in the JOPE over a 20-year period, from 1988 to 2008 (which also almost coincides with the history of the RAE). This difference may be indicative of the perceptions of the RAE among the community(-ies) of philosophers of education. In the journal, the distribution is much more even, and the more traditional philosophical themes, such as the aims and meaning of education and moral education, take a more central position. Philosophy of educational research had a more prominent place in the journal than in the RAE 2001 descriptors – a situation which has changed by RAE 2008, in the submissions to which philosophy of education research has the largest single share in the list of topics. Readership data from the publishers Wiley-Blackwell (whose support in gaining access to these data is gratefully acknowledged) show that, among the ten most downloaded UK-authored JOPE articles in 2007, four covered issues in the philosophy of educational research; two, moral education; two, difference and equality; and one each on well-being and philosophy and education.

Approaches

The most detailed data available to us on how philosophers describe their work or 'approach' come from RAE 2001, because of the unique feature of that exercise of requiring all entrants to specify (in a designated 'text field') the main approach or methodology used in each paper submitted. This requirement posed, somewhat unsurprisingly, particular problems to the philosophy submissions, and often generated very ambiguous descriptors of their approach. An overwhelming proportion of the papers described their approach as generally 'philosophical' (of which some further specified that the work consisted mostly of 'analysis', 'critique' and 'review and synthesis' of literature and evidence). A further 9 per cent combined such approach with empirical work. Some 14 per cent described their work as 'cross-disciplinary' in approach. A final 8 per cent described their main approach by reference to named authors or schools of thought, which they either took forward, or challenged and responded to, including post-structuralism, Popper, Wittgenstein, Habermas, Hegel, Heidegger, Kant and Marx.

'Approach' or 'methodology' was not a required field in the submissions to RAE 2008. However, in the 'text boxes' accompanying each item of output entered, some people made reference to their methodology, usually in support of a claim for the rigour of the piece of work. These responses echoed the descriptors recorded in RAE 2001.

Audiences

The papers submitted to RAE 2001 claimed to be almost equally aimed at an audience of practitioners and researchers (37–38 per cent, although the frequencies calculated were not adjusted by taking into account the order in which different types of audience were listed in each submission). A further 20 per cent of mentions of intended audience consisted of policy-makers and politicians, and managers and administrators; while work aimed at students and at the general public (including parents) only accounted for 5 per cent of the total. There was no equivalent to these data in the submissions to RAE 2008.

Further information comes from circulation and readership data of the JOPE, which show an international audience. In terms of institutional access (through both traditional subscriptions and library consortia), UK institutions accounted for about 3 per cent of the total in 2007, in comparison to the totals for Europe (28 per cent), USA (17 per cent), Australia and New Zealand (4 per cent), and Japan (4 per cent). Among traditional subscriptions only, the UK's share rose to 16 per cent, i.e. the third largest regional share, after Europe (23 per cent) and the USA (18 per cent). The shares of institutional access for the UK and Europe had decreased from 2005 to 2007, while institutional access from the USA and from Japan had increased since 2005 (largely due to increased access via consortia in these regions).

Funding

There is no established major UK funding organisation supporting work in philosophy of education. Over the past year the Economic and Social Research Council (ESRC) and the Arts and Humanities Research Council (AHRC) made no award on topics of philosophy of education, except for the occasional seminar series or, indirectly, the review of the epistemological basis of educational research findings, led by David Bridges and commissioned by the Teaching and Learning Research Programme (TLRP). There has been some funding from charities, but we were unable to find detailed and systematic data on topics and the level of funding. The Philosophy of Education Society of Great Britain (PESGB) has also made small grants and awards. However, overall it seems that work in philosophy of education is generally an indirectly or internally funded activity, either something that philosophers do as part of their job, or something that they do privately, or on the back of external funding for empirical work, in which philosophers of education may be engaged and on which philosophical thinking is brought to bear. This raises questions about whether, in the current era of research metrics and assessment of performance, philosophy of education will remain an attractive career choice for new researchers, or a strategic area of work to nurture and develop for HE departments of education.

Capacity building

In 2005, the ESRC issued a set of revised guidelines for postgraduate training, which included a requirement for all disciplines to provide the students with a background in, at least, the epistemological 'positions' that form the context for research in their field. In addition, and specifically for the field of education (unlike some other fields, such as demography), the guidelines required that 'in addition to the generic research training, the student in Education should have training in philosophical issues in educational research' – including epistemological and ontological issues relevant to education and to education research, as well as an understanding of the ethics and politics of research (ESRC, 2005, F5, 3.1).

However, on our evidence, relatively few departments are equipped to provide the contribution of the philosophy of educational research to research methods courses required by the ESRC guidelines. According to Pring (2007), the ESRC requirement is 'honoured more in the letter than in the spirit' in the general preparation of postgraduate education researchers, as, more often than not, the philosophical training on offer to research students in education consists in fact of philosophy of social science courses in other departments in the same university (e.g. sociology). Out of the 15 (of a total of 22) departments with full ESRC recognition for their postgraduate research training provision which had responded to a survey by Pring in 2001, only seven had an identifiable philosophy component (mostly consisting of research ethics). Our informal, and less systematic, survey of 16 university departments of education with high research rankings in November 2007 showed no indications of improvement.

A crucial issue for the development of philosophical preparation in education research and in teacher education is that, as the RAE 2008 figures presented above indicated, very few departments have the capacity to foster and develop new philosophers of education and to put in place appropriate teaching and supervision provision for them. In addition, a wider context of excessive emphasis on experimental designs, quantifiable outputs and 'what works' questions (welcome as they may be in some areas and for some purposes) may have discouraged young researchers from engaging philosophically with issues of practice and research, and from publishing philosophical papers and monographs. Standish (2007b) goes as far as describing the current research training culture as one that reflects an 'impoverished' conception of education research (p. 340). Beginning philosophers may struggle to fulfil the requirements, and reap the benefits, of short-term training schemes that allow little time for independent reading and reflection and for learning as a form of apprenticeship, or immersion in a research culture (see Suissa, 2006). Researcher development programmes need to allow for less instrumental ways of initiation of researchers in the field.

Philosophy of education: looking forward

Even cursory examination of, for example, the recent pages of the JOPE provides warnings against any attempt to predict the future direction of writing in philosophy of education. It is remarkably diverse, and the originality of many of its contributions is indicated by the unpredictability of the philosophical sources and educational themes which they bring into play and their sideways takes on the subject matter. While a fairly solid group of contributions address issues which are central in contemporary educational policy discourse, they are certainly not ruled by the external agenda, so this too fails to provide a very helpful predictor of what will appear in the coming months or years.

Nevertheless, in September 1997 the Philosophy of Education Society initiated a major review of its position in the British and international educational community. This recognised a number of key relationships which the philosophy of education community needed to develop – and these may provide some clues as to future developments. We shall conclude this chapter with a brief discussion of each of these in turn.

Philosophy of education and the teacher-education communities

We have already observed how the fortunes of the subject have risen and then waned in the last 40 years in fairly direct relationship with the place that it has or has not occupied in the education of teachers. (Of course the change of discourse from 'education' to 'training' itself signalled a conscious narrowing of the cognitive perspective on the practice of teaching.) A major priority for the discipline must be to re-engage with that practice and with the teacher education which underpins it. To this end the Society will be seeking closer engagement with bodies like the Universities Council for the Education of Teachers (UCET), the General Teaching Councils, and (in England) the Teacher Development Agency. The new Master's level Postgraduate Certificates of Education ought to provide an opportunity not just for training new teachers in empirical research methods but also for introducing them (at least) to the disciplined form of educational enquiry which is philosophy. The increasing number of students on BA programmes in Education (i.e. degree programmes which allow the study of Education without the requirements laid down for practical training in teaching) provide another opportunity, if university departments are prepared to seize it, for initiating some early study of philosophical issues and resources applied to Education.

Philosophy of education and the wider educational research communities

Since, in particular, the special issue of the *Cambridge Journal of Education* on 'Philosophy and educational research' edited by Bridges *et al.* (1997), there has been a succession of publications through which philosophers of education have offered perspectives on key issues in educational research methodology, ethics and application (see, for example, Pring, 2000; Bridges, 2003; McNamee and Bridges, 2002; Oancea, 2005, 2007; and Biesta and Burbules, 2003), but these are easily ignored by research practitioners locked into the modern treadmills of research productivity or the requirements of sponsors ruled by a naive technocratic positivism.

Attracting the interest of education research communities, again, has its institutional requirements: for example, engagement of philosophers of education with the mainstream educational research associations like the BERA and the Scottish Educational Research Association and their Special Interest Groups (and not just the Philosophy of Education Special Interest Group, though its establishment and presence is also important). It also invites scholarly contributions to the generic educational research journals and other speciality journals, not just to those that primarily address the philosophy of education community itself.

There are many in the wider research community who are themselves intrigued by the complexities and problematics of the research endeavour and many who do indeed take the wider intellectual context of their work seriously, people who see theory as a friend rather than an extraneous indulgence, people who engage with their work philosophically even if they do not describe themselves as philosophers – and these provide natural allies whom the professional philosophical community should embrace.

Philosophy of education and the 'mainstream' philosophy communities

We described in our opening section examples of the intimate inter-relationships between philosophy of education and what we are still inclined to refer to as 'mainstream philosophy', even if this seems to acknowledge a distance we would prefer not to be there. Intellectually, this relationship is an extremely close one, as we hope we have illustrated. Institutionally there is still something of a divide, which the Philosophy of Education Society is anxious to break down.

Such relationships are not always easy. Too often when 'mainstream' philosophers contribute to debates about education, they seem to lose all philosophical caution and fall back on the prejudices formed by their own experience as a pupil or student, or as a teacher. Such encounters serve to demonstrate the importance of contributions to educational debate *and*, we suggest, philosophical enquiry, of people who bring not just philosophical scholarship but also familiarity with the wider field of critical and empirical educational research and of seriously examined experience.

Philosophy of education and the educational policy community

A recurring theme of discussion in educational research communities at large has reflected, on the one hand, the frustration of policy-makers with the failure of educational researchers to provide them with the answers they needed, and, on the other hand, the frustration among the wider educational research communities with the failure of the policy-makers to take any notice of what it has been contributing. Philosophy of education is party to both sides of this frustration.

A recent issue of the JOPE featured papers issuing from a rare ESRC/ TLRP-sponsored piece of work on the epistemological bases of educational policy, which has extensive discussion of the relationship between research, scholarship and policy (Bridges *et al.*, 2008). In addition, we have already noted the particular initiative taken by the PESGB through its *Impact* pamphlets (e.g. White, 2007). These are serious pieces of work written at a length and in a style intended to make them reasonably accessible to non-philosophers working in the area of educational policy. The pamphlets are launched at a symposium in which the author is joined by people from policy arena and the press.

Individual philosophers of education will, of course, also contribute more directly through their personal participation in regional and national policy communities. It has been said, with relevance to technology transfer to industry, that knowledge transfer 'works best on two legs', i.e. by intellectually equipped people taking their academic insights into working environments – and this probably applies as forcefully to educational research and scholarship as to any other field.

This is, of course, not a new observation: over 2,000 years ago (here is the tradition again) Plato explained to his 'dear Glaucon' that 'there will be no end to the troubles of the states, or indeed … of humanity itself till philosophers become kings in this world or till those we now call kings and rulers really and truly become philosophers' (Richards, 1960, pp. 473c–d). We live in hope.

References

Bain, A. (1897) *Education as a science* (New York, Appleton).

Biesta, G.J.J. and Burbules, N.C. (2003) *Pragmatism and educational research* (Lanham, MD, Rowman & Littlefield).

Blake, N., Smeyers, P., Smith, R. and Standish, P. (2000) *Education in an age of nihilism* (London, Falmer Press).

Blake, N., Smeyers, P., Smith, R. and Standish, P. (eds) (2003) *The Blackwell guide to the philosophy of education* (Oxford, Blackwell).

Bridges, D. (1997) Philosophy and educational research: a reconsideration of episte-mological boundaries, *Cambridge Journal of Education*, 27(2), 177–189.

Bridges, D. (2003) *'Fiction written under oath'? Essays in philosophy and educational research* (Dordrecht, Kluwer).

Bridges, D., Carr, W. and Griffiths, M. (eds) (1997) Philosophy and educational research, special issue, *Cambridge Journal of Education*, 27(2).

Bridges, D., Smeyers, P. and Smith, R.D. (eds) (2008) Evidence based education policy: What evidence? What basis? Whose policy?, *Journal of Philosophy of Education*, 42, supplementary issue 1.

Carr, D. (2006) The moral roots of citizenship: towards a virtue ethical reconcili-ation of principle and character in education for effective citizenship, *Journal of Moral Education*, 35(4), 443–456.

Carr, D. (2007) Virtue ethics and the influence of Aristotle, in D. Fasko and W. Willis (eds) *Contemporary philosophical and psychological perspectives on moral develop-ment and education* (Creskill, NJ, Hampton Press).

Carr, D., Halstead, M.J. and Pring, R. (2008) *Liberalism, education and schooling: essays by T.H. McLaughlin* (Exeter, Imprint).

Carr, W. (2004) Philosophy and education, *Journal of Philosophy of Education*, 38(1), 55–73.

Carr, W. (2006) Philosophy, methodology and action research, *Journal of Philosophy of Education*, 40(4), 421–435.

Cavell, S. (1979) *The claim of reason: Wittgenstein, skepticism, morality, and tragedy* (New York, Oxford University Press).

Cavell, S. (2004) The *Investigations'* everyday aesthetics of itself, in J. Gibson and W. Huemer (eds) *The literary Wittgenstein* (London, Routledge), 21–33.

Davis, A. (2005) Learning and the social nature of mental powers, *Educational Philo-sophy and Theory*, 37, 635–647.

Dewey, J. (1916) *Democracy and education: an introduction to the philosophy of education* (New York, Macmillan).

Dunne, J. (2002) Alasdair MacIntyre on education: in dialogue with Joe Dunne, *Journal of Philosophy of Education*, 36(1), 1–19.

Elliott, J. (1987) Educational theory, practical philosophy and action research, *British Journal of Educational Studies*, 25,149–169.

Elliott, J. (2000) Doing action research, doing philosophy, *Prospero*, 6, 82–100.

ESRC (2005) *Postgraduate training guidelines* (Swindon, ESRC).

Halstead, J.M. and McLaughlin, T.H. (eds) (2004) *Philosophy, education and compara-tive education: a special issue of Comparative Education*, 40(4), 467–594.

Hand, M.J. (2003) The meaning of spiritual education, *Oxford Review of Education*, 29(3), 391–401.

Hardie, C.D. (1942/1962) *Truth and fallacy in educational theory* (Columbia, Teachers College Columbia with Cambridge University Press).

Haydon, G.D. (2004) Values education: sustaining the ethical environment, *Journal of Moral Education*, 33(2), 115–129.

Hirst, P. (1966) Educational theory, in J.W. Tibble (ed.) *The study of education* (London, Routledge & Kegan Paul).

MacIntyre, A. (1985) *After virtue* (London, Duckworth).

McLaughlin, T.H. (1995) Wittgenstein, education and religion, in P. Smeyers and J. Marshall (eds) *Philosophy and education: accepting Wittgenstein's challenge* (Dor-drecht, Kluwer).

McLaughlin, T.H. and Halstead, J.M. (1999) Education in character and virtue, in J.M. Halstead and T.H. McLaughlin (eds) *Education in morality* (London and New York, Routledge).

McNamee, M. and Bridges, D. (eds) (2002) *The ethics of educational research* (Oxford, Blackwell).

Oakeshott, M. (1962) The voice of poetry in the conversation of mankind, in *Rationalism in politics* (London, Methuen).

Oancea, A. (2005) Criticisms of educational research: key topics and levels of analysis, *British Educational Research Journal*, 31(2), 157–183.

Oancea, A. (2007) From Procrustes to Proteus: trends and practices in the assessment of education research, *International Journal for Research and Methods in Education*, 30(3), 243–269.

Oancea, A. and Furlong, J. (2007) Expressions of excellence and the assessment of applied and practice-based research, *Research Papers in Education*, 22(2), 119–137.

Peters, R.S. (1966) The philosophy of education, in J.W. Tibble (ed.) *The study of education* (London, Routledge & Kegan Paul).

Peters, R.S. (ed.) (1967) *The concept of education* (London, Routledge & Kegan Paul).

Phillips, D.C. (2007) The contested nature of empirical research (and why philosophy offers little help), in D. Bridges and R.D. Smith (eds) *Philosophy, methodology and educational research* (Oxford, Blackwell).

Pring, R. (2000) *Philosophy of educational research* (London and New York, Continuum).

Pring, R. (2001) The virtues and vices of an educational researcher, *Journal of Philosophy of Education*, 35(3), 407–422.

Pring, R. (2007) Reclaiming philosophy for educational research, *Educational Review*, 59(3), 315–330.

Pring, R., Hayward, G., Hodgson, A., Johnson, J., Keep, E., Oancea, A., Rees, G., Spours, K. and Wilde, S. (2009) *14–19 education and training: looking to the future* (Oxford, Routledge).

Richards, I.A. (ed.) (1960) *Plato's Republic* (Cambridge, Cambridge University Press).

Saito, N. (2006) Philosophy as education and education as philosophy: democracy and education from Dewey to Cavell, *Journal of Philosophy of Education*, 40(3), 345–356.

Smeyers, P. (2006) 'What it makes sense to say': education, philosophy and Peter Winch on social science, *Journal of Philosophy of Education*, 40(4), 463–485.

Smeyers, P. and Burbules, N. (eds) (2008) Wittgenstein's legacy for education, *Educational Philosophy and Theory*, 40(5).

Smeyers, P., Smith, R. and Standish, P. (2007) *The therapy of education* (Basingstoke, Palgrave Macmillan).

Standish, P. (2006) Uncommon schools: Stanley Cavell and the teaching of Walden, *Studies in Philosophy of Education*, 25(1–2), 145–157.

Standish, P. (2007a) Rival conceptions of the philosophy of education, *Ethics and Education*, 2(2), 159–171.

Standish, P. (2007b) Claims of philosophy: education and research, *Educational Review*, 59(3), 331–341.

Suissa, J. (2006) Shovelling smoke? The experience of being a philosopher on an educational research training programme, *Journal of Philosophy of Education*, 40(4), 547–562.

Tibble, J.W. (1966) *The study of education* (London, Routledge & Kegan Paul).

White, J.P. (2007) *What schools are for and why* (London, Philosophy of Education Society of Great Britain, Impact Publication).

Wilson, J. (1965) *Thinking with concepts* (Cambridge, Cambridge University Press).

Wilson, J. (1998) Philosophy and educational research: a reply to David Bridges *et al.*, *Cambridge Journal of Education*, 28(3), 129–133.

Winch, C. (2000) *Education, work and social capital* (London, Routledge).

Winch, P. (1958) *The idea of a social science and its relation to philosophy* (London, Routledge & Kegan Paul).

Wittgenstein, L. (1958) *Philosophical investigations*, trans. G.E.M. Anscombe (Oxford, Blackwell).

Zagzebski, L.T. (1996) *Virtues of the mind: an inquiry into the nature of virtue and the ethical foundations of knowledge* (Cambridge, Cambridge University Press).

5   The history of education

A curious case?

Joyce Goodman and Ian Grosvenor

Curious, *adj.* anxious to learn: inquisitive: showing great care or nicety (*obs*): solicitous: skilfully made: singular: rare – *n.* **curiosity** state or quality of being curious: inquisitiveness: that which is curious; anything rare or unusual.

(Chambers, 1972)

Introduction

The backdrop to this chapter is a symposium at the European Conference on Educational Research (ECER) 2008 in Gothenburg that highlighted the challenges of discussing intellectual fields and subsequently raised for us the relation of intellectual fields to processes of disciplinarisation. Discussion at the symposium ranged over the boundaries of intellectual networks, how intellectual networks are fluid yet nonetheless have a core, methodologies for tracing intellectual networks, and theoretical frames through which to view, analyse and challenge how intellectual networks are written about and theorised (Verbruggen and Carlier, 2008; Goodman, 2008a). As authors, we 'recognised' our practice as historians of education over the last 20 years in the discussion that ensued. We have developed our practice in networks that have drawn together core members while being unbounded and reaching outward to other networks and across national borders, a position which engenders our particular orientations to history of education.[1] We acknowledge the importance of intellectual networks in the construction of history of education as discipline, in its ebbs and flows, and its continued development in what we term *moments of organic growth*. The ECER symposium also formed a catalyst for understanding what we term *moments of insecurity* in history of education. These occur when scholars articulate insecurities around the place of their discipline in the broader discipline of education. Here we unpack how those *moments of insecurity* have been framed. Analysis of *moments of insecurity* and of *moments of organic growth* provide the basis of our arguments about the contributions of history of education to the development of education in the future and underpin our recommendations for how future researchers can be produced.

There has been considerable debate around the question of history of education as a discipline (Depaepe, 1993; Peim, 2001; Lowe, 2002). In this chapter we focus our gaze on scholarship that deals with education in historical settings. We do not begin with 'a settled definition' of history of education (Fitzgerald and Gunter, 2005). Rather, our focus on *moments of curiosity* signifies the blurring of disciplinary boundaries and of institutional and non-institutional structures. Further, as our concern is essentially with the present and future status of the discipline we have chosen not to focus directly on past achievements. In the first section of the chapter we use a loose form of content analysis of a limited selection of journal articles and conference presentations between 2004 and the end of 2008 to exemplify instances of current contributions to the study of education in the past. We draw on these instances and on the analysis of journal content and intellectual networks in the argument that follows. We acknowledge that selections of this type are always 'an interpretation, a conscious reworking of the past' and in this case 'a rhetorical attempt to re-shape current thinking', written purposively 'with both hindsight and foresight' (Hamilton, 2002, p. 144). This is followed by documenting *moments of insecurity* alongside *moments of organic growth*. Third, we identify *moments of curiosity* and the new areas of research that they have produced which have emerged alongside *moments of insecurity*. Finally, we look to the future of history of education.

A survey of current key themes in history of education

Overviews of international history of education journals at moments of transition to new journal editors have charted both the substantive foci of journals and methodological and theoretical approaches employed (Goodman and Martin, 2004; Depaepe and Simon, 1996; Lowe, 2004; Coles, 2008; Fitzgerald and Gunter, 2008). While assigning content categories to journal articles is not straightforward, key themes around the history of UK education by UK authors in UK-located journals between 2004 and 2008 can be identified.[2] Prominent themes in *History of Education* (HoE) include education for women and girls and the activities of women educators (Chiu, 2008); history of higher education (Aiston, 2005); religion, morality and citizenship (Wright, 2008); pedagogy – including the ideas of progressive educators (Nawrotzki, 2006); secondary education (Goodman, 2007; McCulloch, 2006a, 2006b); disability (Brown, 2005; Dale, 2007; Armstrong, 2007); colonialism and empire (Oldern, 2008); popular and non-formal education (Woodin, 2005); health and welfare (Sheldon, 2007); elementary education (Middleton, 2005); teachers and teacher training (Gardner, 2007); curriculum (Soler, 2006); and psychology (Hirsch, 2005). While the focus of some UK writers is on education overseas, the majority of UK writers concern themselves with England, with some coverage of Scotland, Wales and Ireland. Chronological coverage in HoE runs from the sixteenth to the twentieth centuries, though authors predominantly focus on the nineteenth and twentieth centuries (for an example of eighteenth-century research, see Dick and Watts, 2008). The introduction of a feature on sources and interpretations in HoE in 2004[3] fostered a focus on historiography and methodology. UK authors have contributed particularly to methodological work around visual (Grosvenor, 2007) and biographical approaches (Martin, 2007). Interest in theory and methodology has also been fostered by special issues of the journal (Burke, 2005d).

Key themes in the *Journal of Educational Administration and History* (JEAH) are identified by Janet Coles as national policy, changes in the nineteenth and early twentieth centuries, national and local reformers and interests, religious interests in educational provision, men as reformers, and papers reflecting the colonial legacy, with most work focusing on secondary and higher education (Coles, 2008). Consistent with the orientation of JEAH towards educational administration, the majority of contributions from UK scholars are located around formal education. The editors point to a reduction in the emphasis on the provision of schooling and in articles concerned with biography and to an increase in articles concerned with feminist issues, gender, history and historiography (Fitzgerald and Gunter, 2008). More explicit theorisation, debates about policy process and about the gendered nature of leadership or administration in more recent material (Fitzgerald and Gunter, 2008) resonates with HoE's increasing emphasis on sources and interpretations and historiography.

Publications in UK journals by authors located outside the UK also shape UK history of education. The majority of articles in HoE by these scholars come from Europe (24), including six from Ireland. This is followed by USA (21), Australia and New Zealand (13), Canada (four), Asia (five) and Israel (four). In articles with a primary history of education focus in JEAH, in contrast, there are two from Ireland. The majority of JEAH contributions from outside the UK come from Australia and New Zealand (16), followed by USA (eight), Asia (four), Canada (three), Israel (two) and South Africa (one).

The relationship between conference presentations and special issues of journals drawn from symposia and conferences held outside the UK forms part of a two-way intellectual exchange. A small contingent of UK scholars regularly present at the International Standing Conference for the History of Education (ISCHE) primarily around education for women and girls and the activities of women educators, religion, morality and citizenship, pedagogy (including progressivism), the visual and technologies (including the media). A smaller number of scholars attend conferences of the Australian and New Zealand History of Education Society (ANZHES), including the joint ANZHES/UK History of Education Society conference held in Sydney in 2008. However, only one UK scholar has contributed (and in 2003) to the (Australian and New Zealand) *History of Education Review* and this article resulted from the joint History of Education Society UK/Australia and New Zealand History of Education Society conference held in the UK at Swansea in 2002 (McDermid, 2003). AERA has been a focus for a small number of historians of education. Again, this has led to little publication in journals located in America or Canada. In the last five years there has been one article originating in the UK in *History of Education Quarterly* (Byford, 2008) and none in *Historical Studies in Education*.

The key journal outside the UK for UK historians of education is *Paedagogica Historica*, which has direct links with ISCHE. Of the 188 articles published between 2004 and the end of 2008, 23 are by UK authors, of which two are by philosophers of education addressing methodological issues (Smith, 2008; Standish, 2008). If we exclude those articles directly linked to the ISCHE conferences, key themes addressed include history of school design and environment (Armitage, 2005; Goodman, 2005; Peim, 2005), the materiality of schooling (Burke, 2005a; Grosvenor, 2005), gender relations (Martin, 2008; Goodman, 2008b), educational sciences (Aldrich, 2004; Brehony, 2004; Lawn, 2004), past childhoods (Grosvenor, 2007; Grosvenor, 2009; Fink, 2008) and empire, postcolonialism and social change in history of education (Watts, 2009; Myers, 2009). The majority of these articles addressed new ways or new sources for understanding and conceptualising the educational past.

UK scholars contribute to the wider domain of history through the affiliation of ISCHE to the Congress of Historical Sciences, and more recently through the European Social Science History Congress. The small number of scholars who have published in both history of education and history journals demonstrates that publication in both UK-based history of education and history journals is comparatively rare (Martin, 2005; Myers and Brown, 2005; Jacobs, 2007), but is most prevalent in scholarship on the history of women's education. *Women's History Review* included a special issue entitled *Earning and Learning* (Pullin and Spencer, 2004). The *Journal of Historical Sociology* carried four articles concerned with special education, sexuality and professionalisation. Analysis of *Past and Present* and *Journal of Contemporary History* revealed authors with an interest in education in historical settings but no articles between 2004 and 2008 where history of education was the prime focus.

The survey of journals for this chapter included five general UK educational journals: *British Education Research Journal*, *British Journal of Educational Studies*, *Educational Review*, *Oxford Review of Education* (ORE) and *Cambridge Journal of Education*. There are historical articles or articles with a strong historical dimension in all five journals (e.g. Furlong, 2004; Taylor, 2005; White, 2005; Ruddock and Fielding, 2006; Smith and Exley, 2006; Jephcote and Davies, 2007; Thomas *et al.*, 2007). However, several of these articles were in special themed issues which offered an historical perspective – The University and Public Education (Judge, 2006); Blair's Legacy (Walford, 2008) – and only three articles are by researchers who would describe themselves primarily as historians of education (McCulloch, 2006b; Richardson, 2007a; Vickers in Kan *et al.*, 2007).

A number of trends are apparent from this survey exercise. First, a growing interest among UK historians of education in new methodological approaches, and in enquiry focused around the 'black box' of the school that pays attention to space, place, the visual and the body and which is geared to understanding the everyday experience of classrooms, pupils and teachers. Second, there is a focus on the education of women and girls and the activities of women educators. In her scholarly overview of the 'gendering' of history of education, Ruth Watts concluded that without being unique among modern historians, historians of gender and women's history have been in the vanguard and have stimulated much thought among all kinds of historians (Watts, 2005). Third, an interdisciplinary focus that blurs boundaries; fourth, a more recent and developing interest from UK scholars in transnational approaches (Lawn, 2004); fifth, a tendency of historians of education to confine themselves overly to specialised journals and a predetermined audience; and finally, the readiness of educational researchers who are not historians of education to adopt an historical dimension in their work. What the survey does not show is the value placed by the academic community on the quality of what has been produced by UK historians of education. The Subject Overview Report for Education in the 2008 Research Assessment Exercise (RAE, 2008) commented on the 'original and high quality theoretical, scholarly and critical work in ... history of education'. This high-quality research has been published despite concerns (*moments of insecurity*) about the place of history of education as discipline, which have been debated.

Moments of insecurity

Moments of insecurity in history of education have been signposted by a number of UK authors and have been mirrored by historians of education in Australia, New Zealand and the USA. This Anglo-Saxon signposting is framed through a dominant paradigm that suggests that (1) there is a recognisable core that constitutes history of education that is under attack and (2) that in response to external forces of change, a concerted strategic decision is necessary to put in place something 'different' in the discipline, or for historians of education to locate themselves 'differently' in relation to contemporary education. *Moments of insecurity* flowed in particular from the aftermath of the debates provoked by David Hargreaves, James Tooley and Chris Woodhead in the late 1990s around the contention that the 'gap between researchers and practitioners' constituted the 'fatal flaw in educational research' (Hargreaves, 1996; Tooley and Darby, 1998; Woodhead, 1998). The 'Hargreaves debate' coincided with a range of structural changes in the institutionalisation of teacher education, educational studies and higher education that held ramifications for the disciplines of education and were instrumental in defining parameters of debate in the run up to RAE 2001 (Lowe, 2002).

Manoeuvres around what constituted educational research around the 'Hargreaves' debate' in advance of RAE 2001 are illustrated by Gary McCulloch's defence of the disciplines of education in response to Michael Bassey's contentions about educational research. In 1999 Bassey distinguished between 'critical enquiry aimed at informing educational judgements and decisions in order to improve educational action' and disciplinary research conducted in educational settings that aimed 'critically to inform understandings of phenomena pertinent to the discipline in educational settings' (Bassey, 1999). In a robust defence, McCulloch argued that on the basis of this somewhat rigid distinction a dependence on the disciplines could be seen both as unduly theoretical and tenuous in its connections with educational concerns and as restrictive in holding back the growth of an independent field of enquiry. For McCulloch, grounding in the disciplines was essential as a means of understanding educational theories and practices, given that the disciplines stimulated a pluralist and eclectic approach to the study of education. He contrasted this pluralism with the notion of a unitary and autonomous field of knowledge represented as 'educational research' (McCulloch, 2002).

William Richardson (2002) argued that the heterogeneity in research techniques that had enriched and enlarged the field of education studies had done little to clarify its epistemology. For Richardson, debate around educational studies demonstrated that the conceptual underpinnings of educational research remained 'uncertain and fragile' with 'a lack of accepted theoretical underpinning for educational studies'. What was needed most, argued Richardson, was 'a conceptual framework for education in which theory and practice are fused and closely related to a broad understanding of the workings of society' that was 'neither imperious or doctrinaire'. In his view, this was necessary 'to release educational studies from its problematic status as an integrated field and to offer educators a disciplinary framework of firm pedagogic principles within which to practice their craft, consolidate their values, and prosecute their ideals' (Richardson, 2002). Richardson's more recent work suggests a history of education in which 'traditionalists', whose work is 'painstaking', and 'scientific' and constitutes 'expert history', are counter-posed to postmodernists and post-structuralists whose 'lumpen condemnation' constitutes a threat by questioning the very history project itself (Richardson, 2007b). This proposes distinctions that are absolute (see Aldrich's 2003 comments on Richardson, 1999), whereas shades of grey characterise debate. It is an interpretation that frames feminist (Goodman, 2008b; Martin, 2008) or overtly political approaches to the past (Simon, 1965, 1971, 1991; Jones, 2003) as equally problematic for the traditional history project, however that might be defined.

In surveying history of education in Australia, Campbell and Sherington reiterate the view that the flowering of history of education associated with the new social history harboured challenges for the discipline (Campbell and Sherington, 2002). Their analysis exemplifies the common response of a call to reconnect with teachers and teaching practice by a return to histories of the classroom and by making historical studies essential to the development of good policy. The return to present-minded 'usefulness' is not an approach uniformly endorsed. In arguing that it is the historian of education's duty not to abuse or misuse the record of the past to advance contemporary causes, Aldrich cites Depaepe's view that:

> The relevance of the history of education for educators of the 21st century can in my view only be the relevance of an intrinsic nature, i.e. one that is critical and inevitably unconformable ... For what can the professional competence of the practical educator consist other than in critical reflection on his [sic] activities past and present.
>
> (Aldrich, 2003, p. 136, citing Depaepe, 2001, p. 640; see also Fendler, 2008)

The debate about present-mindedness (utility) and the conditions of the production of the discourse of insecurity both lie partly within conditions of intellectual production and institutional change.

There has been institutional stability as well as disappearance and growth. Since its formation as the London Day Training College, the Institute of Education has been a constant institutional location for history of education, under the leadership of successive professors of education and latterly through the establishment of the Brian Simon chair. Roehampton has a longstanding reputation for research around Froebel and Early Childhood. But the removal of history of education modules from teacher education and the closure of key departments teaching history of education, including at the universities of Leicester, Leeds and Liverpool, have had an impact that is recognisable

Moments of organic growth

Alongside the stability of the London University Institute of Education and Roehampton University (formerly Froebel College and the Froebel Institute) as centres for history of education, newly created institutional bases have developed. These include the Domus Centre at the University of Birmingham which was launched following Birmingham's hosting of the ISCHE conference in 2001. The centre is concerned with promoting interdisciplinary research and the development of a new historiography around education and schooling and it brought together people with shared interests, not all of whom were historians of education. A significant body of published research is associated with the centre, particularly in relation to the development of new methodologies (visual), new areas of research (gender and the history of science, materiality of schooling) and new synergies (heritage education, cultural learning). It continues to promote interdisciplinary work but under a broadened title: Centre for Interdisciplinary Research in

Histories of Education and Childhood. The Centre for the History of Women's Education at the University of Winchester grew into a recognised centre as a direct response to capacity building through successful competition for institutional grants to appoint PhD students and university-funded and externally funded research grants. Again, the centre has been associated with special issue publications of an inter-disciplinary nature that have included *Women's History Review*. The University of Cambridge Department of Education has developed as a centre for history of education around research into teachers' lives and work and has become known for expertise in oral history. These centres for research in history of education have links with the History of Education Society (HES) through committee membership and organisation of conferences, both for the HES and for organisations like ISCHE, the European Educational Research Association and the Women's History Network. All the centres have a commitment to postgraduate study and an active seminar series, plus access to research collections. These examples from Birmingham, Winchester and Cambridge exemplify cycles of topical interest in history of education and orientations to new ways of working as the discipline moves and develops.

Alongside the visibility of centres oriented to research in history of education is the range of departments with scholars working on education in historical settings who do not identify as historians of education. This was illustrated at the 2005 conference on 'Education and Culture in the Long Eighteenth Century' where presentations were given by scholars working on topics around education in historical settings who primarily identified with university departments of philosophy and literature, as well as history and cultural studies. This provides a challenge for capacity and capability building in history of education. It demonstrates both the vibrancy of the discipline and the 'hybridity' that Nick Peim warned constituted a vulnerability (Peim, 2001, p. 654).

The HES's mapping of research theses completed in 2004 and 2005 revealed 65 theses with a primary focus on education in historical settings, and a further 50 where education in historical settings formed a secondary focus. Of the 65 where education in historical settings formed a primary focus, 19 only were coded in *Index to Theses* as educational history. Five of the remainder were coded as Education, five in subject codes related to English Literature, 28 in subject codes of History, five under subject codes of Religion and three in the category Other. Those with a secondary focus on education in historical settings fell under subject codes related to English, History, Philosophy, Religion and Other.[4]

The 65 theses with a primary focus on education in historical settings were produced by research students in 34 institutions. This distributed pattern runs alongside the lack of teaching of the English 'tradition' of history of education research, which is taught only in isolated instances, a partial result of the removal of history of education from teacher education. As a consequence, research students don't have ready access to the development of a common understanding of historiography, theory and methodology on which to draw (and from which to diverge). It also holds consequences for understandings of historians working in social and cultural history about the ways in which historians of education work, and the advances in the discipline.

This is not to argue for research selectivity, but for a system more akin to that existing in Belgium, where there is investment in new researchers and their supervisors and a stress on attendance and presentation at international conferences. Because of the way that research functions in Belgium, students are taught the 'tradition' which develops a shared understanding of historiography and theory that facilitates intellectual exchange and cross-disciplinary work. Belgian students are linked to funded projects, which require (and fund) them to present at international conferences, with the result that students are integrated into the international peer community of researchers from an early stage. In the UK, there are few bursaries for full-time study in history of education and success with grants that include funded studentships or for early career fellowships from the major funding bodies are less likely. This mirrors the situation in Education more generally, where only 4 per cent of studentships were funded by research councils between 2001 and 2007. As the RAE 2008 Education panel noted, this is of significance for ensuring the long-term future of the discipline.

To support the development of history of education, the HES engages in capacity building through research training and networking of the type to which the Education RAE 2008 sub-panel referred. The HES runs an annual research student conference and a strand for postgraduate researcher students in the Society's main annual conference, and also offers bursaries to postgraduate researcher students to attend. The Society links with ISCHE via financing a competition for a fully funded bursary to the ISCHE conference wherever the ISCHE conference is held in the world. The Society has recently invested in its first research fellowship. Through its journals it also mentors new researchers through the peer review process to publish alongside the more experienced. EERA is also moving towards supporting new researchers via a pilot European summer school for research students in history of education in 2010 and 2011 developed in partnership with the Universities of Gent, Edinburgh, Winchester, Cambridge and Birmingham and the *Stichting Paedagogica Historica*.

Moments of curiosity and emergent tributaries

Moments of insecurity encourage disciplines to focus on what constitutes the parameters of the discipline, to interrogate the particular discipline's ways of working and to reach outward to collaborate with other disciplines and across national borders (see the self-referential theories of Luhmann in Schriewer, 1988, pp. 64–65). Rather than seeing *moments of insecurity* as stages of disintegration, they can constitute moments of opportunity when disciplines reach out to spaces shared with other disciplines to develop inter-disciplinary ways of working, as has been the case with cultural historians, historians of women's education and historians working across international borders. Indeed, historians of education are well placed to 'confront the crisis' through analysis of the way in which the field of educational research functions.

Running alongside *moments of insecurity, moments of curiosity* have funda-mentally enriched the development of the discipline. They have occurred on the basis of intellectual exchange and curiosity and in a dialogic way within networks, rather than being a direct outcome of concerted strategic decisions in the face of *moments of insecurity* with their accompanying desire to put in place something 'different' in the discipline or to relate 'differently' to con-temporary education. *Moments of curiosity* have resulted in organic growth linking historians of education to others outside the discipline of history of education in the larger academic community and beyond. They have built on the openness of historians of education to insights and practices from other disciplines and have resulted in new publications that have raised issues for the discipline's focus, methods and ways of working, specifically around the development of visual research and material histories (Grosvenor *et al.*, 1999; Meitzner *et al.*, 2005; Lawn and Grosvenor, 2005; Lawn, 2008, 2009). This is not coherent growth. Rather, it is associational, located with networks, and particularly with co-operative networks of scholars which are themselves unbounded. The openness to new perspectives that accompanies associational growth of this nature has led to the development of some new models, here termed 'tributaries', of which three examples are cited below.

One tributary is from the 'long eighteenth century' and cultural history, exemplified by the conference, 'Education in the Long Eighteenth Century', held at Cambridge University in 2007 that resulted in an edited collection of innovative research (Hilton and Shefrin, 2009). Here researchers spanned a range of disciplines: history of education, of childhood, of religion, of science; literary studies and book history; biography; material culture; the visual; feminist and gender studies. Scholars discussed ideas, practices and forms of culture as diverse as music, dance and architecture. The conference organisers were explicit about their aim to place education at the heart of the cultural history of the long eighteenth century and set out to redefine educa-tion as a cultural practice. This was a history of representations as well as of structures and processes. Researchers demonstrated the innovative work that is possible outside conventional disciplinary boundaries in the conceptual space constituted through education. The sources drawn on were multifari-ous: treatises, tales for children, novels, poems, sermons, works of celebration and explanation of the natural world, published and unpublished letters and artefacts such as toys, pictures and pedagogical games that stimulated instruction and conversation. The conference pointed to just how complex were the ideas, practices and institutions deemed educational and just how fluid and shifting were the ideas and positions of educators. It also demonstrated the rich potential in drawing together insights and practices from educational history and eighteenth-century history to the benefit of both.

A second tributary might be termed the social movement version of history of education, exemplified by women's history and histories of disability and education. Watts (2005) demonstrates how research into women's education and gender and education has raised questions about historical educational issues in new ways, including the inter-relationships of colonialism and national identities and of feminism and imperialism; women as social agents, affected but not determined by their context; the significance of religion as well as of class; and the uses of oral, family and literary history. Watts notes that contributions to this work have come from historians other than those who might call themselves historians of education. To find or restore women, historians of gender and of women's history sought fresh sources and methods and this altered or challenged the historical record. Watts concludes that this work has moved far beyond the mere restoring of women to the historical record. Inter-disciplinary crossings and links particularly with feminist scholars in Australia, New Zealand, India and the USA has enriched this work: 'Without being unique among modern historians, they have been in the vanguard and have stimulated much thought among all kinds of historians' (Watts, 2005).

The third example might be termed the network-of-scholars movement. Historians of education are also benefiting from collaborative organisational links with other societies, with a mutual exchange of agendas. This is exemplified by the link from ISCHE with the International Society for History Didactics, the Society for the History of Children and Youth and the Disability History Society, and the formalised joint conference and symposia agreed for 2012 in Geneva in which the three societies will work as partners.

Looking to the future

In the 1970s the American historian of education Sol Cohen identified three legitimate activities for history of education: the discovery of new source materials; evaluating the impact of new theories, new methods, new academic disciplines; and the asking of new or different kinds of questions of the historical data, old or new (Cohen, 1973). These legitimate activities still remain. Despite the quality of history of education research (RAE 2008 UoA 45 subject overview report), in pursuing these activities historians of education have rarely been seen as part of the mainstream, whether mainstream be defined in relation to history or to the field of education more generally. Historians of education have, in part, contributed to this 'statelessness' through their tendency to publish predominantly in specialised journals and for a pre-determined audience; a state of affairs that must be collectively addressed. While some educational researchers are not unsympathetic to the historical dimension in educational research and its potential for providing contextual understanding of contemporary issues, a general lack of attention to this dimension has also continued to prevail.

That said, in recent years the boundaries of history of education as discipline have become more porous. Institutional and policy change in UK universities, strategic decisions by the HES and ISCHE, the establishment and activities of Network 17 *Histories of Education* of EERA over the last ten years, the promotion of interdisciplinary research in the UK and the growth in opportunities for funded collaborative activity have all contributed to this phenomenon. This porosity has resulted in some historians of education being able to demonstrate that contemporary educational research can be immeasurably enriched by attention to the historical dimension.

A good example of this claim for enrichment is Burke's research on educational spaces. Burke's research on architecture developed from conversations within Network 17 and a curiosity about the history of spaces, places and school design, rather than in response to an externally generated agenda. This incorporated a number of facets of interest to researchers other than historians, including, for example, the concern with children's voice, and with women and society. This research impacted beyond the EERA space, was supported financially by both the HES and the British Academy and in terms of knowledge transfer was taken up by RIBA architects. Outside the academic community it has linked with a whole range of issues to do with the conservation of schools, new school design (with RIBA) and meeting the broader framework of educationists. This provides one example of researchers using their interests strategically to seize opportunities when they arise to declare that there is an issue on which historians of education can enrich contemporary concerns (Burke, 2005a, 2005b, 2005c, 2007a, 2007b, 2007c, 2009; Burke and Grosvenor, 2003, 2007, 2008).

Burke's research suggests that historians (individually or collectively) might develop an eye for 'intelligence' to link their interests with current challenges and point to lacunae in current practice. It illustrates, first, the possibilities for reframing engagements between policy-makers and historians of education that in the past were formally institutionalised via reports of government commissions and a stress on nation building. Second, it offers a connection to a research tradition where historians of education have acknowledged the complex relationship between the historical and the contemporary, have explored the social relations of education (professional identities, knowledge formation, institutional structures, power relations), have produced reconstructive histories which connect the past and the present and argued forcefully for the role of education in civil society. In particular, we are thinking here of the work of Brian and Joan Simon, David Reeder and Malcolm Seaborne and the ongoing contributions of Harold Silver which have been documented and celebrated elsewhere. It addresses lacunae identified by Silver (1992), who flagged the 'enormous' literature around schools in systems and their growth, the careers and organisation of teachers, gender differences, control and organisation, testing and sorting processes, and the characteristics of 'effective' schools; but 'silences' around classrooms, 'experience' and education (in contrast to educational context and curriculum history) – 'there are no classrooms, no children, no learning, no teaching' (Silver, 1992, p. 105). Silver called for a paradigm shift away from conceptions of social structure, the state, political processes and versions of policy defined in narrow political terms that disregarded the people who inhabited the structures and the locations, forms, dimensions and meaning of their experiences. As Burke's work demonstrates, this linkage can strengthen rather than sever the relationship between historians of education and policy-makers. Burke's work also offers a concrete example of knowledge transfer, an activity increasingly stressed by the research councils and one with which historians of education should more directly engage. One such area of engagement might be the ethics of educational research. Here historians of education currently working with images (still or moving) are able to explore ethical issues distanced in time, which may provide a location to work through otherwise difficult issues and to explore questions about ethical relationships between researchers and research. This strategic approach is far removed from one that runs the risk of disciplining the discipline through a utilitarian approach that sees history of education serving agendas to which historians of education must explicitly turn their attention.

Finally, we recognise the need to acknowledge that another story could have been told if we took as our starting point the discipline of history rather than education. For example, if we had taken history as our starting point we could have identified from the Royal Historical Society's bibliographical database (www.rhs.ac.uk/bibl/dataset.asp) an additional 40 journals that carried articles on history of education in 2008. The database also includes most but not all of the articles we have cited. Our concern and our analysis have been about 'history of education' as a branch of educational research rather than as a branch of cultural and social history. The picture we paint therefore is inevitably partial but our aim is to make claims for our sub-discipline which need to be heard by other members of the community of educational researchers. As to the community of historians, to which in a janus-faced way we also belong, we need to turn around and open a new dialogue.

Notes

1 Our locations in the field span former and current editors of two foremost international journals in the field (*History of Education* and *Paedagogica Historica*). We are office-holders in a range of learned societies (president of the UK History of Education Society, former secretary of ISCHE, general secretary of EERA, and founding convenor of ECER Network 17 (Histories of Education)). What follows constitutes a personal view and should not be taken as representative of the views of these organisations or journals.

2 Thanks to Dr Andrea Jacobs, University of Winchester, for compiling the data on journal articles underlying the analysis.
3 This resulted from the incorporation of the *Journal of Sources and Methodology*, produced previously in microfiche form.
4 Thanks to the HES for permission to use data from commissioned research based on abstracts in *Index to Theses* compiled by Helen Loader, University of Winchester.

References

Aiston, S. (2005) A Maternal Identity: The Family Lives of British Women Graduates Pre- and Post-1945, *History of Education*, 34, 4, 407–426.

Aldrich, R. (2003) The Three Duties of the Historian of Education, *History of Education*, 32, 2, 133–143.

Aldrich, R. (2004) The Training of Teachers and Educational Studies: The London Day Training College, 1902–1932, *Paedagogica Historica*, 40, 5, 617–631.

Armitage, M. (2005) The Influence of School Architecture and Design in Education on the Outdoor Play Experience within the Primary School, *Paedagogica Historica*, 41, 4–5, 535–554.

Armstrong, F. (2007) Disability, Education and Social Change: Purpose and Pursuit, *History of Education*, 36, 4–5, 551–568.

Bassey, M. (1999) *Case Study Research in Educational Settings* (Buckingham: Open University Press).

Brehony, K. (2004) A New Education For a New Era: The Contribution of The Conferences of The New Education Fellowship to the Disciplinary Field of Education, 1921–1938, *Paedagogica Historica*, 40, 5–6, 733–755.

Brown, A. (2005) Ellen Pinsent: Including the 'Feebleminded' in Birmingham, 1900–1913, *History of Education*, 34, 5, 535–546.

Burke, C. (2005a) Contested Desires: The Edible Landscape of School, *Paedagogica Historica*, 41, 4–5, 571–588.

Burke, C. (2005b) Personal Journeys: An Examination of the Use of the Concept of Time Travel in Constructing Knowledge of Past Educational Spaces, in U. Mietzner, K. Myers and N. Peim (eds) *Visual History: Images of Education* (London: Peter Lang).

Burke, C. (2005c) Light in the History of Schooling, in M. Lawn and I. Grosvenor (eds) *Materialities of Schooling* (Oxford: Symposium).

Burke, C. (ed.) (2005d) Containing the School Child: Architectures and Pedagogies, Special Issue *History of Education*, 41, 4–5, 489–643.

Burke, C. (2007a) The View of The Child: Releasing 'Visual Voices' in The Design of Learning Environments, *Discourse*, 28, 3, 359–372.

Burke, C. (2007b) Inspiring Spaces: Creating Creative Classrooms, *Curriculum Briefing*, 5, 2, 35–39.

Burke, C. (2007c) *Conversations between Architects and Educators on Post War School Design*, British Academy-funded film.

Burke, C. (2009) Inside Out: A Collaborative Approach to Designing Schools in England, 1945–72, *Paedagogica Historica*, 45, 3, 421–434.

Burke, C. and Grosvenor, I. (2003) *The School I'd Like* (London: Routledge).

Burke, C. and Grosvenor, I. (2007) Designed Spaces and Disciplined Bodies: E.R. Robson's Grand Architectural Tour, in G. Timmerman, N. Bakker and J.H. Dekker (eds) *Cultuuroverdracht als pedagogisch motief. Historische en actuele perspectieven op onderwijs, sekse en beroep* (Groningen: Barkhuis).

Burke, C. and Grosvenor, I. (2008) *School* (London: Reaktion).

Byford, A. (2008) Psychology at High School in Late Imperial Russia (1881–1917), *History of Education Quarterly*, 48, 2, 265–297.

Campbell, C. and Sherington, G. (2002) History of Education: The Possibility of Survival, *Change: Transformations in Education*, 5, 1, 46–64.

Chiu, P. (2008) A Position of Usefulness: Gendering History of Girls' Education in Colonial Hong Kong (1850s–1890s), *History of Education*, 37, 6, 789–806.

Cohen, S. (1973) New Perspectives in the History of American Education 1960–1970, *History of Education*, 1–2, 79–96.

Coles, J. (2008) The JEAH and the Millennium, *Journal of Educational Administration and History*, 40, 1, 49–53.

Dale, P. (2007) Special Education at Starcross before 1948, *History of Education*, 36, 17–44.

Depaepe, M. (1993) Some Statements about the Nature of the History of Education, in K. Salimova and E.V. Johanningmeier (eds) *Why Should We Teach History of Education?* (Moscow: International Academy of Self Improvement), 31–36.

Depaepe, M. (2001) A Professionally Relevant History of Education for Teachers, Does It Exist? A Reply to Jurgen Herbst, *Paedagogica Historica*, 37, 3, 629–640.

Depaepe, M. and Simon, F. (1996) *Paedagogica Historica*: Lever or Mirror in the Making of the History of Education, *Paedagogica Historica*, 32, 2, 421–450.

Dick, M.M. and Watts, R. (eds) (2008) Eighteenth Century Education: Discourses and Informal Agencies, *History of Education*, 37, 4, 506–619.

Donato, R. and Lazerson, M. (2000) New Directions in American Educational History: Problems and Prospects, *Educational Researcher*, 29, 4–15.

Fendler, L. (2008) The Upside of Presentism, *Paedagogica Historica*, 44, 6, 677–690.

Fink, J. (2008) Inside a Hall of Mirrors: Residential Care and the Shifting Constructions of Childhood in Mid-twentieth-century Britain, *Paedagogica Historica*, 44, 3, 287–308.

Fitzgerald, T. and Gunter, H. (2005) Trends in the Administration and History of Education: What Counts?' *Journal of Education Administration and History*, 37, 2, 127–136.

Fitzgerald, T. and Gunter, H. (2008) Educational Administration and History Part 2: Academic Journals and the Contribution of JEAH, *Journal of Educational Administration and History*, 40, 1, 23–40.

Furlong, J. (2004) BERA at 30. Have We Come of Age?, *British Educational Research Journal*, 30, 3, 343–358.

Gardner, P. (2007) The Life Long Draft: From Learning to Teaching and Back, *History of Education*, 36, 4–5, 465–482.

Goodman, J. (2005) A Cloistered Ethos? Landscapes of Learning and English Secondary Schools for Girls: An Historical Perspective, *Paedagogica Historica*, 41, 4–5, 589–604.

Goodman, J. (2007) Social Change and Secondary Schooling for Girls in the 'Long 1920s': European Engagements, *History of Education*, 36, 4–5, 497–514.

Goodman, J. (2008a) Transnational Networks, Intellectual Co-operation and Women's International Organisations, unpublished paper, ECER 2008, Gothenburg.

Goodman, J. (2008b) Conservative Woman or Woman Conservative? Complicating Accounts of Women's Educational Leadership, *Paedagogica Historica*, 44, 4, 415–428.

Goodman, J. and Martin, J. (2004) Editorial: History of Education – Defining a Field, *History of Education*, 33, 1, 1–10.

Grosvenor, I. (2005) The Art of Seeing: Promoting Design in Education in 1930s England, *Paedagogica Historica*, 41, 4–5, 507–534.

Grosvenor, I. (2007) From the Eye of History to a 'Second Gaze': The Visual Archive and the Marginalized in the History of Education, *History of Education*, 36, 4–5, 607–602.

Grosvenor, I. (2008) Seen but Not Heard: City Childhoods from the Past into the Present, *Paedagogica Historica*, 43, 3, 405–430.

Grosvenor, I. (2009) Geographies of Risk: An Exploration of City Childhoods in Early Twentieth Century Britain, *Paedagogica Historica*, 45, 1–2, 215–234.

Grosvenor, I., Rousmaniere, K. and Lawn, M. (1999) *Silences and Images: The Social History of The Classroom* (New York: Peter Lang).

Hamilton, D. (2002) Noisy, Fallible and Biased Though It Be (on the Vagaries of Educational Research), *British Journal of Educational Studies*, 50, 1–2, 144.

Hargreaves, D. (1996) *Teaching as a Research-based Profession: Possibilities and Prospects* (London: TTA).

Hilton, M. and Shefrin, J. (eds) (2009) *Educating the Child in Enlightenment Britain* (Aldershot: Ashgate).

Hirsch, P. (2005) Apostle of Freedom: Alfred Adler and his British Disciples, *History of Education*, 35, 5, 473–482.

Jacobs, A. (2007) Examinations as Cultural Capital for The Victorian Schoolgirl: 'Thinking' with Bourdieu, *Women's History Review*, 16, 2, 245–261.

Jephcote, M. and Davies, B. (2007) School Subjects, Subject Communities and Curriculum Change: The Social Construction of Economics in the School Curriculum, *Cambridge Journal of Education*, 37, 2, 207–227.

Jones, K. (2003) *Education in Britain 1944 to the Present* (Cambridge: Polity Press).

Judge, H. (ed.) (2006) The University and Public Education: The Contribution of Oxford. Special Issue *Oxford Review of Education*, 32, 1, 1–165.

Kan, F., Vickers, E. and Morris, P. (2007) Keepers of the Sacred Flame: Patriotism, Politics and the Chinese History Subject Community in Hong Kong, *Cambridge Journal of Education*, 37, 2, 229–247.

Lawn, M. (2004) Reflecting the Passion: Mid-century Projects for Education, *History of Education*, 33, 4, 505–514.

Lawn, M. (ed.) (2008) *An Atlantic Crossing? The Work of the International Examination Inquiry, Its Researchers, Methods and Influence* (Oxford: Symposium).

Lawn, M. (ed.) (2009) *Modelling the Future: Exhibitions and the Materiality of Education* (Oxford, Symposium).

Lawn, M. and Grosvenor, I. (eds) (2005) *Materialities of Schooling* (Oxford: Symposium).

Lowe, R. (2002) Do We Still Need History of Education: Is It Central or Peripheral? *History of Education*, 31, 6, 491–504.

Lowe, R. (2004) Editorial Trends in the Administration and History of Education, *Journal of Educational Administration and History*, 36, 1, 3–8.

McCulloch, G. (2002) 'Disciplines Contributing to Education?' Educational Studies and the Disciplines, *British Journal of Educational Studies*, 50, 1, 100–119.

McCulloch, G. (2006a) Education and the Middle Classes: The Case of the English Grammar Schools, 1868–1944, *History of Education*, 35, 6, 689–704.

McCulloch, G. (2006b) Cyril Norwood and the English Tradition of Education, *Oxford Review of Education*, 32, 1, 55–69.

McCulloch, G. (2007) Forty Years On: Presidential Address to the History of Education Society, *History of Education*, 36, 1, 1–15.

McDermid, J. (2003) Gender and Geography: The Schooling of Poor Girls in the Highlands and Islands of Nineteenth-Century Scotland, *History of Education Review*, 32, 2, 30–45.

Macdonald, A.M. (ed.) (1972) *Chambers Twentieth Century Dictionary*, new edn (Edinburgh: W&R Chambers Ltd).

Martin, J. (2005) Mary Bridges Adams and Education Reform, 1890–1920: An Ethic of Care, *Women's History Review*, 13, 3, 467–487.

Martin, J. (2007) Thinking Education Histories Differently: Biographical Approaches to Class Politics and Women's Movements in London 1900s to 1960s, *History of Education*, 36, 4, 515–533.

Martin, J. (2008) Engendering City Politics and Educational Thought: Elite Women and the London Labour Party, 1914–1965, *Paedagogica Historica*, 44, 4, 397–413.

Meitzner, U., Myers, K. and Peim, N. (eds) (2005) *Visual History* (London: Peter Lang).

Middleton, J. (2005) Thomas Hopley and Mid-Victorian Attitudes to Corporal Punishment, *History of Education*, 34, 6, 599–616.

Myers, K. (2009) Immigrants and Ethnic Minorities in the History of Education, *Paedagogica Historica*, 45, 6, 801–816.

Myers, K. and Brown, A. (2005) Mental Deficiency: The Diagnosis and After-care of Special School Leavers in Early Twentieth Century Birmingham, *Journal of Historical Sociology*, 18, 1–2, 72–89.

Nawrotzki, K. (2006) Froebel is Dead: Long Live Froebel. The National Froebel Foundation and English Education, *History of Education*, 35, 2, 209–224.

Oldern, A. (2008) Opposition to Government Education: R.E. Ellison and the Berbera School Affair 1938–1940, *History of Education*, 37, 1, 71–90.

Peim, N. (2001) The State of the Art or the Ruins of Nostalgia? The Problematics of Subject Identity, Its Objects, Theoretical Resources and Practices, *Paedagogica Historica*, 37, 3, 653–662.

Peim, N. (2005) Towards a Social Ecology of the Modern School: Reflections on the Histories of the Governmental Environment of Schooling, *History of Education,* 41, 4–5, 627–639.

Pullin, N. and Spencer, S. (eds) (2004) Earning and Learning in Women's History, *Women's History Review*, 13, 3, 341–509.

RAE (2008) *Sub-Panel 45 Education: Subject Overview Report*. Available online at www.rae.ac.uk/pubs/2009/ov.

Richardson, W. (1999) Historians and Educationists: The History of Education as a Field of Study in Post-war England, Part 1: 1945–72, *History of Education*, 28, 1, 1–30.

Richardson, W. (2002) Educational Studies in the United Kingdom, 1940–2002, *British Journal of Educational Studies*, 51, 1, 3–56.

Richardson, W. (2007a) Public Policy Failure and Fiasco in Education: Perspectives on the British Examinations Crises of 2000–2002 and Other Episodes since 1975, *Oxford Review of Education*, 33, 3, 143–160.

Richardson, W. (2007b) British Historiography of Education in International Context at the Turn of the Century, 1996–2006, *History of Education*, 36, 4–5, 569–593.

Ruddock, J. and Fielding, M. (2006) Student Voice and the Perils of Popularity, *Educational Review*, 58, 2, 219–231.

Schriewer, J. (1988) The Method of Comparison and the Need for Externalisation: Methodological Criteria and Sociological Concepts, in J. Schriewer and B. Holmes (eds) *Theories and Methods in Comparative Education* (Frankfurt: Peter Lang).

Sheldon, N. (2007) The School Attendance Officer 1900–1939: Policeman to Welfare Worker, *History of Education*, 36, 6, 735–746.

Silver, H. (1992) Knowing and Not Knowing in the History of Education, *History of Education*, 21, 1, 97–108.

Simon, B. (1965) *Education and the Labour Movement, 1870–1920* (London: Lawrence & Wishart).

Simon, B. (1971) *The Politics of Educational Reform, 1920–1940* (London: Lawrence & Wishart).

Simon, B. (1991) *Education and the Social Order: British Education since 1944* (London: Lawrence & Wishart).

Smith, R. (2008) To School with the Poets: Philosophy, Method and Clarity, *Paedagogica Historica*, 44, 6, 635–646.

Smith, G. and Exley, S. (2006) The Influence of Overseas Examples on DES Policy-making for the School System in England, 1985–1995, *Oxford Review of Education*, 32, 5, 575–597.

Soler, J. (2006) Renegotiating Cultural Authority: Imperial Culture and the New Zealand Primary School Curriculum in the 1930s, *History of Education*, 35, 1, 11–26.

Standish, P. (2008) Chroniclers and Critics, *Paedagogica Historica*, 44, 6, 661–676.

Taylor, R. (2005) Lifelong Learning and the Labour Governments 1997–2004, *Oxford Review of Education*, 31, 1, 101–118.

Thomas, S., Peng, W.J. and Gray, J. (2007) Modelling Patterns of Improvement over Time: Value Added Trends in English Secondary School Performance across Ten Schools, *Oxford Review of Education*, 33, 3, 261–295.

Tooley, J. and Darby, D. (1998) *Educational Research: A Critique* (London: Ofsted).

Verbruggen, C. and Carlier, J. (2008) Transnational Networks of Feminists, Progressive Educationalists and Other Intellectuals at the Eve of the First World War, unpublished paper, ECER, 2008, Gothenburg.

Walford, G. (ed.) (2008) *Blair's Educational Legacy? Special Issue Oxford Review of Education*, 34, 6, 637–765.

Watts, R. (2005) Gendering the Story: Change in the History of Education, *History of Education*, 34, 3, 225–241.

Watts, R. (2009) Education, Empire and Social Change in Nineteenth Century Britain, *Paedagogica Historica*, 45, 6, 773–786.

White, J. (2005) Puritan Intelligence: The Ideological Background to IQ, *Oxford Review of Education*, 31, 3, 423–442.

Woodhead, C. (1998) Too Much Research, or Not Enough?, the *Independent*, 9 April.

Woodin, T. (2005) More Writing than Welding: Learning in Worker Writer Groups, *History of Education*, 34, 5, 561–578.

Wright, S. (2008) 'There Is Something Universal in Our Movement Which Appeals Not Only to One Country But to All': International Communication and Moral Education 1892–1914, *History of Education*, 37, 6, 807–824.

6 The contribution of the economics of education to education

Lorraine Dearden, Stephen Machin and Anna Vignoles

Introduction

During the recent Research Assessment Exercise, the strength and quality of economic research in UK universities was confirmed, with economics securing the highest rate of 4* grades compared to any other discipline. Within this vibrant discipline, an important sub-discipline, the economics of education, has also burgeoned in recent years. Although the economics of education effectively emerged as a field of its own in the 1960s, it is only in recent decades that there has been a resurgence of new research by economists on education issues and education policy. This follows a relatively fallow period when (with the exception of continued work on education by US economists) research in the area was much less active, at least as compared to the initial heydays of the field in the 1960s and 1970s. In this chapter we argue that this increased popularity of the economics of education has come about for a number of reasons: the desire by policy-makers to have robust quantitative and policy-relevant academic research that can inform education policy-making, better availability of rich data with which to undertake more methodologically challenging research and the development of new econometric techniques that lend themselves to the analysis of education issues. We explore these developments in this chapter, giving reasons why there has been a recent increase in interest in this field, providing supporting empirical evidence for our hypotheses and highlighting key research and approaches that have been a feature of this research.

Put starkly, the economics of education is about how best to allocate scarce resources in education. It can help us understand how education can best be produced, who gets more (or less) education and the economic impact of education on individuals, firms and society as a whole. There are many key approaches and findings that have become commonplace, not just in academic research but also in policy areas and in general day-to-day discussions. These include: the idea of education acquisition as an investment (the human capital approach of Becker, 1964); the notion of economic returns to education in the form of improved labour market outcomes (the earnings function of Mincer, 1958, 1974); arguments about cost efficiency and effectiveness applied to education policy options; and many others.

We make the case that the economics of education as a research field has had a significant impact on both the theoretical and empirical evidence base on education across the world and that it is now an exciting, rapidly advancing field with enormous influence on policy-making in many countries. We begin in the next section by placing the economics of education research field into its appropriate historical context. We also show bibliometric evidence from economics about the upsurge of research in the area, in terms of increased numbers of publications in the top economics journals. The following section then discusses some of the key theoretical advancements in the field. The fourth section considers methodological innovations, while the discussion in the fifth section considers wider impacts of the economics of education research field. The final section concludes by highlighting key contributions of the field and by assessing future prospects in the area.

The origins and resurgence of economics of education research

Historical context

Many of the basic core principles of the economics of education can be dated back a long way, at least as far as Adam Smith in his *Wealth of Nations* treatise published in 1776. Certainly, he alluded to the idea that one might invest in education to increase the productive capacity of society. However, the founding father of the economics of education is arguably Gary Becker, who wrote the enormously influential *Human Capital* in 1964.[1] Becker set out the principles of what became known as human capital theory, which purports to explain why individuals invest in education and training in a manner analogous to investments in physical capital, i.e. to earn a financial return. Human capital theory has become and remained the dominant paradigm in the economics of education today, despite challenges along the way in the early days from commentators who were concerned with the notion that people (like machines) can be viewed as capital, and from economists doubting the key proposition of the human capital approach that education in and of itself is productive (Spence, 1973; Blaug, 1976). In fact, it is quite striking the extent to which human capital theory and its basic principles are readily discussed and accepted by economists and non-economists alike.

Not least because of the huge impact of human capital theory on academic and public discourse in the early days, the heyday of the economics of education is seen by some as the 1960s and 1970s. Classic writings emerged in the field at that time, many of them challenging, extending or applying human capital theory (like Blaug, 1972, 1976; Freeman, 1976; Layard and Psacharopoulos, 1974; Psacharopoulos, 1973; Spence, 1973; and Schultz, 1961, 1963). That said, it is during recent decades that the principles of the economics of education have been so widely applied in education policy-making, thus raising the profile of the field both academically and to the wider public.

Significant developments were also made on the empirical side of things at that time. Mincer's (1958, 1974) highly influential work developed the earnings function (also known as the Mincer earnings equation) that seeks to model the relationship between (log) earnings and an individual's schooling and work experience. This is one of the most widely used tools among empirical economists and lies at the cornerstone of a vast array of empirical research done in many areas of economics. It is used very heavily in the economics of education field to provide estimates of the labour market value of different types of schooling and qualifications. There is now a large body of micro-economic research that has focused on the core elements of the Mincer equation and attempted to both establish and quantify the causal impact of education on earnings (Card, 1999).

The current upsurge

During the 1960s and 1970s therefore, the economics of education emerged as a distinct field of economics. It was during this early period that much of the theoretical developments in the field were first published, and we return to these important theories below. However, despite this period being particularly fertile in terms of developing economic theories with which to analyse education issues, there was a subsequent significant decline in research activity in the economics of education, especially outside the USA. More recently, this decline has been reversed and there has been a huge upsurge of interest in the field: in the UK and USA at least, it has been accompanied by an increase in the use of economic evaluation in educational reform and policy-making.

Table 6.1 shows these trends using bibliometric evidence. The table shows the number of publications per year with the word 'education', 'schooling' or 'school' in the title of papers published in leading mainstream economics journals across six decades beginning in the 1950s.[2] The table shows a very clear pattern. In the 1950s hardly any education papers were published. In the 1960s 3.4 papers per year appeared in the most prestigious journals and this almost doubled to 6.3 in the 1970s. After this, however,

Table 6.1 Education publications in mainstream economics journals

	Decade					
	1950s	*1960s*	*1970s*	*1980s*	*1990s*	*2000s*
Papers per year	0.2	3.4	6.3	2.5	5.2	9.7
Non-North American papers per year	0.0	0.4	0.7	0.5	1.2	3.2

Notes
Reproduced from Machin (2008a). Publications with the word Education, Schooling or School in the title in the following list of journals: *American Economic Review*; *Economic Journal*; *Econometrica*; *Economica*; *Journal of Political Economy*; *Quarterly Journal of Economics*; *RAND Journal of Economics*; *Review of Economic Studies*.
Source: JSTOR, Ingenta Connect, Business Source Premier, Blackwell Synergy.

there was a sharp fall in the 1980s (down to 2.5 papers per year), something of a pick up in the 1990s (up to 5.2 a year, although with a lot of these towards the end of the decade) and then a very sharp increase to 9.7 a year in the 2000s, the highest level in all the decades considered.[3]

There is another very marked feature of this recent upsurge in academic interest in the economics of education. The second row of the table shows the number of papers with authors from outside North America. For this group the trend upwards over time is striking. Hardly any education papers were published by this group until recently and the 2000s sees 3.2 papers per year published. Given that the majority of the journals in the list are American, this trend is very notable, and reveals that the economics of education is currently a thriving field beyond the USA and particularly in Europe where many of the authors of these papers are from.

Theoretical contributions to the field of education

Economics has contributed to the field of education in a number of major ways. We choose to focus in detail on two of these: first, economists' theoretical contributions to our understanding of education issues, and second, the contribution made by economists to important methodological developments in the field of education. We start by focusing on theory and specifically economists' role in introducing economic ideas and the principles of the market to the field of education. We then move on to consider how the economics of education literature has made significant methodological contributions to quantitative research methods in education, particularly in the area of education policy evaluation.

A strength of the economics of education is that it has clear theoretical underpinnings, as of course do the other disciplines of education discussed in the other chapters of this volume. There is a well-known set of core principles that offer a research framework that is more structured than other areas. Economists utilise and apply robust, precisely specified theoretical models to questions that are of policy relevance. Economics produces testable hypotheses in the field of education that can then be subjected to rigorous (generally quantitative) analysis. Indeed one explanation as to why economics has increased its influence as a discipline in a wide range of fields, and in particular in education, is that it provides answers to policy questions in quantifiable terms. This is clearly hugely appealing to policy-makers who have to justify resource allocations. Furthermore, since economics is the science of scarcity, it is no wonder that its influence in fields such as education and health has been huge. In the public sector, with limited resources, the analytical tools of economics are enormously useful in providing answers that help policy-makers decide where, given scarce resources, they should invest next.

It is, of course, difficult to select specific examples from the economics of education literature to illustrate the contribution of the discipline without appearing partial. However, there are several broad areas of research where economics has made a clear contribution. The first is in improving our understanding of the impact of education on individuals and the economy as a whole. Certainly most practitioners in the economics of education field subscribe, at least partially, to the notion that individuals and governments invest in education to earn a return on their investment. This return is generally in the form of higher earnings but may be in the form of non-monetary benefits, such as job quality.

With the right data, and the right methods, economists can measure this rate of return to different types of education investment. This area of research has burgeoned since the 1960s and key contributions have clearly shown that more education significantly raises individuals' wages (Card, 1999; Harmon and Walker, 1995; Dearden, Mcintosh et al., 2002; Blundell et al., 2005a), although there is less agreement among economists on the contribution of education to economic growth (see Sianesi and Van Reenen, 2003). The rate of return literature has also moved beyond estimating the impact of an additional year of schooling on individuals' earnings (5–10 per cent) to establish how economic returns to education investments vary by qualification type, level, subject area and over time (see, for example, Dearden, Mcintosh et al., 2002; Blundell et al., 2005a; and Machin, 2003, 2008b).

Another key area in which economists have made an impact is in modelling education production (see, *inter alia*, Todd and Wolpin, 2007, or Haveman and Wolfe, 1995). Although this may be anathema to some, the process of producing education can be analysed in a similar way to the production of other goods and services. If we accept the premise that the production of education is a process with inputs and outputs, we can then move on to consider issues about efficiency (i.e. the amount of input produced from a given level of input), as well as distributional issues, such as how the education that is produced is distributed across the population. There have been a number of major contributions to the field in this area, including estimates of the impact of additional resources (for example, smaller class sizes) on pupil achievement and/or the impact of teachers on pupil achievement (e.g. Angrist and Lavy, 1999; Dearden, Ferri et al., 2002; Rivkin et al., 2005). This evidence suggests that, unless the reductions are sizeable and hence extremely costly, reducing class sizes has little effect on achievement and that spending money on improving teacher quality is likely to be more effective than reducing class sizes.

Further, there has been a growing (sometimes controversial) literature on the role of education in promoting or preventing social mobility and inequality (Blanden et al., 2005, 2007, 2008; Ermisch and Nicoletti, 2007; Eriksson and Goldthorpe, 2008). This work on educational inequality tends to show that education has had a disequalising impact on mobility, since it has disproportionately benefited individuals from richer families and therefore reinforced, rather than countered, existing inequalities (Blanden and Machin, 2005). The work in this area has been of huge policy importance and continues to be a major theme pursued by all major political parties in the UK and indeed elsewhere.

We have been necessarily selective (and somewhat UK-centric) here, but, in summary, a major way that economics has contributed to the field of education has been by clarifying and measuring the effect of state and private investments in education on pupil outcomes.

Of course, the strength of economic analyses is their reliance on quantifying effects in ways that are appealing to policy-makers. This may equally be a potential weakness. One illustration of this point is in the application of human capital theory to the analysis of education investments. Human capital theory has been the dominant theory in the economics of education for more than 40 years. Its strength is its clarity and simplicity in analysing investments in education in an analogous way to investments in physical capital, such as new tube lines or rail links. This enables policy-makers to compare the economic return on investments in education with the economic return to other physical investments and make sensible resource-allocation decisions from these types of data. However, education investments, and indeed other forms of human capital, are of course not exactly the same as physical capital. Education has potentially unquantifiable benefits, such as giving individuals a greater sense of self-worth or a more active interest in society. Education also has knock-on or 'spill-over' effects, which are benefits to education that accrue beyond the individual acquiring the education. For instance, a more educated manager may make all the members of his team more productive because of the way he/she manages them or because he/she passes on his knowledge to them. This spill-over from his/her education will not necessarily be translated into higher earnings for the manager: rather, it may also show up as greater profits for the firm or higher earnings for co-workers. Thus a narrow economic estimate of the impact of education on an individual's earnings may miss part of the real (wider) economic and non-economic value of education.

Economists have responded to this criticism and many have started to try to quantify non-monetary benefits arising from education, for example, some studies have investigated the impact of early education interventions and education participation on crime rates or levels of civic participation (for crime, see Lochner and Moretti, 2004; Feinstein and Sabates, 2005; or Machin and Vujic, 2005; for evidence on civic participation, see Brehm and Rahn, 1997; Bynner and Egerton, 2001; Bynner and Parsons, 1997; or Dee, 2004). Such exercises are useful and may aid policy-makers in making the case for different types of education investment and once again they have the appeal that they produce quantifiable impacts. However, they essentially force the analyst or the educationalist to put some kind of monetary value on all benefits arising from education. This is of course a difficult (probably impossible) task. Too narrow an approach to the potential benefits of education then alienates economists from researchers in other disciplines, such as psychologists or sociologists, who take a broader perspective on these issues. However, this is not to say that economists do not think that these wider (unquantifiable) benefits are not important, just something that they cannot directly quantify. Moreover, if even this somewhat narrow approach taken by economists shows that the measureable benefits of education outweigh the costs then this is useful information to use alongside the findings from other disciplines.

Methodological innovations from the economics of education

A second main contribution of the economics of education has been to make major methodological contributions to the field of education. In particular, economists bring with them techniques that improve the quantitative rigour of analyses in the field of education. There is, of course, a long tradition of quantitative research in education and reliance on quantitative methods in education. However, this has increased dramatically over the last 10–20 years with the ever-increasing availability of high-quality survey data, particularly longitudinal survey data. More recently, quantitative education research has also been relying on the ever-increasing numbers of administrative education data-sets in a large number of countries, particularly the UK, which has world-class data in this regard.

A range of social scientists currently research education issues seeking to address relatively similar substantive research questions that are of current policy interest. How can we improve the cognitive skills of young people? How can we reduce the socio-economic gap in education achievement? Should we reduce class sizes or spend more on teaching assistants? And the list goes on. So what is different about the methodologies that economists use? The economics of education generally takes a very clear starting point when applying quantitative methods of analysis to educational issues. The key question for those working in the economics of education is: what is the *causal impact* of education qualifications, or an education initiative, or school quality or class size or some other type of 'educational treatment' on some outcome of interest? That is, the natural question for an economist to ask is: what is the outcome if a person receives a particular educational treatment versus the outcome if they had not? The problem is that we never observe the missing counterfactual, that is the outcome a person would have got if they had not gone to university, or not had a good teacher, or not been in a smaller class.

In medical research, and sometimes in social research, randomised control trials are used to estimate the causal impact of an intervention. In this instance the counterfactual is derived from random assignment to the intervention (or not). But in the education area it is much more difficult to use randomised control trials to investigate most (though not all) educational questions. For instance, the notion of randomly allocating pupils to schools or to higher education institutions is not a credible approach to estimating the causal impact of schooling or higher education. So the economics of education has spent a lot of time developing other analytical methods that

estimate this missing counterfactual in a convincing manner. In many circumstances, just using simple, or even sophisticated, multivariate regression
techniques will not be sufficient to do this.

Why are economists so concerned with finding causal impacts? It is
simply the fact that unless one can establish a causal impact, rather than a
simple correlation, incorrect policy conclusions will be drawn. If participants
in an educational intervention or treatment are systematically different from
non-participants in observable and/or unobservable ways and these factors
also affect the outcome of interest, a phenomenon economists refer to as
selection bias, then the outcome observed for non-participants does not represent a good approximation to the counterfactual for participants. For
instance, if students with challenging behaviour are allocated to smaller class
sizes, we will observe a positive correlation between class size and pupil
achievement. Larger classes will appear to be more effective. This is only
because we cannot take account of the fact that children in the smaller classes
may be more difficult to teach. Even if we have information on pupils' prior
achievement, this may not be enough to allow for the unobserved characteristics of pupils in the smaller classes that cause them to have lower achievement. This is what economists call selection bias or endogeneity and has
been a particular focus of the economics of education.

For instance in November 2002, Margaret Hodge, the then minister for
Education and Skills, in justifying the introduction of fees for higher education stated that a graduate earned a £400,000 premium over their working
life because of undertaking higher education. However, this figure was
obtained by just comparing the earnings of graduates versus non-graduates
in the Labour Force Survey and completely failed to take into account the
other differences between graduates and non-graduates (such as prior education, ability and family background). The Department for Children, Schools
and Families now says 'Over the working life, we believe that the average
graduate premium remains comfortably above £100,000 in today's valua-
tion, compared to what a similar individual would have earned if they just
had A levels.' In terms of policy development, whether the average lifetime
return to undertaking higher education is £400,000 or £100,000 makes a
big difference in terms of developing higher education funding policy.

Economists are also concerned with distribution effects. For example, we
also know that the impact of higher education for those who undertake it is
far from homogeneous and for some individuals the return will be much
larger and for others much smaller (or even negative). It is important that
policy also takes this into account (see Dearden *et al.*, 2002, for a full discussion of these issues).

So how do economists deal with selection bias (the potential endogeneity
of the educational intervention)? There is no 'one size fits all' solution to
finding the causal impact of an educational treatment on an outcome of
interest, and the economics of education has come up with a number of
innovative ways which analysts may or may not be able to use in order to

find the causal impact of an educational treatment. The most appropriate methodological approach will depend on a number of factors and it is important to assess these factors each time a new policy question arises.

There are six distinct but related approaches that economists generally take (see Blundell *et al.*, 2005a, and Blundell and Costa Dias, 2009). These are:

1   social experiments;
2   natural experiments/difference-in-difference methods;
3   instrumental variable methods;
4   control function methods;
5   matching methods;
6   regression discontinuity design.

Each of these approaches involves different assumptions and the decision of which approach to use depends crucially on the question being considered.

The social experiment is the social scientists' version of a clinical trial in that it relies on some randomised assignment rule that determines whether people receive an educational treatment or not. Social experiments have been used to evaluate a number of educational interventions in a number of countries including the UK. The most well-known social experiment in education is the Tennessee class-size experiment which randomly allocated children in Tennessee to different class sizes (and randomly allocated teachers to teach these classes). The results from this experiment suggested that large class size reductions in early schooling would yield significant gains in terms of pupil achievement (Card and Krueger, 1992).[4] In the UK random experiments in education are rare. More common are pilot schemes, where the results of an educational intervention can be compared to a control group that did not experience the intervention (e.g. the Education Maintenance Allowance (EMA) scheme, see Dearden *et al.*, 2009). Social experiments could be used more widely in the UK by combining pilot schemes with randomisation, for instance by randomly phasing in new educational initiatives rather than introducing a new initiative right across the country at the same time.

Natural (or quasi) experiments rely on some 'natural' randomisation to estimate the impact of an educational intervention. It involves finding some naturally occurring event which changes the policy environment for one group but not another (e.g. a change in rules for one group of individuals but not another, or in one jurisdiction but not another). We can then estimate the impact of the policy change by comparing the two groups before and after the change (the so-called difference-in-difference estimator). Of course, to use this type of approach one needs longitudinal data or repeated cross-sections where samples are drawn from the same population before and after the intervention. Dynarski (2003) used this approach to estimate the impact of college grants on college participation (by exploiting a change in law in the USA in 1982 which abolished college grants for children from families where one parent had died). Thus she investigates whether a sudden change in the grants available to these families had any impact on the higher education participation of the children. Machin and McNally's (2008) study of the literacy hour in England, where children in some schools were exposed to up to two years on introduction of the policy and others were not, similarly adopts a difference-in-difference type approach. The crucial assumption is that any unobserved characteristics of the treatment group that might influence outcomes (e.g. their socio-economic disadvantage) remain unchanging over time and are therefore taken account of in the modelling.

The instrumental variable approach has similarities to the natural experiment approach in that it relies on finding something (an instrument) that causes a 'natural' variation in an educational treatment but that has no impact on the outcome of interest, other than through its impact on the educational treatment. For instance, Harmon and Walker (1995) use changes in the compulsory school leaving age as an instrument to estimate the causal impact of education on earnings. The idea is that because of the law change, individuals who would have normally left school at 15 in 1972 would have been forced to stay at school until 16 in 1973 (the year of the law change). This allows us to estimate the impact of extra education for this group who were forced to stay on at school. If the impact of education is the same for all individuals then this estimate will tell us the causal impact of an additional year of education. If it is not, it will only tell us the return for those who were forced to switch behaviour which may be very different to those who would have stayed at school both before and after the change in law.

Matching methods involve comparing the group that gets the educational intervention with a control group that is very similar, on the basis of characteristics observed in the data. Technically this means that matching methods involve re-weighting the control group so that it looks the same as the treatment group so as to mimic the experimental setting. Matching may be a powerful approach but it relies on the researcher being confident that he/she has data on all the important characteristics of individuals or groups. So, for example, if the researcher is evaluating the impact of an intervention such as an after-school club on pupil achievement, the data needs to include information on all the characteristics of pupils that affect both whether they make use of the after-school club in the first place and that might also determine their academic outcomes (e.g. their socio-economic background, prior achievement, parental education level). If there are unobservable characteristics that determine both whether the pupils enrol in the after-school club *and* their outcomes (e.g. their attitude towards being in school) the matching method will not necessarily work. So even with rich data on observable characteristics, the treatment and control groups are often so different because of selection that no re-weighting scheme or matching can make the two groups look comparable. However, with good data and careful selection of control groups it can be a reliable way of estimating causal impact. It is commonly used in evaluations in the UK. The evaluation of the EMA scheme is just one example of the use of matching methods (see Dearden *et al.*, 2009).

Finally, regression discontinuity design relies on some discontinuity in policy design that provides a source of randomisation that can be explored to estimate the impact of an educational intervention. Examples of this in the education field include exploiting the rigid school years rules that operate in England to look at whether it is better to start school younger or older (children born on 31 August start school up to a year earlier than those born a day later on 1 September in England). From this research we see that in England it is much better starting school at an older age than a younger age and this negative effect of starting school young continues into higher education (see Crawford, Dearden and Meghir, 2009). It has also been used to look at the impact of class size in Israel where the number of teachers per class is decided using a strict rule of no more than 40 pupils per teacher. Hence, if there is a class of 40 and an extra pupil arrives, another teacher has to be allocated to a second class (Angrist and Lavy, 1999).

So where have these distinct methods made a contribution in education? One example is the issue of whether additional resources in schools lead to better pupil achievement, as mentioned above. This has been subject to study for many decades, largely by educationalists from a wide range of discipline backgrounds, working on issues of school effectiveness and school improvement (e.g. Nutall *et al.*, 1989; Gray *et al.*, 1996; Thomas *et al.*, 2007, to name but a few). In recent years, however, researchers in the field of economics of education have started to make a major contribution in this area of research (Angrist and Lavy, 1999; Card and Krueger, 1992; Dearden, Ferri *et al.*, 2002). In particular, they have applied most of the methods outlined above to the same question and come up with ways of trying to determine a genuinely causal relationship between resources, such as class size, and pupil achievement.

Economists have also used these techniques to become more involved in specific government evaluations of particular education programmes. For instance, in the USA major education investment programmes, such as HeadStart[5] have been subject to rigorous evaluation by economists, using statistical and econometric methods. Likewise here in the UK, quantitative evaluations of government education investments are often carried out by those working in the economics of education, as well as educationalists and those from other disciplines. The evaluation of the Excellence in Cities programme (Machin *et al.*, 2007), the EMA scheme (Dearden *et al.*, 2009) and the Literacy Hour (Machin and McNally, 2008) are all (selected) examples of this genre of contemporary research.

It is only after establishing genuine casual impact that we are able to assess the true costs and benefits of a particular education policy or intervention and compare the return with other investments. This is crucial for sound policy decision-making.

Wider impacts of the economics of education

As has been already discussed, the main route by which economics has recently been influential is via its influence on education policy. This is particularly the case in the USA and indeed the UK, where there has been greater emphasis on the economic aspects of education, both in terms of designing policies for the education system and from the perspective of evaluating the impact of policy on student outcomes.

The increased marketisation of education in the UK (Adnett and Davies, 2002) is just one example of the important role economists have played in education policy-making. It is, however, perhaps one of the most illuminating examples of the wider impact of economics in education. In the 1980s and 1990s, the then Conservative government of the UK adopted a more ostensibly economic approach to education, introducing some market mechanisms into the UK education system.[6] These quasi-market mechanisms included parental choice, parent representation on governing bodies and linking school funding with student enrolment numbers. Alongside this, publicly available test-score information was made available with which parents could compare the performance of one school with another.[7] These quasi-market reforms were designed with an explicit aim to improve pupil achievement, drawing heavily on the economic principles of incentives and competition. More recently, further legislation has been introduced, following the Department for Education and Skills White Paper, *Higher Standards, Better Schools for All* (2006), with the purpose of further increasing school autonomy and parental choice. Thus, for more than 20 years education policy-making in the UK has increasingly looked to economics to provide guidance as to how to improve the efficiency of the education system.

Such economic concepts have not, of course, been applied without limits and the economics of the market are not allowed to run rife through the UK education system. For instance, in the UK schools are generally not allowed to go 'bankrupt', i.e. exit from the market. Furthermore, there continue to be many market failures. For example, many parents still lack full information on the quality of schools. These limitations clearly weaken the incentive for schools to improve and may reduce the impact of economically motivated reforms designed to raise standards. Yet despite this, policy-makers' commitment to the basic tenet that incentives and competition can improve school quality has remained firm.

Of course, policy-makers have also become increasingly aware of the need for better understanding of the exact nature of the incentives faced by schools, recognising that teachers and head-teachers often have conflicting objectives and that market principles sometimes sit uneasily in schools. Thus, as Besley and Ghatak (2003) state, the critical issue has been to work out the best means by which the economic principles of competition, incentives and accountability can be brought together to enhance educational outcomes in the broadest sense. Economists and policy-makers have recognised the difficulties in applying economic principles to education (Le Grand, 2003) but there has as yet been no backlash against the notion that the efficiency of the system can be improved by applying such principles.

It must also be acknowledged, of course, that the evidence on the impact of the reforms on pupil performance suggests only limited positive effects of choice and competition on pupil achievement, at least in the UK (Bradley *et al.*, 2001; Gibbons *et al.*, 2008). The evidence (mainly from the USA, e.g. Hoxby, 2000, 2003a, 2003b) also shows that while increased competition among schools and moves to decentralise school finance can enhance attainment, it can raise inequality because richer parents are better able to take advantage of a more market-oriented system. This potential trade-off between efficiency in the school system and equity has long been recognised by economists (Le Grand, 2001, 2003). It is interesting, however, that in response to concerns about inequality in the UK school system, the current government has responded, not by reducing the marketisation of education, but by trying to mitigate its potentially negative effects on equality. This is exemplified by major initiatives such as the Every Child Matters agenda and the Children Act (2004), which seek to consider the achievement and welfare of all children, including those who are most vulnerable and those who are currently under-achieving. Whether or not such attempts will be successful remains an open question as such initiatives have generally not been evaluated, as yet. However, we would argue that economists have therefore played a major and increasing role in the design of a range of different education reforms across a number of countries during the last 20 years.

Key contributions and future prospects

There are a number of challenges facing education as we move through the twenty-first century. While economists certainly do not have all the answers, they can provide guidance on a whole range of important issues. For example, educationalists continue to grapple with the key question facing practitioners, policy-makers and parents, namely how do we raise pupil achievement, particularly the achievement of those currently lagging behind? In fact, economics has already provided a partial answer to that question. For instance, economists have determined that teacher quality is central to any attempt to improve school quality and raise standards and that teacher pay in turn plays a huge role in determining the quality of the teacher work-force. Much more needs to be done from a research perspective, however, to better understand the link between teachers, teaching and pupil achievement and on what kinds of education policies (whether targeted or universal) can deliver cost-effective improvements in education delivery and performance.

A question that is likely to become pressing in the face of economic downturn and rising educational participation is whether our continued emphasis on education and in particular qualifications really has a genuine

positive effect on individuals' lives. For example, despite increased investments in education over time, why does inequality in educational and cognitive achievement emerge so early (Feinstein, 2003) and why, in the UK at
least, do we have more or less as unequal a society now as we did 20 years
ago (Blanden and Machin, 2004; Blanden *et al.*, 2005; Machin and Vignoles,
2004)? As we encourage more and more young people to invest in degrees,
will this genuinely provide them with economic benefits and a route to
better-quality jobs and greater life satisfaction? Or will it simply lead to
'qualification inflation' as it becomes the norm for everyone to have a degree,
even for lower-level jobs? Indeed, the most fundamental question of all is
whether our education investments always benefit society as a whole and can
we really say how many graduates our economy needs?

We have also made the case that economists play a key role in the field of
education research as a whole. Of course statisticians and others have also
increasingly been involved in quantitative evaluation of education policy.
However, the contribution of economists is distinct. First, economists take a
different theoretical perspective and therefore may be more focused on incentives and other related issues trying to distinguish between benefits and costs
more precisely than other disciplines. Furthermore, from a methodological
perspective, economists bring a wide range of tools to bear on evaluations.
For instance, while the randomised control trial remains the 'gold standard'
of evaluation, it is increasingly recognised that randomised control trials are
not possible in all circumstances and that we must rely on other statistical
methods to evaluate the impacts of programmes in non-randomised settings
and, most importantly, to go beyond simply identifying correlations. Economists provide a range of methods that can be applied in a non-experimental
setting, as we outlined above.

It is also of note that such quantitative rigour was historically seen as
sorely lacking by those working within the education research establishment
(as summarised in Furlong and Oancea, 2005). Whether economics has contributed to improved methodology in education (for example, by introducing more robust econometric models to the field of education) or whether it
is the case that economists have simply taken over parts of the education
field is an arguable point. It is, however, an important distinction. Clearly
economics has the potential to offer theoretical models and methodological
rigour to the study of education. However, the contribution made by economists may be limited if the economics of education is seen as quite distinct
from the other disciplines working in the field of education. Economists are
often seen as positivist in their approach and simplistic in their analysis of
complex education issues. Furthermore, since economists generally use quantitative methods of analysis, antagonism towards quantitative methods is
often intertwined with suspicion about the real contribution that economists
can make to the field. Economists do need to work side by side with the
other major disciplines in the field of education if their contribution to the
field is to be maximised, particularly in terms of improved methodology.

In summary, in assessing the future prospects for the economics of education as a research field, it is evident that it is now a thriving and burgeoning part of education research. Education is now widely recognised to be an important determinant of economic and social outcomes. There is now much richer data available to do high-quality quantitative research in the areas and for such work to have high contemporary policy relevance. Thus it would seem that study of education acquisition and its economic and social impact in the economics of education research area is very likely to remain a fertile research ground.

Acknowledgement

This work was supported by the Centre for the Economics of Education at the Institute of Education, University of London.

Notes

1 Commentators on the origins of the economics of education as an independent field of research (e.g. Teixeira, 2001) also refer to Theodore Schultz's presidential address to the 1960 American Economic Association (Schultz, 1961) and to the Special Issue of the 1962 *Journal of Political Economy* edited by Schultz entitled 'Investment in Human Beings' as early instances of the start of the rise of the subject.

2 The journals are the following: *American Economic Review, Economic Journal, Econometrica, Economica, Journal of Political Economy, Quarterly Journal of Economics, RAND Journal of Economics, Review of Economic Studies.*

3 Of course, the number of papers per journal may well have also risen through time (especially in those journals that now have more issues per year than in the past), but not by enough to explain the scale of the recent upsurge. Similarly specialist journals that were set up in this period and that have published a lot of economics of education papers (e.g. *Journal of Human Resources, Economics of Education Review* and *Journal of Labor Economics*) were not considered in this suggestive analysis.

4 The magnitude of the effects was such that this evidence does not contradict the general notion that reductions in class size are not the most cost-effective way of improving pupil achievement.

5 An early-years policy intervention to help children in poor families akin to Sure Start in the UK (see the Effective Provision of Pre-School Education (EPPE) Project: Final Report, a longitudinal study funded by the DfES, 1997–2004).

6 Many of these policies were only introduced in England and Wales, and the Scottish education system is, in any case, differently structured. We refer to England and Wales where a particular policy does not apply to Scotland. Much of the evidence presented does, however, include Scotland.

7 A growing literature shows significant value attached to these school performance tables with parents willing to pay significant sums of money through the housing market to live near a better-performing school (see, *inter alia*, Cheshire and Sheppard, 2004, and Gibbons and Machin, 2003, 2006, 2008). This also has impacted on the policy debate, and the wider debate in the media, with talk of 'selection by mortgage' and discussions of school admissions reform.

References

Adnett, N. and P. Davies (2002) *Markets for Schooling*, Routledge, London.

Angrist, J. and V. Lavy (1999) Using Maimonides' Rule to Estimate the Effect of Class Size on Scholastic Achievement, *Quarterly Journal of Economics*, 114, 533–576.

Becker, G. (1964) *Human Capital: A Theoretical Analysis with Special Reference to Education*, Columbia University Press, New York.

Besley, T. and M. Ghatak (2003) Incentives, Choice, and Accountability in the Provision of Public Services, *Oxford Review of Economic Policy*, 19, 235–249.

Blanden, J. and S. Machin (2004) Educational Inequality and the Expansion of UK Higher Education, *Scottish Journal of Political Economy*, Special Issue on the Economics of Education, 51, 230–249.

Blanden, J., P. Gregg and S. Machin (2005) Educational Inequality and Intergenerational Mobility, in S. Machin and A. Vignoles (eds) *What's the Good of Education? The Economics of Education in the United Kingdom*, Princeton University Press, Princeton.

Blanden, J., P. Gregg and L. MacMillan (2007) Accounting for Intergenerational Persistence, *Economic Journal*, 117, C43–C60.

Blanden, J., P. Gregg and L. MacMillan (2008) *Intergenerational Persistence in Income and Social Class: The Impact of Increased Inequality*, CMPO mimeo.

Blaug, M. (1972) *An Introduction to the Economics of Education*, Penguin, Harmondsworth.

Blaug, M. (1976) The Empirical Status of Human Capital Theory: A Slightly Jaundiced Survey, *Journal of Economic Literature*, 14, 827–855.

Blundell, R. and M. Costa Dias (2009) Alternative Approaches to Evaluation in Empirical Microeconomics, *Journal of Human Resources*, 44(3), 565–640.

Blundell, R., L. Dearden and B. Sianesi (2005a) Evaluating the Impact of Education on Earnings: Models, Methods and Results from the NCDS, *Journal of the Royal Statistical Society Series A*, 168(3), 473–512.

Blundell, R., L. Dearden and B. Sianesi (2005b) Measuring the Returns to Education, in S. Machin and A. Vignoles (eds) *What's the Good of Education? The Economics of Education in the United Kingdom*, Princeton University Press, Princeton.

Bradley, S., G. Johnes and J. Millington (2001) School Choice, Competition and the Efficiency of Secondary Schools in England, *European Journal of Operational Research*, 135, 527–544.

Brehm, J. and W. Rahn (1997) Individual-Level Evidence for the Causes and Consequences of Social Capital, *American Journal of Political Science*, 41, 999–1023.

Bynner, J. and M. Egerton (2001) *The Wider Benefits of Higher Education*, Higher Education Funding Council For England, London.

Bynner, J. and S. Parsons (1997) *It Doesn't Get Any Better: The Impact of Poor Basic Skills on the Lives of 37 year Olds*, Basic Skills Agency, London.

Card, D. (1999) The Causal Effect of Education on Earnings, in O. Ashenfelter and D. Card (eds) *Handbook of Labor Economics*, vol. 3A, Elsevier, Amsterdam.

Card, D. and A.B. Krueger (1992) Does School Quality Matter? Returns to Education and the Characteristics of Public Schools in the United States, *Journal of Political Economy*, 100 (February), F1–F40.

Cheshire, P. and S. Sheppard (2004) Capitalising the Value of Free Schools: The Impact of Supply Characteristics and Uncertainty, *Economic Journal*, 114, F397–F424.

Dearden, L., C. Emmerson, C. Frayne and C. Meghir (2009) Conditional Cash Transfers and School Dropout Rates, *Journal of Human Resources*, 44(4), 827–857.

Dearden, L., J. Ferri and C. Meghir (2002) The Effect of School Quality on Educational Attainment and Wages, *Review of Economics and Statistics*, 84, 1–20.

Dearden, L., S. Mcintosh, M. Myck and A. Vignoles (2002) The Returns to Academic and Vocational Qualifications in Britain, *Bulletin of Economic Research*, 54, 249–274.

Dee, T. (2004) Are There Civic Returns to Education?, *Journal of Public Economics*, 88, 1697–1720.

Department for Education and Skills (2005) *Higher Standards, Better Schools for All: More Choice for Parents and Pupils*, Cm 6677.

Dynarski, S. (2003) Does Aid Matter? Measuring the Effect of Student Aid on College Attendance and Completion, *American Economic Review*, 93(1), 279–288.

Erikson, R. and J. Goldthorpe (2008) *Income and Class Mobility between Generations in Great Britain: The Problem of Divergent Findings from British Birth Cohort Studies*, Nuffield College mimeo.

Ermisch, J. and C. Nicoletti (2007) Intergenerational Earnings Mobility: Changes across Cohorts in Britain, *B.E. Journal of Economic Analysis and Policy*, 7(2), article 9.

Feinstein, L. (2003) Inequality in the Early Cognitive Development of British Children in the 1970 Cohort, *Economica*, 70, 73–97.

Feinstein, L. and R. Sabates (2005) *Education and Youth Crime: Effects of Introducing the Education Maintenance Allowance Programme*, Centre for Research on the Wider Benefits of Learning Research Report No. 14.

Freeman, R.B. (1976) *The Overeducated American*, Academic Press.

Furlong, J. and A. Oancea (2005) *Assessing Quality in Applied and Practice-based Educational Research: A Framework for Discussion*, University of Oxford, Department of Educational Studies, www.bera.ac.uk/pdfs/Qualitycriteria.pdf.

Gibbons, S. and S. Machin (2003) Valuing English Primary Schools, *Journal of Urban Economics*, 53, 197–219.

Gibbons, S. and S. Machin (2006) Paying for Primary Schools: Admissions Constraints, School Popularity or Congestion, *Economic Journal*, 116, C77–C92.

Gibbons, S. and S. Machin (2008) Valuing School Quality, Better Transport and Lower Crime: Evidence from House Prices, *Oxford Review of Economic Policy*, 24, 99–119.

Gibbons, S., S. Machin and O. Silva (2008) Choice, Competition and Pupil Achievement, *Journal of the European Economic Association*, 6, 912–947.

Gray, J., H. Goldstein and D. Jesson (1996) Changes and Improvements in Schools' Effectiveness: Trends over Five Years, *Research Papers in Education*. 11, 35–51.

Harmon, C. and I. Walker (1995) Estimates of the Economic Return to Schooling for the United Kingdom, *American Economic Review*, 85, 1278–1286.

Haveman, R. and B. Wolfe (1995) The Determinants of Children's Attainments: A Review of Methods and Findings, *Journal of Economic Literature*, 33, 1829–1878.

Hoxby, C. (2000) Does Competition among Public Schools Benefit Students and Taxpayers?, *American Economic Review*, 90, 1209–1238.

Hoxby, C. (2003a) *The Economics of School Choice*, Chicago, Chicago University Press.

Hoxby, C. (2003b) School Choice and School Competition: Evidence from the United States, *Swedish Economic Policy Review*, 10, 9–66.

Layard, R. and G. Psacharopoulos (1974) The Screening Hypothesis and the Returns to Education, *Journal of Political Economy*, 82, 985–998.

Le Grand, J. (1991) *Equity and Choice*, HarperCollins, London.

Le Grand, J. (1993) *Quasi-markets and Social Policy*, Macmillan, London.

Le Grand, J. (2001) The Theory of Government Failure, in *Economic Theory and the Welfare State*, Edward Elgar, Cheltenham.

Le Grand, J. (2003) *Motivation, Agency, and Public Policy: Of Knights and Knaves, Pawns and Queens*, Oxford University Press, Oxford.

Lochner, L. and E. Moretti (2004) The Effect of Education on Criminal Activity: Evidence from Prison Inmates, Arrests and Self-Reports, *American Economic Review*, 94, 155–189.

Machin, S. (2003) Wage Inequality since 1975, in R. Dickens, P. Gregg and J. Wadsworth (eds) *The Labour Market under New Labour*, Palgrave Macmillan, Basingstoke.

Machin, S. (2008a) The New Economics of Education: Methods, Evidence and Policy, *Journal of Population Economics*, 21, 1–19.

Machin, S. (2008b) An Appraisal of Economic Research on Changes in Wage Inequality, *Labour*, 22, 7–26.

Machin, S. and S. McNally (2008) The Literacy Hour, *Journal of Public Economics*, 92, 1441–1462.

Machin, S. and A. Vignoles (2004) Educational Inequality: The Widening Socio-Economic Gap, *Fiscal Studies*, 25, 107–128.

Machin, S. and A. Vignoles (2005) (eds) *What's the Good of Education? The Economics of Education in the United Kingdom*, Princeton University Press, Princeton.

Machin, S. and S. Vujic (2005) *Crime and Education in the United Kingdom*, Centre for Economic Performance, draft paper.

Machin, S., S. McNally and C. Meghir (2007) *Resources and Standards in Urban Schools*, Centre for the Economics of Education Discussion Paper 76.

Mincer, J. (1958) Investment in Human Capital and Personal Income Distribution, *Journal of Political Economy*, 66, 281–302.

Mincer, J. (1974) *Schooling, Experience and Earnings*, Columbia University Press, NBER, New York.

Nutall, D.L., H. Goldstein, R. Prosser and J. Rasbash (1989) Differential School Effectiveness, *International Journal of Education Research*, 13, 769–776.

Psacharopoulos, G. (1973) *Returns to Education: An International Comparison*, Jossey-Bass, Elsevier, Amsterdam.

Rivkin, S.G., E.A. Hanushek and J.F. Kain (2005) Teachers, Schools, and Academic Achievement, *Econometrica*, 73(2), 417–458.

Schultz, T. (1961) Investment in Human Capital, *American Economic Review*, 51, 1–17.

Schultz, T. (1963) *The Economic Value of Education*, Columbia University Press, New York.

Sianesi, B. and J. Van Reenen (2003) The Returns to Education, *Macroeconomics*, 17, 157–200.

Spence, M. (1973) Job Market Signalling, *Quarterly Journal of Economics*, 87, 355–374.

Teixeira, P. (2001) The Economics of Education: An Exploratory Portrait, *History of Political Economy*, Annual Supplement, 257–287.

Thomas, S., Peng, W.J. and Gray, J. (2007) Modelling Patterns of Improvement over Time: Value Added Trends in English Secondary School Performance across Ten Cohorts, *Oxford Review of Education*, 33, 261–295.

Todd, P. and K. Wolpin (2007) The Production of Cognitive Achievement in Children: Home, School, and Racial Test Score Gaps, *Journal of Human Capital*, 1, 91–136.

7 Comparative and international education

Policy transfer, context sensitivity and professional development

Michael Crossley and Keith Watson

Introduction

Comparative and international education (CIE) has a long and distinguished history. Along with other disciplines of education, however, it has faced repeated challenges as times and professional agendas and priorities have changed. Recent years have, nevertheless, seen a sustained and creative revitalisation of the field, driven by a strengthened research base, growing awareness of cross-cultural issues in teacher education and increased recognition of the importance of global and comparative perspectives across the social sciences. These shifts are captured in earlier work (Crossley and Watson, 2003, p. 19), in the following quotation and throughout the chapter itself.

> At a time such as the present, when profound changes are occurring in the whole structure of global economic, social and cultural relations, and the role of education in these changes is coming to be recognised as fundamental, all countries can only benefit from knowing more about the cultural premises of each other's education.
>
> (UNESCO, 1993, p. 89)

Historical and paradigmatic foundations

The origins of systematic comparative studies of education can be traced back to seminal European initiatives in the early nineteenth century when French scholars such as Marc-Antoine Jullien called for research on the nature and impact of foreign education systems. The motive for this was to help shape the reform, and competitiveness, of education in France itself. This is a familiar rationale for change – and one that demonstrates the continuity of long-held assumptions about the potential of comparative studies to help decision-makers to better understand the workings, needs and priorities of their home system. Reflecting the scientific turn that characterised the early nineteenth century, Jullien argued that the careful comparison of international and statistically grounded data on student enrolments, numbers of teachers, administrative systems and educational finance would help 'to deduce true principles and determined routes so that education would be transformed into an almost positive science' (1817, cited in Fraser, 1964, p. 20). Jullien is recognised as the first to use the term 'comparative education', and many writers regard him as its founding father. Today, the positivistic influence of Jullien's proposals can be seen in the statistical work of many international organisations and large-scale cross-national studies, such as those pioneered by the International Association for the Evaluation of Educational Achievement (IEA) (Goldstein, 1998; Postlethwaite, 1999), and the more recent Programme for International Student Assessment (PISA) surveys (OECD, 2004).

In the UK, work that Michael Sadler carried out at the outset of the twentieth century is often acknowledged as the foundation for systematic comparative research in education (Higginson, 1979, 1995). Sadler's impact was, however, very different in nature to that inspired by Jullien, representing distinctively socio-cultural and interpretivist paradigmatic perspectives and principles. Sadler's sensitivity to differences in culture and context represented a challenge to the scientific aspirations embodied in Jullien's search for the 'best' way forward for education. It also inspired a philosophically and historically informed tradition for comparative studies. This generated tensions between different approaches to comparative research that continue to the present day. Crossley *et al.* (2007) document the emergence of this socio-cultural tradition in comparative education in ways that demonstrate its influence upon British teaching, research and scholarship over the past 40 years. We will return to these issues and tensions later. It is pertinent to note, however, that Sadler's influence also drew increased attention to the multi-disciplinary demands of comparative research in education by emphasising that 'In studying foreign systems of education, we should not forget that the things outside the schools matter even more than the things inside the schools, and govern and interpret the things inside' (Sadler, 1900, p. 49).

A multi-disciplinary field

It is perspectives such as these that have long emphasised the contributions to be made to comparative studies by disciplines as diverse as philosophy, history, psychology, sociology and economics. Indeed, while many writers refer to the 'discipline' of comparative education (Heath, 1958), others believe it can be helpfully conceptualised as a 'multi-disciplinary field'. Not only does a multi-disciplinary perspective convey the complexity and demands of such work, but it also reflects and encourages the creative involvement of a diversity of scholars and helps to legitimise the close relationship between the two sub-fields of comparative and international studies of education.

As Wilson (1994) and Epstein (1994) argue, the twin fields of CIE have different epistemological, disciplinary and professional origins and characteristics, but they are often mutually supportive enterprises. Epstein, for example, maintains that while 'comparativists ... are primarily scholars interested in explaining why educational systems and processes vary and how education relates to wider social factors and forces', international educators 'use the findings derived from comparative education to understand better the educational processes they examine and thus to enhance their ability to make policy relating to programmes such as those associated with international exchange and understanding' (Epstein, 1994, p. 918). Thus, for Epstein, comparative education 'is primarily an academic and interdisciplinary pursuit' (1994, p. 918), while international education is more applied in nature, concerned with international development and ways of fostering 'an international orientation in knowledge and attitudes' (1994, p. 918). Indeed, for many writers, attention to educational policy and practice in low-income countries best characterises the parameters of international education.[1] Here it is appropriate to note how researchers often focus their attention on a combination of comparative *and* international studies; and many have incorporated both terms in the titles adopted for research centres and national societies. This is demonstrated by contributions to a recent volume devoted to the histories of comparative education societies, including the British Association (Masemann *et al.*, 2007). This returns our attention to the significance of comparative contributions to educational studies within the UK.

Early contributions, mechanisms and sites of production

Academic and applied contributions

Early contributions to educational studies in the UK reflect the intellectual positionings adopted by different proponents of CIE noted above. As indicated previously, positivistic influences played a significant role in shaping the orientation and statistical work of international agencies, such as the International Bureau of Education (IBE) that was established in Geneva in 1925. This led to the compilation of the first annual international education reports and statistics, and influenced the subsequent emergence of other international agencies and research centres following the Second World War. These include bodies that now play leading roles in global educational research and development, such as the United Nations Development Programme (UNDP); the United Nations Educational, Scientific and Cultural Organisation (UNESCO); the UNESCO International Institute for Educational Planning (IIEP); and the Organisation for Economic Co-operation and Development (OECD). British comparativists have played significant roles in such organisations and UK researchers have contributed to the development of what have become the largest and most influential cross-national studies of education in the form of the IEA, PISA and other related surveys of student achievement. It will later be argued that the contemporary impact of such comparative studies, and the controversies they generate, represent

some of the most significant educational issues for attention by both theorists and practitioners today.

Within the UK, the influence of the Sadlerian tradition was especially
significant as the field sought to establish academic legitimacy in the early–
mid twentieth century. As the biographical research of Higginson (1979,
1995) and Sislian (2003) testifies, Sadler's personal impact, as the Director of
the Office of Special Inquiries and Reports of the Committee (later Board) of
Education in England, made a recognised contribution to European and
colonial policy deliberations. Most notably this challenged earlier preoccupations with the uncritical international transfer of educational policy and
practice from one context to another. Sadler (1900) also drew attention to
ways in which comparative studies can assist researchers to understand their
own home systems. It was in such ways that many of the comparativists that
followed Sadler aimed to both contribute to socio-cultural theorising and to
guide educational policy development. The field thus simultaneously
developed academic and applied aspirations, and engaged with agendas for
post First and Second World War reconstruction and development at home
and abroad.

Writers such as Kandel (1933) pioneered the field in the USA from the
1930s, emphasising historical antecedents and the centrality of disciplined
scholarship focused upon analysis and explanation. Hans (1964), at King's
College, London, built upon such work, but stressed the reformative element
of comparative studies. So too did Mallinson, at the University of Reading,
and King (King's College, London). The engagement of the international
constituency of the field in educational planning throughout the developing
world made what was, perhaps, a more direct impact upon actual practice
(Parkyn, 1977; Watson, 1998). The 1960s and 1970s are, therefore, recognised as a time when CIE was enjoying what many see as a 'golden age' in
terms of its popularity and influence in educational studies throughout the
UK. King's (1979) best-selling book ran through five editions, demonstrating this popularity and advancing the socio-cultural paradigm. The influence of the 'scientific' approach also remained strong, however, and the
paradigm wars of the 1960s and 1970s were clearly visible in the methodological tensions and debates surrounding the publication of Holmes's (1965)
arguments articulating a neo-positivistic, problem-based approach to comparative education and the influential American text, *Toward a Science of
Comparative Education*, published by Noah and Eckstein (1969).

Centres for teaching and research

The first department in the UK to focus upon what is now called CIE was
established at the University of London, Institute of Education (ULIE) in
1927 (Little, 2004). This was the Colonial Department, introduced initially
to meet the training needs of the colonial administration. In subsequent
years, this was re-named the Department of Education in Tropical Areas

(1952–1973), and the Department of Education in Developing Countries (1973–1985). Comparative education courses at the Institute were begun in 1947, under the leadership of Joseph Lauwerys, though the intellectual differences between these international and comparative units often inhibited close professional collaboration. The ULIE thus made a seminal contribution to the development of the combined field. This was reinforced by the contribution made by King's College, under the influence of Hans and King. Other notable pre-Second World War university centres for specialist study in the field included Oxford and Reading – to be followed after the war by Bristol, Birmingham, Cardiff, Edinburgh, Glasgow, Hull, Leeds, Manchester and Newcastle. By the 1960s, academics with a declared interest in CIE were also running specialist courses at Cambridge, Durham, Hull, Liverpool and Ulster at Coleraine. Equally important for the field, most of the UK colleges of education also ran courses in comparative education for prospective teachers undertaking initial teacher training. This, as Watson (1982) argues, was a heyday for specialist teaching in CIE. Enrolments were growing, staffing was robust and the future looked bright. Such optimism was expressed by participants at a benchmark conference on 'The Place of Comparative Education in the Training of Teachers', held at the University of Reading in 1965 (Mercier, 1966). This was to translate into follow-up initiatives that created the forerunner of the British Comparative Education Society (BCES).

The emergence of a national society and core journals

The Comparative Education Society in Europe (CESE) was formed in 1961 and, enthused by the 1965 Reading conference, a British section of CESE was established at a second Reading conference held in 1966. The British section of CESE, led by combinations of university and college academics, initially thrived in a buoyant higher education climate characterised by growth in student and teacher numbers, and major reforms in secondary education. The new society convened annual conferences with themes that focused upon key questions and developments of the day (Sutherland *et al.*, 2007). Active support for the founding of the World Council of Comparative Education Societies (WCCES), in Ottawa (1970), was generated, and, emerging from an early newsletter, the society's official journal, *Compare*, was launched in 1970. These developments, along with the regular publication of conference proceedings, strengthened the influence of CIE throughout teacher education, within national and international policy arenas and in academia at home and abroad. This is reflected in comments made by Peterson (1964) when, in launching *Comparative Education*, the first British-based journal in the field, he wrote:

> We hope to serve the cause and attract the interest not only of comparative education and comparativists, but of education as a whole and its administrators or practitioners … The continuing need for this kind of

practical approach is surely clear at a time when governments are at last beginning to realise the true importance of education in the social and economic structure. As the demand for social planning increases and the techniques of sociological enquiry improve, it becomes both more urgent and more practicable to consider the educational problems of different types of society as a whole.

(Peterson, 1964, p. 20)

As the early volumes of *Comparative Education* demonstrate, the focus of CIE at the time was upon 'the processes of educational planning, higher and secondary education – in the north and the south – and, to a lesser extent, studies of teacher training and the pertinence of selected school subjects' (Crossley *et al.*, 2007, p. 4). At the same time, global decolonisation processes generated considerable demand for the training of educational personnel, and consultancy advice, for newly independent national systems of education; the international constituency of the field played a significant role in this process. The British Council, for example, designated ten UK university departments of education, with comparative and international expertise and experience, as centres of excellence for the training of Commonwealth scholars in educational administration, science education, English as a foreign/second language and rural/community development. Capturing these priorities and focusing specifically upon education in the developing world, a third British-based journal, the *International Journal of Educational Development* (IJED), was established in 1979 and, in the same year, the British section of CESE was formally re-designated as the British Comparative Education Society (BCES).

Challenging times

The buoyant times portrayed above were short-lived. Changes in British political and educational policy contexts during the mid-1970s began to challenge the role played by many of the core disciplines in education – including CIE – in the preparation of teachers. Despite the growth of education that was envisaged in the White Paper 'A Framework for Expansion' (DES, 1972), the next few years saw the closure or amalgamation of many colleges of higher education. This was influenced by predictions of a fall in population growth, and by questions raised about the kinds of education needed for a post-industrial future. Prime Minister Callaghan launched the Great Education Debate in 1976, and further challenges emerged as the 1977 financial crisis hit the UK. This led to a squeeze on funding for higher education, including teacher education, and the beginning of tighter regulations for the education of teachers. The impact of these developments upon CIE is documented in Watson's (1982) survey of the 'state of comparative education in British teacher education'. Watson examined questionnaires from 106 higher education institutions, and revealed that comparative education was being forced out from courses in colleges of education and was struggling to survive in some universities. There had, he suggested:

> been a crisis of confidence in the value of comparative education as well as its place in educational institutions ... For far too many teachers and administrators, comparative education is regarded as an interesting luxury, a 'frill', but an unnecessary ingredient for a common core teacher education curriculum.
>
> (1982, p. 197)

Schweisfurth (1999) and O'Sullivan (2008) provide more recent analyses of the place of CIE in UK teacher education, and in doing so reinforce Watson's 1980s argument that influential global trends, inspired by neo-liberal philosophies, increasingly focused teacher-education programmes 'on the development of specific teaching competencies ... that are related to actual performance in the classroom' (O'Sullivan, 2008, p. 138). This was the start of the 'practical turn' that challenged, and continues to challenge, many of the disciplines of education to the present day. To cite McGrath's (2001, p. 392) related analysis of the political economy of British CIE:

> In the educational sphere, globalisation leads to the hegemony of the view that education is about economic competitiveness. This privileges human resources over liberal or critical perspectives of education and privileges the market over all other areas ... The stress is on essential competencies and, as can be seen from the curriculum of teacher training across Britain, non-essential perspectives (historical, religious, international) are marginalised or ignored.

Methodological and theoretical developments

The decline of college and undergraduate teaching in CIE that characterised the 1980s had a detrimental effect upon the influence of the field and upon the membership of the BCES. As Raggatt (1984, p. 3) pointed out: 'In 1971/72 some 130,000 students were enrolled in colleges of education ... by 1980/81 college enrolment had fallen to some 38,000.' Similar concerns were shared by the other disciplines of education at the time, where efforts to regroup were inevitably prioritised.

Organisationally, one revitalisation strategy pursued led to closer relations between those who saw themselves as primarily 'comparativists' or as 'internationalists'. This led to the renaming of the national society as the British Comparative and International Education Society (BCIES) in 1983. This reflected the growth of the international development constituency and the changing geopolitical realities of the 1980s. This was aided by the increasing influence of the processes of globalisation on the international transfer of educational policy – and of the potential for CIE to play a central role in the critical interrogation of such developments. The research dimension of the field thus emerged more prominently as policy-makers and social science researchers became more international in outlook. This had an impact upon the quality and status of publications within the field, with the editor for *Compare* in 1988 arguing that:

> Circulation has held up but has also gone more 'up market'. There are fewer readers in exclusively under-graduate teaching institutions. A greater number of major centres of educational policy-making and research in a wider range of countries now take the journal.

Similarly, changes visible in the journal *Comparative Education* demonstrate how a shift towards the research base of the field was reflected in the nature and improved academic quality of articles published in the journal (Crossley *et al.*, 2007). Increased attention was paid to a readership of researchers and policy-makers, and critical studies challenging the global impact of Western neo-liberal models featured increasingly prominently in *Comparative Education* throughout the 1980s. IJED, notably, focused much critical attention on the implications of dependency and modernisation theories.

Methodologically, the field's traditional focus upon the nation-state encountered sustained challenges on a variety of fronts. Moreover, the traditional preoccupation of many comparativists with policy studies was increasingly seen to suffer from a lack of critical engagement with educational practice in context. New generations of researchers that pioneered the revitalisation of the field thus made significant contributions to the development and application of qualitative approaches in educational research during this period – informed by traditional respect for the significance of cultural and contextual differences. Stenhouse (1979), for example, explored the potential for empirically grounded, qualitative case studies in comparative education. This demonstrated a clear challenge to past practices that tended to focus upon policy studies and the nation-state as the primary unit of analysis. It also helped to open the way for new units of analysis, and to revitalise hermeneutic and interpretivist approaches to comparative research. For Stenhouse (1979, p. 5), comparative education was seen to 'deal in insight rather than law as a basis for understanding', and this, in tune with contemporary advances in the 'new sociology of education', inspired many subsequent researchers to develop their work at the micro-level, located in the world of lived experience and professional practice.

The impact of such methodological changes can be seen in the trajectory of much British research carried out in the following decades, and in the impact of this on both the comparative and international dimensions of the field. It is reflected, for example, in influential work by researchers, such as Broadfoot and Osborn, on perceptions of teaching in England and France (Broadfoot *et al.*, 1993), and on the experiences of young learners in England, France and Denmark (Osborn *et al.*, 2003), where emphasis was given to case studies, classroom observations and in-depth interviews. While this work also explores the potential to be gained from 'mixed methods', its deep grounding in comparativists' traditional concerns for cultural and contextual influences underpins its ongoing significance within the broader field of educational studies today.

Similarly, the 1980s saw the influence of qualitative research play a role worldwide in challenging the dominance of positivistic assumptions, and the prevalence of the uncritical international transfer of educational policy and practice, in the international development arena. This can later be seen in challenges to the impact of World Bank policy raised by a special issue of IJED (1996). Indeed, the CIE research community mounted a concerted challenge to what many now see as the hegemony of positivistic assumptions and neo-liberal philosophies and principles in the international education policy arena. Inspired by Stenhouse, detailed case studies of educational reform in isolated schools throughout Papua New Guinea were carried out in this spirit by one of the current writers during the early 1980s (Crossley, 1984). Similarly grounded fieldwork by other British researchers can be seen in contexts as diverse as East Asia (Bray, 1996), India (Dyer and Choksi, 1997), Sri Lanka (Little, 1999), Ghana, South Africa and Indonesia (Stephens, 2007).

While the influence of the qualitative paradigm is now well represented within the development discourse, its place in influencing policy and practice remains contested. More recently, Vulliamy (2004, p. 277) has also warned that while:

> A concern for sensitivity to cultural context has been a key part of the field of comparative education in England – all the way from its pioneers ... to current exponents ... Such concern for cultural context also pervades sociological traditions underpinning the development of qualitative research ... The challenge for future comparative and international researchers in education is to harness the symbiosis of these two traditions to resist the increasing hegemony of a positivist global discourse of educational research and policy-making.

This helps to return our attention to theoretical developments within the field that continue to hold contemporary significance. Dale (2001) and Apple (2001), for example, prioritise the development of global perspectives, at the macro-level, that 'pay particular attention to some of the most important dynamics surrounding globalisation in education' (Apple, 2001, p. 409), and 'lay bare the nature and the reasons for the different impacts globalisation has had' (Dale, 2001, p. 493). Here it is argued that CIE is especially well placed to pursue such work given its early engagement with world systems theories (Arnove, 1980), the tradition of multi-disciplinarity that connects with related advances across the social sciences, and a long history of research challenging uncritical international transfer (Crossley and Watson, 2003, pp. 50–69).

Traditional concerns with the significance of culture and context upon both educational policy and educational research also position the field well for critical engagement with postmodern and postcolonial understandings of educational and social development. American researchers such as Carnoy (1974) and Altbach and Kelly (1978) made early contributions in this respect, and in the UK work by Watson (1998) and Crossley and Tikly (2004) has also helped to develop the way for postcolonial theorising. In this, it can be seen how history – one of the foundational disciplines for the field – is re-emerging in ways that demonstrate the contemporary relevance that Kazamias (2001) values and highlights for the future of CIE.

Reconceptualising for the future

In looking to the future, it is argued that CIE is well positioned to contribute to the ongoing development of both educational studies and professional practice. The developments discussed above indicate why this might be so, and help to demonstrate the scope and nature of this potential. It is argued elsewhere that concerted attention needs to be given to the ongoing 'reconceptualisation' of the field (Crossley, 1999), but here we explore the potential for a reconceptualised field to strengthen the contemporary relevance and quality of educational studies, improve relations between the 'disciplines of education', bridge the worlds of professional practice, theory and research and contribute to higher education in ways that will help advance future teaching, research and professional development.

In 1997, the British Association for International and Comparative Education (BAICE) was formed from the amalgamation of BCIES and BATROE (British Association for Teachers and Researchers in Overseas Education). This merger continued earlier efforts in the UK to bring comparativists closer together with their 'internationally' and development-oriented colleagues and students. In the early 1990s, efforts had been made to co-ordinate the 'British resource of expertise' (Watson and King, 1991) in international education through the creation of an umbrella organisation that came to be known as the United Kingdom Forum for International Education and Training (UKFIET). This brought together professional bodies, non-government organisations and agencies such as the Commonwealth Secretariat and British Council along with BCIES/BAICE itself. The success of UKFIET in strengthening the presence, profile and influence of the collective British resource can be seen in its active role in advising government agencies, in supporting research capacity building and in the impact of the biennial UKFIET International Conference on Education and Development that has been held at the University of Oxford since 1991 (see www.ukfiet.org). BAICE was formally launched at an inaugural conference held at the University of Reading in September 1998 (Watson, 2001). The first keynote sessions at this conference adopted the theme of 'Reconceptualising Comparative and International Education', recognising that while a revitalisation of the field was a positive sign in the UK, if this renewed investment was to meet the needs of the twenty-first century, fundamental organisational, theoretical and methodological changes were essential.

The revitalisation that characterised the 1990s was stimulated by changing geopolitical relations, the acceleration of globalisation, advances in ICT and paradigmatic shifts across the social sciences. The response was also worldwide with the creation, or re-invigoration, of research centres, publications and national societies, both in the UK and abroad. This is documented in institutional surveys carried out by Dyer and King (1993) and Altbach and Tan (1995); and ongoing momentum can be seen in more recent studies by Schweisfurth (1999), Wilson (2005), Masemann *et al.* (2007) and Wolhunter *et al.* (2008). To cite the editors of the recent *Histories of the World Council of Comparative Education Societies and Its Members*:

> The WCCES was founded in 1970 in Ottawa, Canada. It evolved from an International Committee of Comparative Education which had been convened in 1968 ... and brought together the four national societies and one regional society for comparative education then existing. Over the decades, additional societies joined, and by 2007 the WCCES had 36 member Societies.
>
> (Masemann *et al.*, 2007, p. 1)

This indicates healthy growth for the field worldwide and provides a supportive framework for future generations. As more and more UK researchers have built international dimensions into their studies, the potential size of the home constituency has also grown. Membership of BAICE, for example, has steadily increased since the turn of the millennium, and this includes the increased engagement of young doctoral and post-doctoral researchers (Sutherland *et al.*, 2007). University departments and research centres, however, continue to face financial and staffing challenges in a context characterised by intense competition for external funding.

Such challenges are especially prominent in the current higher education sector which is suffering the protracted impact of the latest world economic crisis across many fields and disciplines. Moreover, as efforts are made to respond to the tightening of financial resources, there are signs that old divisions could, once again, be in danger of opening within CIE, as individuals and groups compete for position and influence. Thus, in addition to the resurgence of positivistic research noted earlier, there are indications that comparative studies of educational policy are beginning to re-emerge in ways that prioritise the status and esteem of theoretical positioning at the expense of research grounded in the in-depth experience of educational practice. Ironically this raises new dangers that the former divisions between theorists and practitioners, between academic 'tribes and territories', could return to challenge the future coherence and policy impact of the field. As King (1965, p. 147) long ago warned, if comparativists do not pay attention to the links between academic scholarship, the work of practitioners and applied social science, then 'other people will [and] they may not then call their work comparative education, but will nevertheless, work over our proper concerns without benefit of our insights'. These dangers are especially significant in times of budgetary constraint when key leaders in the field are often not replaced when they retire or move on, leaving the field itself weakened and diminished. Such trends can, indeed, be seen within and beyond the UK, though Wolhunter *et al.*'s (2008) recent international review of the field, combined with WCCES's growth, reveals more reassuring patterns throughout China, Japan, South East Asia and Southern Africa – where both the theoretical and applied dimensions of the field are being pursued in mutually supportive ways.

Returning to the UK, research councils and bodies, such as DFID, are, nevertheless, taking increased interest in supporting high-quality comparative and international studies (Lewin, 2007). This form of competitive external funding now plays a strategically important part in maintaining and renewing a sustainable research community. The Economic and Social Research Council (ESRC), for example, funded an influential UK programme of comparative education seminars between 1997 and 1999. This resulted in publications that highlighted the current need for work on innovative comparative methodologies and for more disciplined comparative studies of pedagogy, the processes of learning, pupil achievement and the professional development of teachers (Alexander *et al.*, 1999).

Throughout the last decade, DFID has also devoted increased resources to research (Allsop, 2000), including a joint funding scheme in collaboration with the ESRC. The products of this can be seen in a now extensive series of theoretically informed, but policy-oriented, *Education Papers* (www.DFID. gov.uk/education). Building upon this experience, along with developments in the organisation of large-scale research in other disciplines, DFID funding has made recent contributions that are in tune with the BAICE reconceptualisation rationale. In an effort to bring together researchers from education (and other disciplines) in the north and the south, to focus research funding upon international development priorities (such as the Millennium Development Goals), and to strengthen the development of comparative/international research capacity, three large-scale Research Programme Consortia have been established with substantial DFID funding. The administrative centres for these groups are located at the Universities of Cambridge, Bristol and Sussex. In each of these cases, bridges are being built between northern and southern research organisations/universities (Crossley, 2008), research priorities are being identified collaboratively, comparative principles and perspectives are informing the nature of critical analysis, multi-disciplinary teams are being forged and the building of research capacity (north and south) is integral to the rationale for each consortia (www.create-rpc.org; www.edqual.org; www.recoup.educ.cam.ac.uk). Collaboration between researchers in the north and south also holds future potential for the further

development of postcolonial perspectives in ways that previously marginalised voices – the poor, women and girls, indigenous communities, 'the
Other' – may challenge new forms of imperialism (Tikly, 2004) and
contribute to advances in both theory development and policy applications.

Initiatives such as these are, therefore, making significant contributions to
innovative forms of empirically grounded and thematically/problem-oriented
research that are very different to the types of nation-state policy studies
pursued by earlier generations of comparativists. The audience for such work is
also wider, including researchers working across the social sciences, comparativists in other fields and disciplines (Schriewer, 2006), mainstream educationalists and general readers concerned with, for example, the relationships
between education and the processes of international development. Grek and
colleagues (2009) identify another priority issue for critical attention in their
analysis of the impact of the results of cross-national studies of student achievement upon education policy formation in a range of European systems. Other
emergent questions relating closely to teacher education and the education disciplines that would benefit from future comparative study include critically
informed research on the role and influence of international league tables; the
nature and impact of globally influential policy agendas; differing conceptions
of pedagogy; accountability and the quality of education; relationships
between educational success, culture and identity; the impact of climate
change and challenges to global security on education; and implications of the
internationalisation of higher education. While it is not the intention to construct a definitive list of research priorities here, it is argued that issues such as
these could be best approached by researchers with a deep, multi-disciplinary
grounding in comparative perspectives, methodologies and sensitivities.

A final issue that we prioritise returns the analysis to the dilemmas of
international transfer. This relates directly to Vulliamy's challenge to the
uncritical global transfer and impact of 'systematic review methodology and
its associated privileging of quantitative research strategies, such as randomised controlled trials in evidence-based policy' (Vulliamy, 2004, p. 261).
Here is an issue that warrants careful consideration by the educational
research and international development communities if the uncritical transfer of policies, practices *and research methodologies* is not to perpetuate the
questionable 'borrowing' (Phillips and Schweisfurth, 2006) of models and
what Noah (1984) long ago warned of as the 'abuse' of comparative education. St Claire and Belzer (2007) explore such issues in their study of the
political economy of educational research in the USA and the UK, and
Furlong (2004, p. 343) concurs with Vulliamy by arguing that the educational research community needs 'to defend a rich and diverse range of
approaches to research, promoting debate about quality within different sub-
communities and encouraging open discussion across epistemological and
methodological boundaries'. For comparativists, where differences in world
views and cultures add to the complexities and philosophical possibilities,
such questions are even more timely and revealing.

Conclusions

The questions and debates outlined above identify new challenges and point to ways forward for future research. They also hold potential for the reconceptualisation of postgraduate teaching, with additional implications for the future of teacher education and educational studies as a whole. In a related study of the teaching of CIE (Tikly and Crossley, 2001), it was acknowledged that undergraduate studies and courses for prospective teachers had been progressively squeezed out of higher education by the 'practical turn' referred to earlier. It was also argued that the revitalisation of the research dimension of the field had supported renewed growth in the form of postgraduate studies, notably at the Master's and Doctoral levels. The teaching of such courses currently contributes to the development of future generations of researchers and what Schweisfurth (1999) refers to as the 'resilience' and 'responsiveness' of specialist research centres.

Given that the internationalisation of higher education now impacts upon all teaching programmes – including those with a distinctively practical orientation – it can be argued that comparative perspectives and international content have a valuable role to play within many future course offerings. This could help to inject a more critical, reflective and context-sensitive dimension into continuing professional development for teachers. In sum, it is argued that:

> while there is a strong case for comparative and international education to maintain its status as a specialism within education studies, there is also an urgent need for comparativists to become active change agents in the broader transformation of their institutions – if they are to better meet the contemporary challenges posed by globalisation, changing geopolitical relations, and reform in the higher education sector.
>
> (Tikly and Crossley, 2001, p. 562)

Finally, writers such as Wilson (2005), O'Sullivan (2008) and Planel (2008) have begun to develop such arguments in ways that open up renewed possibilities for CIE in initial teacher education. To cite Planel (2008, p. 386), who recognises how global migrations now bring multiple cultures into many classrooms:

> at a time when classroom cross-cultural encounters are on the increase, it is comparative pedagogy, that area of comparative education which is concerned with cultural values and meanings that lie behind teaching and learning, that is most relevant to teachers.

Indeed, the UK Universities Council for the Education of Teachers (UCET) is currently preparing a discussion document on 'The Internationalisation of Teacher Education' that aims 'to broaden and deepen experiences of international and global dimensions in the professional development of teachers, which encompasses all phases, including post-compulsory, from initial teacher education through to continuing professional development' (UCET, 2008, p. 1). In doing so, it is argued that 'the international and global dimension must feature much more prominently in teacher education programmes' (2008, p. 4), and that 'the internationalisation of teacher education is a key strategic challenge for education in the coming years' (2008, p. 5). Similar arguments to this were made by Watson and Williams (1984) in previous decades, but, today, a wider range of stakeholders, many working beyond the comparative field, are now in strong agreement. The boundaries between comparativists and other researchers have also blurred considerably over recent years, in ways that greatly increase the possibilities and potential to be gained from increased collaboration between the field, other disciplines of education and the wider social sciences. While new challenges are emerging for education, CIE provides a strategically important foundation for the production of innovative, timely and globally significant research – and for the disciplined development of future researchers with much to offer to educational studies and the social sciences as a whole.

Acknowledgements

With thanks to Mark Bray, for comments on an earlier draft of this chapter.

Note

1 'International education' is also often associated with the International Schools movement; with teaching international students; and with improving international understanding.

References

Alexander, R., Broadfoot, P. and Phillips, D. (eds) (1999) *Learning from Comparing: New Directions in Comparative Education Research – Contexts, Classrooms and Outcomes* (Oxford: Symposium).

Allsop, T. (2000) 'The Department for International Development: knowledge generation after the White Paper', in Alexander *et al.* (eds) (2000) *Learning from Comparing: New Directions in Comparative Education Research – Policy, Professionals and Development* (Oxford: Symposium).

Altbach, P.G. and Kelly, G.P. (eds) (1978) *Education and Colonialism* (New York: Longmans).

Altbach P.G. and Tan, J. (1995) *Programs and Centre in Comparative and International Education: A Global Inventory* (Buffalo: State University of New York Press).

Apple, M. (2001) 'Comparing neo-liberal projects and inequality in education', *Comparative Education*, 37, 4: 409–423.

Arnove, R.F. (1980) 'Comparative education and world systems analysis', *Comparative Education Review*, 24, 1: 48–62.

Bray, M. (1996) *Counting the Full Cost: Parental and Community Financing of Education in East Asia* (Washington, DC: World Bank).

Broadfoot, P., Osborn, M., Gilly, M. and Bucher, A. (1993) *Perceptions of Teaching: Primary School Teachers in England and France* (London: Cassell).

Carnoy, M. (1974) *Education as Cultural Imperialism* (New York: Longman).

Crossley, M. (1984) 'Strategies for curriculum change and the question of international transfer', *Journal of Curriculum Studies*, 16, 1: 75–88.

Crossley, M. (1999) 'Reconceptualising comparative and international education', *Compare*, 29, 3: 249–267.

Crossley, M. (2008) 'Bridging cultures and traditions for educational and international development: comparative research, dialogue and difference', *International Review of Education*, 51, 3–4: 319–336.

Crossley, M. and Tikly, L. (eds) (2004) *Postcolonialism and Comparative Education*, Special Issue of *Comparative Education*, 42, 2.

Crossley, M. and Watson, K. (2003) *Comparative and International Research in Education: Globalisation, Context and Difference* (London and New York: Routledge-Falmer).

Crossley, M., Broadfoot, P. and Schweisfurth, M. (2007) 'Introduction: changing educational contexts, issues and identities', in *Changing Educational Contexts, Issues and Identities. 40 Years of Comparative Education* (London: Routledge), 1–15.

Dale, R. (2001) 'Constructing a long spoon for comparative education: charting the career of the "New Zealand" model', *Comparative Education*, 37, 4: 493–500.

Department of Education and Science (1972) *A Framework for Expansion* (London: Her Majesty's Stationery Office).

Dyer, C. and Choksi, A. (1997) 'North–south collaboration in educational research: reflections on Indian experience', in Crossley, M. and Vulliamy, G. (eds) *Qualitative Educational Research in Developing Countries* (New York: Garland), 267–293.

Dyer, C. and King, K. (1993) *The British Resource in International Training and Education: An Inventory* (Edinburgh: University of Edinburgh).

Epstein, E.H. (1994) 'Comparative and international education: overview and historical development', in Husen, T. and Postlethwaite, T.N. (eds) *The International Encyclopaedia of Education*, 2nd edn (Oxford: Pergamon Press), 928–923.

Fraser, S.E. (1964) *Jullien's Plan for Comparative Education 1816–1817* (New York: Bureau of Publications, Teachers College, Columbia University).

Furlong, J. (2004) 'BERA at 30: have we come of age?', *British Educational Research Journal*, 30, 3: 343–358.

Goldstein, H. (1998) 'Introduction', Special Issue *Assessment in Education* on *The IEA Studies*, 3, 2: 125–128.

Grek, S., Lawn, M., Lingard, B., Ozga, J., Rinne, R., Segerholm, C. and Simola, H. (2009) 'National policy brokering and the construction of the European education space in England, Sweden, Finland and Scotland', *Comparative Education*, 45, 1, 5–21.

Hans, N. (1964) *Comparative Education* (London: Routledge & Kegan Paul).

Heath, K.G. (1958) 'Is comparative education a discipline?', *Comparative Education Review*, 12, 2: 31–32.

Higginson, J.H. (ed.) (1979) *Selections from Michael Sadler: Studies in World Citizenship* (Liverpool: Dejall and Meyorre).

Higginson, J.H. (1995) 'Michael Sadler's groundwork as research director', *Compare*, 25, 2: 109–114.

Holmes, B. (1965) *Problems in Education* (London: Routledge & Kegan Paul).

International Journal of Educational Development (1996) Special Issue: *The World Bank's Education Sector Review: Priorities and Strategies for Education*, 5, 3.

Kandel, I.L. (1933) *Studies in Comparative Education* (Boston: Houghton and Mifflin).

Kazamias, A.M. (2001) 'Re-inventing the historical in comparative education: reflections on a protean epistome by a contemporary player', *Comparative Education*, 37, 4: 439–449.

King, E.J. (1965) 'The purpose of comparative education', *Comparative Education*, 1, 3: 147–159.

King, E.J. (1979) *Other Schools and Ours*, 5th edn (London: Holt, Rinehart and Winston).

Lewin, K.M. (2007) 'Diversity in convergence: access to education for all', *Compare*, 37, 5: 577–599.

Little, A.W. (1999) *Labouring to Learn: Towards a Political Economy of Plantations, People and Education in Sri Lanka* (New York and London: Macmillan and St. Martin's Press).

Little, A.W. (2004) 'Seventy-five years of education partnerships with developing countries'. Paper written for the 75th anniversary of the Institute of Education's work with developing countries in *Education and Developing Countries, 75 Years*. London: Institute of Education, University of London.

Masemann, V., Bray, M. and Manzon, M. (eds) (2007) *Common Interests, Uncommon Goals: Histories of the World Council of Comparative Education Societies and Its Members* (Springer/University of Hong Kong).

McGrath, S. (2001) 'Research in a cold climate: towards a political economy of British international and comparative education', *International Journal of Educational Development*, 21, 5: 391–400.

Mercier, P.J. (ed.) (1966) *The Place of Comparative Education in the Training of Teachers* (Reading: University of Reading, Institute of Education).

Noah, H.J. (1984) 'The use and abuse of comparative education', *Comparative Education Review*, 28, 4: 550–562.

Noah, H.J. and Eckstein, M.A. (1969) *Toward a Science of Comparative Education* (London: Macmillan).

OECD (2004) 'Learning for tomorrow's world: first results from PISA 2003'. Available online at www.pisa.oecd.org.

Osborn, M., Broadfoot, P., McNess, E., Planel, C., Ravn, B., and Triggs, P. (2003) *A World of Difference? Comparing Learners across Europe* (Maidenhead: Open University Press).

O'Sullivan, M. (2008) 'Comparative education in teacher education in the UK and Ireland', in Wolhuter, C. *et al.* (2008) *Comparative Education at Universities Worldwide*, 2nd edn (Sofia: Bureau for Educational Services), 136–142.

Parkyn, G.W. (1977) 'Comparative education research and development education', *Comparative Education*, 13, 1: 87–93.

Peterson, A.D.C. (1964) 'Editorial', *Comparative Education*, 1, 1: 1–3.

Phillips, D. and Schweisfurth, M. (2006) *Comparative and International Education: An Introduction to Theory, Method and Practice* (London: Continuum Books).

Planel, C. (2008) 'The rise and fall of comparative education in teacher training: should it rise again as comparative pedagogy?', *Compare*, 38, 4: 385–399.

Postlethwaite, T.N. (1999) *International Studies of Educational Achievement: Methodological Issues* (Hong Kong: University of Hong Kong).

Raggatt, P. (1984) 'Comparative education: its condition and future', *Compare*, 14, 1: 3–5.

Sadler, M. (1900) 'How far can we learn anything of practical value from the study of foreign systems of education?', in Higginson, J.H. (ed.) (1979) *Selections from Michael Sadler* (Liverpool: Dejall and Meyorre).

St Claire, R. and Belzer, A. (2007) 'In the market for ideas: how reforms in the political economy of educational research in the US and UK promote market managerialism', *Comparative Education*, 43, 4: 471–488.

Schriewer, J. (ed.) (2006) *Comparative Methodologies in the Social Sciences: Cross-disciplinary Inspirations*, Special Issue *Comparative Education*, 42, 3.

Schweisfurth, M. (1999) 'Resilience, resistance and responsiveness: comparative and international education at UK universities', in Alexander, R., Broadfoot, P. and Phillips, D. (eds) *Learning from Comparing: New Directions in Comparative Educational Research – Contexts, Classrooms and Outcomes* (Oxford: Symposium).

Sislian, J. (2003) *Representative Sadleriana, Sir Michael Sadler (1861–1943) on English, French, German and American School and Society* (New York: Nova Science Publishers).

Stenhouse, L. (1979) 'Case-study and comparative education: particularity and generalisation', *Comparative Education*, 15, 1: 5–11.

Stephens, D. (2007) *Culture in Education and Development: Principles, Practice and Policy* (Oxford: Symposium).

Sutherland, M.B., Watson, K. and Crossley, M. (2007) 'The British Association for International and Comparative Education', in Masemann, V., Bray, M. and Manzon, M. (eds) *Common Interests, Uncommon Goals: Histories of the World Council of Comparative Education Societies and its Members* (Springer, University of Hong Kong), 155–169.

Tikly, L. (2004) 'Education and the new imperialism', *Comparative Education*, 40, 2: 173–198.

Tikly, L. and Crossley, M. (2001) 'Teaching comparative and international education: a framework for analysis', *Comparative Education Review*, 45, 4: 561–580.

UNESCO (1993) *World Education Report 1993* (Paris: UNESCO Publishing).

Universities Council for the Education of Teachers (2008) *The Internationalisation of Teacher Education* (draft document), UCET, September 2008.

Vulliamy, G. (2004) 'The impact of globalisation on qualitative research in comparative and international education', *Compare*, 34, 3: 261–284.

Watson, K. (1982) 'Comparative education in British teacher education', in Goodings, R., Byram, M. and McPartland, M. (eds) *Changing Priorities in Teacher Education* (London: Croom Helm), 193–225.

Watson, K. (1998) 'Memories, models and mapping: the impact of geopolitical changes on comparative studies in education', *Compare*, 28, 1: 5–31.

Watson, K. (ed.) (2001) *Doing Comparative Education Research: Issues and Problems* (Oxford: Symposium).

Watson, K. and King, K. (1991) 'From comparative to international studies in education: towards the co-ordination of a British resource of expertise', *International Journal of Educational Development*, 11, 3: 245–253.

Watson, K. with Williams, P. (1984) 'Comparative studies and international awareness in teacher education', *Journal of Education for Teaching*, 10, 3: 249–255.

Wilson, D.N. (1994) 'Comparative and international education: fraternal or Siamese twins? A preliminary genealogy of our twin fields', *Comparative Education Review*, 38, 4: 449–486.

Wilson, M. (2005) 'Regression, Repositioning and Regeneration. Comparative and international education in UK higher education institutions', paper presented at the 8th UKFIET International Conference on Education and Development (New College, Oxford).

Wolhuter, C., Popov, N., Manzon, M. and Leutwyler, B. (eds) (2008) *Comparative Education at Universities Worldwide*, 2nd edn (Sofia: Bureau for Educational Services).

8 Towards a geography of education

Chris Taylor

It seems to me that some of the most stimulating intellectual developments of recent years have come either from new, hybrid places (cultural studies might be an example) or from places where boundaries between disciplines have been constructively breached and new conversations have taken place.

(Massey, 1999, p. 5)

Introduction

The main context to this edited collection is to consider the future of education research in light of the changing demographics, and their consequences, in the field of education (Mills *et al.*, 2006). The proposition that education may lose subject specialists is important given the significance of different disciplines to education research. However, as Doreen Massey, one of the best-known British geographers, reminds us above, the role of different disciplines within the social sciences is not just about 'borrowing' ideas – knowledge, theory and methods – it is also about ensuring there are new and constructive interdisciplinary developments at the interface of different subjects. This distinction is quite important and illustrates, to some extent, the past contributions of geography to the field of education, but also highlights the challenges ahead. As we will see there has been considerable and growing use of geographical ideas in education research. However, this has not been matched with any significant and formal developments at the interface of these two subjects, necessary to both fully exploit the inter-relationship between these two subjects and warrant the existence of recognised sub-disciplines in each subject. While the former suggests there are many exciting questions and areas of research still to be addressed, the absence of the latter makes it difficult to foresee how geography could play a sustained part in the future of education research.

For some current and future education researchers the notion of 'borrowing' geographical ideas may be enough to sustain or offer new insights into the key challenges of education. But throughout this chapter I want to make a case for distinguishing between what Collins and Evans (2007) term interactional expertise and contributory expertise. This is, rather crudely, the difference between education researchers being fluent in the language of geography and education researchers having the tacit knowledge to practice or 'do' geography. As we will see later, much use of geography in education research does not go beyond utilising the language and vocabulary of geography. As Robertson also argues, 'it is not sufficient to simply bring a spatial lexicon to our conceptual sentences (as in "geographies" of classroom emotions; the school as a "place"; communities of practice). This is to fetishize space' (2009, p. 2). Clearly, the practice of 'borrowing' geographical ideas may be more than a matter of linguistics, but nonetheless, contributory expertise suggests something more. And this is important, since, as will be argued later, the key developments in geography that may be of most relevance to education now and in the future are likely to require geographical skills equivalent to contributory expertise. But this is not straightforward either, since it raises wider concerns about inter-disciplinary research and new divisions of labour within an integrated social science academy (Harvey, 1990; Massey, 1999).

The chapter is necessarily organised into four main sections. First it considers the main mechanisms and sites of production of what can be considered the geography of education. Second, I attempt to define and then outline the major contributions of geography to the field of education research, before then presenting what I consider to be the most important developments in geography of relevance to the field of education now and in the immediate future. The chapter concludes by considering what the future might hold for the geography of education, in terms of its intellectual contributions but also in terms of the institutional and practical challenges that this discussion raises.

Before proceeding, however, it is important to outline a number of assumptions and limitations to this discussion. First, my own inter-disciplinary journey may privilege a particular perspective on the issues being addressed in this chapter. Therefore, it is important to declare that the following discussion is likely to be partial and really only provides the basis from which, hopefully, further discussions and debates may follow, in education *and* in geography. This brief 'glance' across the two disciplines is further compounded by the breadth of these two subjects across the three dimensions of knowledge, theory and method.

The next set of limitations to this discussion relates to the boundaries that I place around the two subjects of geography and education. Clearly one of the important ways that geography and education are related is in terms of the process of teaching and learning the subject of geography, particularly in schools and higher education. And of course there are some very important contributions and sites of production for this kind of research (such as the work of the Geographical Association and the *Journal of Geography in Higher Education*). However, in line with the rest of this edited collection, I will largely focus on the contribution geography can make to our understanding of education. In turn this also means the focus is more precisely on the contribution of *human* geography to education. Almost conversely, the discussion considers education research in its broadest definition. While the difference between education research and education*al* research (Whitty, 2006) should be recognised, it would be perhaps be short-sighted at this stage of the discussion to consider only the role of geography on educational research that is solely geared towards improving policy and practice.

Lastly, since this volume is principally about the future of education research in the UK, most of the following examples are largely taken from the UK. However, processes and practices of any social science discipline are now firmly embedded within an international framework; the recent 2008 Research Assessment Exercise demonstrates this. Therefore it is important that the often local practices of education research (say, within the UK) are situated alongside the international development of knowledge, theories and methods. This, as will also be shown, is itself an important way in which geography can contribute to the field of education research, particularly within the higher education sector.

In search of geography's contribution to education

Geography is a very messy subject and has always had a contested tradition. Furthermore, it has changed considerably as a discipline over time, and indeed space, reflecting the shifting social, cultural, economic and political contexts of the UK. Livingstone (1992) provides an excellent journey through the history of geography, while simultaneously gathering together the main characteristics[1] of geography (see also Johnston and Sidaway, 2004). At the turn of the twentieth century, geography was largely characterised by exploration, mapping, imperialism and areal differentiation that lent itself to what Livingstone (1992) called 'regional recitation'. It also laid the important groundwork for inter-disciplinary approaches to studying society and its environments. The focus on describing and understanding the region has remained an important characteristic of geography, but a desire to move beyond the descriptive to a law-making and explanatory science emerged during the highly modernist 1960s and early 1970s. The ensuing quantitative revolution (as in many other social science disciplines) took a central role in geography, focusing on spatial distributions and locational analyses. Unsurprisingly many humanistic geographers challenged the centrality of geographical positivism and quantitative methods during that time. This also coincided with (renewed) interest in Marxist analyses of social justice and inequality (Harvey, 1973). Consequently the prevailing discourse in geography became that of structure and agency and political-economic approaches to geography, followed by the utilisation of Giddens' structuration theory. By the mid-1980s geographers began to recognise the prime significance of locale and place, both in terms of understanding the interplay of structure and agency but also how those relationships themselves shape place; the socio-spatial dialectic (Soja, 1989). This was quickly followed by the 'cultural turn' in geography, allied to postmodernism, feminism, identity politics and language (Barnett, 2002; Johnston and Sidaway, 2004). Geography, often assumed to be a largely empirical discipline, promoted its role in the development of new social theories. As we will see, these most recent advances have certainly helped geography to be considered more seriously by other social science disciplines (Thrift and Walling, 2000). This 'success' has also led to a proliferation of new and highly ranked geographical journals in the last decade (Johnston, 2003). But despite a higher profile outside the discipline many of the changes have led to increased fragmentation, certainly between human and physical geography, but also within human geography. Over ten years ago, Johnston (1991) highlighted increasing specialisation and fewer cross-disciplinary links within geography. Massey (1999) also warned against the dangers of increased divisions of labour within the new social sciences. This led to a flurry of debates within geography about its future within the increasingly integrated social sciences and a search for its 'core principles' (Clifford, 2002; Thrift, 2002; Turner, 2002; Gregson, 2003; Hamnett, 2003). This concern with the future of the discipline has been further exacerbated by the significant decline in the number of students studying geography at GCSE in England (OFSTED, 2008). Despite the apparent uncertainty of what constitutes and characterises 'geography' it remains one of the largest social science disciplines in the UK, with a relatively young age profile of researchers, and continues to have a strong commitment to working across disciplinary boundaries (Mills *et al.*, 2006).

Given the contested nature of the subject and its increasing fragmentation it is difficult to provide a single coherent picture of the way in which geography has contributed to the field of education. It is further complicated for three additional reasons. First, both geography *and* education have always had strong connections with other core social science disciplines, such as sociology, economics and political science. Therefore, the movement and exchange of ideas between geography and education are heavily intertwined with these other social science disciplines (Figure 8.1). Second, the multi-disciplinary nature of the two subjects has also meant that they each have developed strong sub-disciplinary groups around these core social science subjects. The absence of any formally recognised networks or communities of practice at the interface between geography and education is compounded, third, by the presence of very few other sites of production, such as journals or books with a specific focus on geography and education.

The most relevant journals are *Globalisation, Societies and Education* and *Compare*. The former is particularly interested in the nature and effects of globalisation in education, in which geography makes an important contribution. But again, they both tend to represent a particular type of geographical analysis. Other relevant journals (both US-based) are *Urban Education* and the *Journal of Research in Rural Education*. Clearly these journals publish education research that has a particular geographical context, but this does not necessarily extend to geographical or spatial analyses of education.

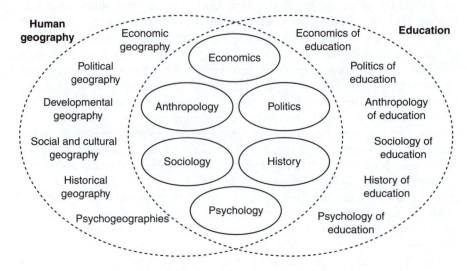

Figure 8.1 The multi-disciplinary foundations of geography and education.

Similarly there are no major tomes or monographs that present or discuss the geography of education. However, there are a number of edited collections that all emerged from informal networks of debate and discussion. Probably the earliest example of this was *Education and Society: studies in the politics, sociology and geography of education* (Bondi and Matthews, 1988), containing ten essays focusing on either the politics of education or social issues in education, but all from a geographical perspective. More recent examples include: a special issue of *Urban Studies* in 2007, a collection of geographical analyses of school choice and education marketisation; *Spatial Theories of Education: policy and geography matters* (Gulson and Symes, 2007), an international set of contributions primarily concerned with identifying 'the possibilities provided by spatial analysis; that current theorising of space helps edify a variety of educational problems, on, and across, a range of scales' (Gulson and Symes, 2007, p. 9); and *Geographies of Knowledge, Geometries of Power: framing the future of higher education* (Epstein *et al.*, 2008), which takes an explicitly inter-disciplinary focus on higher education and globalisation.

But without doubt the main interest in recent years within geography has been to study children as key actors in society and space. The journal *Children's Geographies* reflects this growing research focus. This has also led to the creation of the Geographies of Children, Youth and Families working group within the RGS-IBG. Of course, this important development in geography is part of a wider focus on children and childhood across most of the social sciences (such as sociology, psychology and anthropology). And, although it is interested in children, little of the focus has been so far on children as learners or children within an educational arena.

There is clearly evidence, then, to suggest that new communities of practice examining and debating the interface between geography and education are beginning to appear. Analyses of a number of academic databases (Figure 8.2), key mainstream journals in education and geography (Figure 8.3) and conference presentations (Figure 8.4) demonstrate this. The growth in research presented or published that can be considered to cover both geography and education can easily be seen, both in the UK and international contexts. The very recent growth in this area reflects a wider 'spatial turn' across the social sciences (Gulson and Symes, 2007; Warf and Arias, 2008), which in turn reflects what many commentators see as the changing social, cultural, economic and political landscape of the UK and the rest of the world. As Thrift remarks, 'things are becoming "more geographical"' (2002, p. 291). But despite this increasing geographical attention there is a strong view that much of it does not go further than using the language of geography (Smith and Katz, 1993), as Massey (1999) also notes, 'It is very easy to argue that we should "take space seriously". Everybody says it these days. There has indeed, it is rumoured, been something called "the spatial turn". The rhetoric is everywhere; the content is more elusive' (p. 11). The same can also be said for education more specifically (Gulson and Symes, 2007; Robertson, 2009). Much of this can be attributed to the growing use of education theorists such as Pierre Bourdieu (habitus) and, to a lesser extent, Basil Bernstein (classroom codes). But both of these important authors used spatial language only incidentally, largely as metaphor, and certainly never to examine spatial phenomenon or spatial relations in the education context. There has also been a growing use of the social theorist Henri Lefebvre and the spatial theorist Edward Soja in education research, both of whom stress that space is socially constructed and that social relations are constitutive of that space.

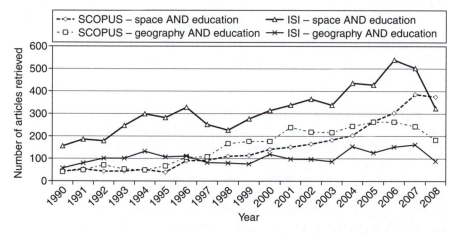

Figure 8.2 Interface between geography and education: analysis of academic databases.

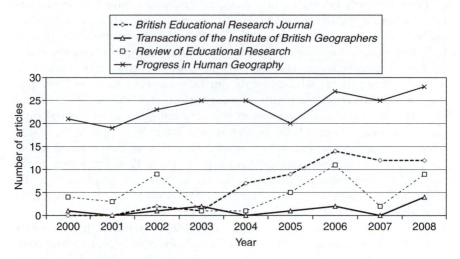

Figure 8.3 Interface between geography and education: analysis of key journals.

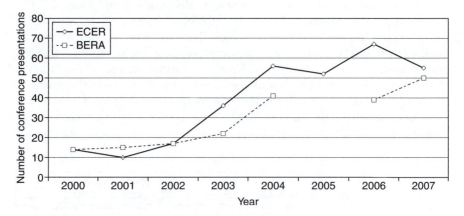

Figure 8.4 Interface between geography and education: analysis of conference presentations.

Despite the apparent 'spatial turn' in education and corresponding 'child-hood turn' in geography, such developments are still at a critical stage; much of the examples given above still involve different groups of scholars with very little overlap, particularly across the education–geography subject divide. It is also the case that very few formal sites of production or dissemination (journals, research networks, etc.) exist. As a result it can be difficult for academic practitioners who work at the interface between education and geography to consider themselves as a coherent community of practice. And it is equally difficult to identify the full contribution that geography has on the field of education. It is also important we keep sight on such developments both in terms of whether they convey interaction expertise – that could characterise much of the spatial turn in education – and/or contributory expertise – that still only occurs rather much on a small-scale and ad hoc basis and within existing (sub-) disciplinary pockets (Collins and Evans, 2007).

The contribution of geography to education

In identifying the main sites of production and dissemination, the major contributions that geography has made and is making to the field of education have already begun to be outlined. The discussion thus far has also highlighted and stressed how complex this is. In order to fully appreciate its contribution I utilise the geographically related concept of *scale* to provide a framework from which we can systematically explore the relationship between geography and education. Figure 8.5 employs the notion of 'operational scale' (Lam and Quatttrochi, 1992) to attempt to illustrate the varying levels of phenomenon and processes that a geography of education would be concerned with. Figure 8.5 also summarises some of the most important examples of geographical research at each of these levels.

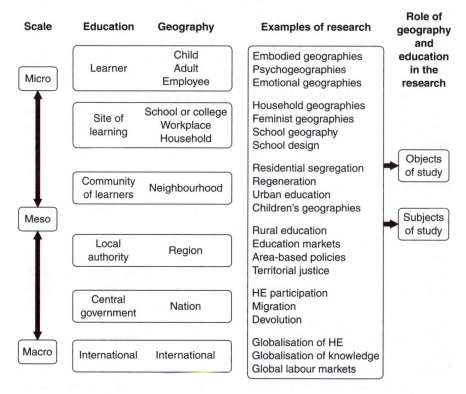

Figure 8.5 Towards a geography of education.

The learner/child

As we have already seen there has been considerable interest in the geographies of children as the primary research subject. However, geography has, until recently, given little attention to the child as a learner. However, there is now growing interest in psycho-geographies, with their emphasis on the relationship between the environment, emotions, fantasies and embodiment of children (Sibley, 2003; Matthews and Tucker, 2006). This has been particularly useful in showing how children demonstrate their agency within the institutional confines of schools (Hemming, 2007) and the role of gender and sexualities in schools (Renold, 2005).

Site of learning/school/household

Of course, what constitutes the site of learning is more complex than simply the confines of the classroom or lecture hall. But the main focus tends to be on the school and the household as two important sites of spatial and social practices. Although most geographical research within and on the household has not been concerned with processes of teaching and learning there are clearly some important ways in which the geography of the home have some bearings on processes of social relations (such as between siblings and/or between parents) – such as in terms of 'good-enough parenting' (Duncan and Smith, 2002), children's use of space within the home (Christensen et al., 2000), or children's relationship with cyber-space (Valentine et al., 2000). There has also been much interest in the geography of the schools, in terms of their design and architecture (e.g. Eggleston, 1977; Woolner et al., 2007), children's use of space within the school (e.g. Gordon et al., 2000; Fielding, 2000), the curriculum (Edwards and Usher, 2003) and inclusion (Armstrong, 2003).

Community of learners/neighbourhood

Probably the greatest contribution of geography to the field of education is in research at the level of community and neighbourhood. For example, there is a relatively long history of community-based studies that have been primarily interested in education as the subject and object of study at the neighbourhood level, dating back to the 1960s era of geography (Young and Willmott, 1962; Jackson and Marsden, 1966; Rex and Moore, 1967; Robson, 1969). Much of this kind of research continued under the genre of urban education, particularly in the USA, where the focus has been on the particular challenges to education within urban and inner-city contexts of concentrated social and economic deprivation and ethnic plurality (e.g. Herbert, 1976; Reay, 2004). Attention has since returned to this level of geographical–education phenomenon and processes with the introduction of quasi-education markets and school choice (Gewirtz et al., 1995; Taylor,

2002) and more specifically residential segregation and gentrification (Taeuber *et al.*, 1981; Taylor and Gorard, 2001; Butler and Robson, 2003; Burgess *et al.*, 2005; Allen, 2007). Furthermore, education and schools are increasingly seen as important features of social geography more generally (Collins and Coleman, 2008), particularly in terms of community or neighbourhood regeneration (Crowther *et al.*, 2003; Gulson, 2005), geographies of children (Holloway and Valentine, 2000a; Spencer and Blades, 2006), neighbourhood environments and processes of learning (Rickinson *et al.*, 2004) and the relationship between educational attainment and neighbourhood (Garner and Raudenbush, 1991; Bell, 2003).

Local authority/region

Again, there has long been a geographical interest in education at the level of the local authority or region. Ever since the introduction of local education authorities and regional governance to education much research has been interested in this form of political geography and territorial justice (Jennings, 1977; Radnor and Ball, 1996). This has generally focused on the uneven provision of education (Benn and Simon, 1970; Coates and Rawstron, 1971; Marsden, 1987; Taylor, 2001), contested policy landscapes (e.g. Coffield *et al.*, 2005) and studies of differential attainment at the local authority level (Byrne and Williamson, 1971; Rees and Rees, 1980; Gray *et al.*, 1984). There are also significant methodological developments within multi-level modelling (O'Connell and McCoach, 2008) that have linked analyses of educational attainment at the neighbourhood and school levels with analyses at the local authority level. Other examples of research at this level include studies on rural education (Green and Letts, 2007) and analyses of area-based education policies (Halsey, 1972; Rees *et al.*, 2007).

Central government/nation

There has been relatively little interest in geographical analyses of education at the national level, beyond policy-oriented research or accounts of national education systems. However, since political devolution in the UK during the late 1990s there has been renewed interest in new national policy developments (Bryce and Humes, 2003; Rees, 2005) and 'home international' analyses of education (Phillips, 2003). Particular attention is often made to higher education at this level (Rees and Taylor, 2006; Rutten *et al.*, 2003).

International

The final scale of phenomenon to be considered here is international. The main attention given to the relationship between schools and school education at an international level used to be international comparisons of educational attainment (Goldstein, 2004). However, as has already been noted, there has been considerable interest in the processes and influences of glo-balisation on education, from an international perspective (Lingard *et al.*, 2005; Robertson, 2007), from a school reform perspective (Lipman, 2004), from higher education (Epstein *et al.*, 2008) and the relationships between skills, training, labour markets and the global economy (Ashton and Green, 1997).

In summarising such research a number of important issues arise. First, the examples reflect a wide variety of types and forms of research, from the descriptive to the predictive, from the polemical to the empirical, from the small-scale to the large-scale and in their emphasis on space, place and locale. Second, there are very few examples of research that transcend the dif-ferent scales outlined in Figure 8.5. Of course, this could be a result of using operational scale as a framework for presenting this body of research. However, it should be evident that there are clearly some educational issues and research questions that are being addressed at a number of different levels of activity, such as differential educational attainment. Third, there is an important contrast to be made between research that, as Bradford (1990) highlights, makes education and/or geography the *objects* of study − where education and/or geography are used to help understand other social, eco-nomic or political processes − and research that makes education and/or geo-graphy the *subjects* of study − where other social, economic or political processes help understand education and geography better. This leads on to the fourth observation, which is that there are considerable differences in the role of geography in these studies. In some examples, geography provides the context in which education phenomena (or other social phenomena) are studied. In other examples the focus of research is in geographical variations in the phenomena studied. And then there are examples, admittedly fewer than the others, of research where geography is considered to be an import-ant determinant of the educational phenomenon being examined.

Key substantive, methodological and theoretical developments of contemporary relevance

Before I go on to discuss the key developments in geography of *contemporary* relevance to education research, it is worth stressing that there are still areas of research where recent or past geographical approaches are still highly rele-vant. Butler and Hamnett (2007) summarise these as: (1) (spatial) differences in educational provision, facilities, teaching, finance or structure of provi-sion; and (2) the effect of concentrations of different groups in different areas in educational outcomes (and distinguishing between composition effects or area effects).

It is also worth re-stating the difficulty in distinguishing between the contribution of geography to the field of education from the contributions of other social science subjects, which in turn make it equally difficult to discuss the future promises and contributions of geography. This difficulty is well illustrated by Robertson's (2009) excellent discussion of 'spatialising' the sociology of education, or even Holloway and Valentine's (2000b) equally stimulating discussion of spatiality and inter-disciplinary studies of children and childhood. In the former, Robertson draws heavily on the work of David Harvey (e.g. 2006) and Henri Lefebvre (e.g. 1991) to progress a particular 'critical spatial analytic' (2009, p. 11) to help the sociology of education come to terms with the importance of spatiality in that particular sub-discipline. Clearly these offer much greater theoretical insight than what can be achieved in this more general overview, but the important point is that (1) it would be impractical to offer this level of insight across all the varying sub-disciplines of education and geography in the space of this chapter, and (2) Robertson's analytic scheme for the sociology of education actually may not be the most appropriate framework for the other sub-disciplines of education. However, Robertson's proposals remind us that past developments in geography, such as Harvey's (1989) grid of spatial practice, distinguishing between material spatial practice (experience), representations of space (perception) and spaces of representation (imagination) are still of value to future education research. Hence, the focus here will be on the most recent contemporary developments in geography that may be of relevance across a wide range of sub-disciplines and operational scales of education.

It has already been noted that the relevance of geography to contemporary British society has increased in recent years (Thrift, 2002). It clearly follows that the field of education will also have to give increasing attention to the geographical nature of education, including the relationships between the curriculum, labour markets and globalisation; education and spatial mobility; and space, environments, learning and physical exercise. These contemporary issues alone will require education research to take geography more seriously.

Furthermore, as the social, cultural, economic and political contexts of education change, 'new' geographies of education will emerge. Some very recent developments in geography have already been highlighted, such as the growing attention given to psychogeographies and geographies of emotion. These are all important aspects of learning, and could offer new insights into impulses, memory and pre-reflexive reactions – 'a bodily logic of sense' (Thrift, 2002, p. 296). Other 'new' geographies that will be of relevance to the field of education are consumption – affecting how learners behave and react to learning as consumers of education – and globalisation – which has already led to significant developments within the field of education.

Another important development within geography is the relationship between space and time (Crang, 2005). Not only does this mean recognising that space is situated and conceived *in* time, but also that space is constituted *through* time (Massey, 1999). Some geographers argue that space cannot be studied without considering its relationship with time – a form of relational approach (Whatmore, 1997). This approach, drawing upon physics' four-dimensional notion of space–time, is already being utilised in epidemiology, transport studies and research into tourism. Again, this would seem to have a particular resonance in education as institutions (e.g. schools or workplaces) tend to operate in space (e.g. classrooms) and time (e.g. lessons); the result is that schools develop a rhythm, which in turn may affect what goes on within a school and on its outcomes. Developments in time–space have strong connections with liminal geographies – the geography of 'betweenness'. This has particular relevance to understanding socio-spatial relationships within education establishments and between home and other formal and informal sites of learning.

Geography has for many years been interested in participatory research and methods, but a further advance that will be of relevance to education research is the growing use of digital maps. It has long been accepted that formal published maps are often quite removed from individuals' understanding of space and place. This is particularly the case for children who tend to have very different conceptions of space, place and scale. The ability to produce digital maps that can be considered in conjunction with other spatial representations, and that can be systematically analysed using spatial tools in a Geographical Information System (GIS), offers an important new methodological and participatory tool for researchers (see developments in the 'public' Google Earth).

Allied to developments in digital mapping and GIS are some significant advances in spatial analysis (Anselin, 1999), made increasingly available due to other ICT and software developments (Rey and Anselin, 2006). There are two main sets of developments to GIS and spatial analysis that will be of particular relevance to the field of education. The first are developments in the visualisation and interactive exploratory analysis of spatial data. Not only can spatial information be made more 'public' and responsive to a wide range of users and researchers, it can also provide new ways of interrogating data (such as through virtual reality). This may be important to education as increasingly larger and more complex datasets are made available. The second set of benefits relate to developments in advanced spatial statistics, particularly in network analysis, space–time analysis, multi-level modelling (and other hierarchical approaches to statistical modelling) and geographically weighted statistical analyses.

One of the most exciting prospects that geography offers in the coming years is the move towards a more spatially integrated social science (Goodchild *et al.*, 2000). This reflects many of the developments that have already been discussed. But it also encompasses the interconnection between education and other aspects of social life and the growing amount of geographical and administrative data available to education (such as the National Pupil Databases in England and Wales). Two relatively large-scale education-related research projects are currently under way to explore the construction and use of more integrated spatial data, Administrative Data: Methods, Inference and Networks (ADMIN) at the Institute of Education, University of London, and the Welsh Institute of Social Economic Data and Methods (WISERD), located across five higher education institutions in Wales. However, Goodchild *et al.* (2000) are keen to stress the importance of developing a research infrastructure to enhance the ability of research to adopt a spatial approach across the *entire* social sciences, to satisfy a growing trend in inter-disciplinary research and to prevent different disciplines from re-inventing the wheel.

The final area of work that is of particular contemporary importance to the field of education is the need to develop projects and analyses that study education issues from multiple scales of influence (Figure 8.5). It is the case that education research has been criticised for being small-scale and sometimes parochial (Hillage *et al.*, 1998). Furthermore, 'educational research is conspicuously weak in its ability to continuously develop and refine a body of knowledge which is quasi-universally acknowledged as well-founded' (OECD, 2007, p. 27). One reason for this, and a challenge for education and all the social sciences, is 'giving due weight to structural opportunities and constraints without making the actions of individuals appear either over-determined or unrealistically free' (Edwards, 2000, p. 308). Geographical research provides a particularly unique way to address this challenge, by transcending scale (Figure 8.5) when studying a given phenomena. This seems implicit in the way in which, for example, the Economic and Social Research Council (ESRC)-funded Teaching and Learning Research Programme has developed a framework to organise its thematic educational research (Pollard, 2006). Clearly, locale is central to most studies of education; it is often used to give importance to the agency of learners and teachers (at a local scale). But this can be at the expense of considering the real structural opportunities and constraints that Edwards (2000) makes reference to. Unfortunately, there are few contemporary developments in geography that provide a ready-made solution to this challenge. This is largely due to a preoccupation within geography, currently, to view scale as relational and socially constructed (Marston *et al.*, 2005). However, a re-focus on 'place', as outlined by Johnston (1991) and, more recently, Cresswell (2004), does offer an alternative methodological approach to studying education issues. This proposes studying 'place' in its full diversity, with a return to the kind of locality studies employed during the 1960s, but that are also (1) firmly situated within and concerned with relevant processes at the regional, national and global level, and (2) concerned with the spatial dimensions (patterns, processes, inequalities, etc.) within those locales. This approach would also suggest the need to use mixed methods; combining qualitative and quantitative data within a spatially integrated framework of analysis. Such a relatively new approach would also see the development of a new regional geography, which would be more responsive to different conceptions of space and the influences of the local and global than the traditional model of regional geography (Johnston, 1991).

Conclusions: looking ahead

It is very timely to be discussing the future contribution of geography to the field of education because of recent debates within geography about its own disciplinary status. It is also timely because of the increased attention to areas of interconnection between education and geography, currently around children and childhood, globalisation and differential educational attainment (e.g. multi-level modelling). Although this chapter has provided only a partial overview, other areas of synergy have also been highlighted as past or potential contributions of geography to the field of education. Hopefully this has begun to demonstrate the many different ways these two subjects can be interconnected.

Rather than identify substantive areas of research in which geography will or should contribute in the future – as has been shown, there are various points of entry into education for geography – I will begin to outline the ways in which geography can contribute that will hopefully prompt further discussion. The first conclusion is that the important concepts of space and place will always be relevant to future studies of education. Admittedly the importance of these two concepts will vary between different areas of education research, but nevertheless, there remain many questions in education that require greater geographical consideration. These include:

- the geography of educational establishments;
- the changing relationship between educational establishments, communities and neighbourhoods;
- the spatial distribution of educational resources and opportunities;
- the social reproduction of localities through educational opportunities and outcomes;
- the relationship between schooling and housing;
- the interconnections between formal sites of learning (e.g. schools, colleges, workplaces) and informal sites of learning (e.g. home), and in the spaces and places 'in-between' those formal and informal sites of learning;
- the socio-political and cultural features of devolved education policy;
- the geography and spaces of knowledge; and
- the use of spatial datasets in studying educational phenomena.

Second, a genuine move to develop the inter-disciplinary space between geography and education must attempt to utilise a wide range of geographical research, theories, methods and authors. This would reflect the contested nature of knowledge in geography,[2] and prevent the over-simplified and inappropriate use of geographical ideas. However, this begins to highlight an important tension between the capacity to bridge the two subjects fully, on the one hand, and the development of specialist expertise within each subject, on the other.

The third conclusion is to make a distinction between at least four geographical 'approaches' to studying education (Figure 8.6): the use of a spatial vocabulary or language in research; the importance of defining and providing context to research; exploring the spatial relationships between phenomenon; and lastly research that considers the importance of space *and* place simultaneously – i.e. research that considers spatial relationships within a deep understanding of their context (at various operational scales). A fifth approach could also be added, that of space–time. This distinction highlights the need to move beyond the use of spatial language, where much education research tends to be situated, to research that actually makes a substantive contribution (back) to the field of geography – the relationship between the two subjects must be two-way. And it is perhaps this contribution of knowledge, theory or method to more than one discipline or field of study that characterises *inter-disciplinary* research more generally. However, this in turn reflects the greater 'geographical' sophistication required to adopt these alternative approaches, perhaps reflecting differences between the interactional expertise and contributory expertise of those involved in such research (Collins and Evans, 2007).

It would seem, therefore, that to enhance and build upon the inter-disciplinary relationships between geography and education it is not sufficient to simply 'borrow' geographical knowledge, theories and methods. Instead there is a clear justification, as Massey (1999) has argued, for giving much greater attention to constructively breaching the subject divide. However, as we have also seen, this will not be an easy task given the complex relationships between the two subjects. One of the main ways of successfully developing a geography of education sub-discipline would be, as the ESRC *Demographic Review* suggests, to 'export/import' geographers into the field of education. Clearly this has some potential, but it would be more realistic, at least in the short term, for more researchers to work and share their ideas across the disciplinary boundaries. But this would require more sophisticated and sustainable conversations to be established across the boundary of geography and education; not least through the creation of formal inter-disciplinary networks, conferences and journals.

A final major challenge would be to consider the issue of research capacity. Even if the boundary between geography and education were constructively breached it would still be difficult to see how individual researchers could develop contributory expertise that spans all areas of overlap between the two subjects (Figure 8.1). Similarly, developing or utilising contributory

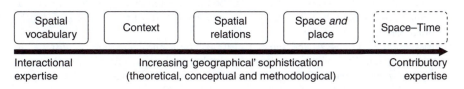

Figure 8.6 Geographical approaches to education research.

expertise in one subject may be at the expense of developing contributory expertise in the other. However, an alternative solution would possibly lead to new divisions of labour within the respective subjects, which in turn may undermine the very foundations from which each subject is based. Instead a balance must be found between exporting/importing expertise and greater collaboration between the two subjects.

Notes

1 Livingstone calls these conversations rather than characteristics.
2 The same could be said for all inter-disciplinary research.

References

Allen, R. (2007) Allocating pupils to their nearest school: the consequences for ability and social stratification, *Urban Studies*, 44, 4, 751–770.

Anselin, L. (1999) The future of spatial analysis in the social sciences, *Geographic Information Systems*, 5, 2, 67–76.

Armstrong, F. (2003) *Spaced Out: Policy, difference and the challenge of inclusive education*, London: Kluwer.

Ashton, D.N. and Green, F. (1997) *Education, Training and the Global Economy*, Cheltenham: Edward Elgar.

Barnett, C. (2002) The cultural turn: fashion or progress in human geography?, *Antipode*, 30, 4, 379–394.

Bell, J.F. (2003) Beyond the school gates: the influence of school neighbourhood on the relative progress of pupils, *Oxford Review of Education*, 29, 4, 485–502.

Benn, C. and Simon, B. (1970) *Half Way There: Report on the British comprehensive-school reform*, Harmondsworth: Penguin Books.

Bondi, L. and Matthews, M.H. (1988) *Education and Society: Studies in the politics, sociology and geography of education*, London: Routledge.

Bradford, M. (1990) Education, attainment and the geography of choice, *Geography*, 75, 1, 3–16.

Bryce, T.G. and Hume, W.M. (eds) (2003) *Scottish Education: Post-devolution*, 2nd edn, Edinburgh: Edinburgh University Press.

Burgess, S.M., Wilson, D. and Lupton, R. (2005) Parallel lives? Ethnic segregation in schools and neighbourhoods, *Urban Studies*, 42, 7, 1027–1056.

Butler, T. and Hamnett, C. (2007) The geography of education: introduction, *Urban Studies*, 44, 7, 1161–1174.

Butler, T. and Robson, T. (2003) *London Calling: The middle classes and the remaking of inner London*, Oxford: Berg.

Byrne, D.S. and Williamson, W. (1971) Some intra-regional variations in educational provision and their bearing on educational attainment: the case of the north-east, *Sociology*, 6, 71–87.

Christensen, P., James, A. and Jenks, C. (2000) Home and movement: children constructing 'family time', in S.L. Holloway and G. Valentine (eds) *Children's Geographies: Playing, living, learning*, pp. 139–155, London: Routledge.

Clifford, N.J. (2002) The future of geography: when the whole is less than the sum of its parts, *Geoforum*, 33, 431–436.

Coates, B. and Rawstron, E.M. (1971) *Regional Variations in Britain*, London: Batsford.

Coffield, F., Steer, R., Hodgson, A., Spours, K., Edwards, S. and Finlay, I. (2005) A new learning and skills landscape? The central role of the Learning and Skills Council, *Journal of Education Policy*, 20, 5, 631–656.

Collins, D. and Coleman, T. (2008) Social geographies of education: looking within, and beyond, school boundaries, *Geography Compass*, 2, 1, 281–299.

Collins, H. and Evans, R. (2007) *Rethinking Expertise*, Chicago: University of Chicago Press.

Crang, M. (2005) Time:space, in P. Cloke and R. Johnston (eds) *Spaces of Geographical Thought*, pp. 199–219, London: Sage.

Cresswell, T. (2004) *Place: A short introduction*, Oxford: Blackwell.

Crowther, D., Cummings, C., Dyson, A. and Millward, A. (2003) *Schools and Area Regeneration*, Bristol: Bristol University Press.

Duncan, S. and Smith, D. (2002) Family geographies and gender cultures, *Social Policy and Society*, 1, 1, 21–34.

Edwards, R. and Usher, R. (eds) (2003) *Space, Curriculum and Learning*, Greenwich, CT: Information Age Publishing.

Edwards, T. (2000) 'All the evidence shows…': reasonable expectations of educational research, *Oxford Review of Education*, 26, 3–4, 299–313.

Eggleston, J. (1977) *The Ecology of the School*, London: Methuen.

Epstein, D., Boden, R., Deem, R., Rizvi and Wright, S. (eds) (2008) *Geographies of Knowledge, Geometries of Power: Framing the future of higher education*, London: Routledge.

Fielding, S. (2000) Walk on the left: children's geographies and the primary school, in S.L. Holloway and G. Valentine (eds) *Children's Geographies: Playing, living, learning*, pp. 230–244, London: Routledge.

Garner, C.L. and Raudenbush, S.W. (1991) Neighbourhood effects on educational attainment: a multilevel analysis, *Sociology of Education*, 64, 4, 251–262.

Gewirtz, S., Ball, S. and Bowe, R. (1995) *Markets, Choice and Equity in Education*, Buckingham: Open University Press.

Goldstein, H. (2004) International comparisons of student attainment: some issues arising from the PISA study, *Assessment in Education*, 11, 319–330.

Goodchild, M.F., Anselin, L., Appelbaum, R.P. and Harthorn, B.H. (2000) Toward spatially integrated social science, *International Regional Science Review*, 23, 2, 139–159.

Gordon, T., Holland, J. and Lahelma, E. (2000) *Making Spaces: Citizenship and difference in schools*, Basingstoke: Macmillan.

Gray, J., Jesson, D. and Jones, B. (1984) Predicting differences in examination results between Local Education Authorities: does school organisation matter?, *Oxford Review of Education*, 10, 1, 45–68.

Green, B. and Letts, W. (2007) Space, equity and rural education: a 'trialectical' account, in K. Gulson and C. Symes (eds) *Spatial Theories in Education: Policy and geography matters*, pp. 57–76, New York: Routledge.

Gregson, N. (2003) Discipline games, disciplinary games and the need for a post-disciplinary practice: responses to Nigel Thrift's 'The future of geography', *Geoforum*, 34, 5–7.

Gulson, K. (2005) Renovating educational identities: policy, space and urban renewal, *Journal of Education Policy*, 20, 2, 147–164.

Gulson, K. and Symes, C. (2007) Knowing one's place, in K. Gulson and C. Symes (eds) *Spatial Theories in Education: Policy and geography matters*, pp. 1–16, New York: Routledge.

Halsey, A.H. (1972) Educational Priority: report of a research project sponsored by the Department of Education and Science and the Social Science Research Council, vol. 1, *E.P.A. Problems and Policies*, London: HMSO.

Hamnett, C. (2003) Contemporary human geography: fiddling while Rome burns?, *Geoforum*, 34, 1–3.

Harvey, D. (1973) *Social Justice and the City*, London: Edward Arnold.

Harvey, D. (1989) *The Condition of Postmodernity*, Oxford: Blackwell.

Harvey, D. (1990) Between space and time: reflections on the geographical imagination, *Annals of the Association of American Geographers*, 80, 418–434.

Harvey, D. (2006) Space as a keyword, in N. Castree and D. Gregory (eds) *David Harvey: A critical reader*, pp. 270–293, Oxford: Blackwell Publishing.

Hemming, P. (2007) Renegotiating the primary school: children's emotional geographies of sport, exercise and active play, *Children's Geographies*, 5, 4, 353–371.

Herbert, D.T. (1976) Urban education: problems and policies, in D.T. Herbert and R. Johnston (eds) *Social Areas in Cities*, pp. 123–158, London: Wiley.

Hillage, J., Pearson, R., Anderson, A. and Tamkin, P. (1998) *Excellence in Research on Schools*, London: HMSO.

Holloway, S.L. and Valentine, G. (eds) (2000a) *Children's Geographies: Playing, living, learning*, London: Routledge.

Holloway, S.L. and Valentine, G. (2000b) Spatiality and the new social studies of childhood, *Sociology*, 34, 4, 763–783.

Jackson, B. and Marsden, D. (1966) *Education and the Working Class*, London: Pelican.

Jennings, R.E. (1977) *Education and Politics: Policy-making in local education authorities*, London: Batsford.

Johnston, R. (1991) *A Question of Place: Exploring the practice of human geography*, Oxford: Blackwell.

Johnston, R. (2003) Geography: a different sort of discipline? *Transactions of the Institute of British Geographers*, 23, 133–141.

Johnston, R. and Sidaway, J. (2004) *Geography and Geographers: Anglo-American human geography since 1945*, 6th edn, London: Arnold.

Lam, N. and Quattrochi, D. (1992) On the issues of scale, resolution and fractal analysis in the mapping sciences, *Professional Geographer*, 44, 88–98.

Lefebvre, H. (1991) *The Production of Space*, Oxford: Blackwell Publishing.

Lingard, B., Rawolle, S. and Taylor, S. (2005) Globalising policy sociology in education: working with Bourdieu, *Journal of Education Policy*, 20, 6, 759–777.

Lipman, P. (2004) *High Stakes Education: Inequality, globalisation and urban school reform*, New York: Routledge.

Livingstone, D. (1992) *The Geographical Tradition*, Oxford: Blackwell Publishing.

Marsden, W.E. (1987) *Unequal Educational Provision in England and Wales: The nineteenth-century roots*, London: Routledge.

Marston, S.A., Jones, J.P. and Woodward, K. (2005) Human geography without scale, *Transactions of the Institute of British Geographers*, 30, 4, 416–432.

Massey, D. (1999) Negotiating disciplinary boundaries, *Current Sociology*, 47, 4, 5–12.

Matthews, H. and Tucker, F. (2006) On the other side of the tracks: the psychogeographies and everyday lives of rural teenagers in the UK, in C. Spencer and M. Blades (eds) *Children and their Environments*, pp. 161–175, Cambridge: Cambridge University Press.

Mills, D., Jepson, A., Coxon, T., Easterby-Smith, M., Hawkins, P. and Spencer, J. (2006) *Demographic Review of the UK Social Sciences*, Swindon: ESRC.

O'Connell, A.A. and McCoach, D.B. (eds) (2008) *Multilevel Modelling of Educational Data*, Greenwich, CT: Information Age Publishing.

OECD (2007) *Evidence in Education: Linking research and policy*, Paris: OECD.

OFSTED (2008) *Geography in Schools: Changing practice*, London: OFSTED.

Phillips, R. (2003) Education policy, comprehensive schooling and devolution in the disUnited Kingdom: an historical 'home international' analysis, *Journal of Education Policy*, 18, 1, 1–17.

Pollard, A. (2006) Challenges facing educational research: Educational Review Guest Lecture 2005, *Educational Review*, 58, 3, 251–267.

Radnor, H.A. and Ball, S.J. (1996) *Local Education Authorities: accountability and control*, Stoke-on-Trent: Trentham Books.

Reay, D. (2004) 'Mostly roughs and toughs': social class, race and representation in inner city schooling, *Sociology*, 35, 4, 1005–1023.

Rees, G. (2005) Democratic devolution and education policy in Wales: the emergence of a national system? *Contemporary Wales*, 17, 1, 28–43.

Rees, G. and Rees, T. (1980) Educational inequality in Wales: some problems and paradoxes, in G. Rees (ed.) *Poverty and Social Inequality in Wales*, pp. 71–92, London: Croom Helm.

Rees, G. and Taylor, C. (2006) Devolution and the restructuring of participation in higher education in Wales, *Higher Education Quarterly*, 60, 4, 370–391.

Rees, G., Power, S. and Taylor, C. (2007) The governance of educational inequalities: the limits of area-based initiatives, *Journal of Comparative Policy Analysis*, 9, 3, 261–274.

Renold, E. (2005) *Girls, Boys and Junior Sexualities: Exploring children's gender and sexual relations in the primary school*, London: RoutledgeFalmer.

Rex, J., and Moore, R. (1967) *Race, Community and Conflict: A study of Sparkbrook*, London: Oxford University Press.

Rey, S.J. and Anselin, L. (2006) Recent advances in software for spatial analysis in the social sciences, *Geographical Analysis*, 38, 1–4.

Rickinson, M., Dillon, J., Teamey, K., Morris, M., Young Choi, M., Sanders, D. and Benefield, P. (2004) *A Review of Research on Outdoor Learning*, Shrewsbury: Field Studies Council.

Robertson, S.L. (2007) Absences and imaginings: the production of knowledge on globalisation and education, *Globalisation, Societies and Education*, 4, 2, 303–318.

Robertson, S.L. (2009) *Spatialising the sociology of education: Stand-points, entry-points, vantage-points*, Bristol: Centre for Globalisation, Education and Societies, University of Bristol. Available online at www.bris.ac.uk/education/people/academic-Staff/edslr/publications/28slr (accessed 20 January 2009).

Robson, B. (1969) *Urban Analysis: A study of city structure with special reference to Sunderland*, Cambridge: Cambridge University Press.

Rutten, R., Boekema, F. and Kujipers, E. (2003) *Economic Geography of Higher Education: Knowledge infrastructure and learning regions*, London: Routledge.

Sibley, D. (2003) Psychogeographies of rural space and practices of exclusion, in P. Cloke (ed.) *Country Visions*, Harlow: Pearson Education.

Smith, N. and Katz, C. (1993) Grounding metaphor: towards a spatialised politics, in M. Keith and S. Piles (eds) *Place and the Politics of Identity*, London: Routledge.

Soja, E. (1989) *Postmodern Geographies: The reassertion of space in critical social theory*, London: Verso.

Spencer, C. and Blades, M. (eds) (2006) *Children and Their Environments: Learning, using and designing spaces*, Cambridge: Cambridge University Press.

Taeuber, K.E., Wilson, F.D., James, D.R. and Taeuber, A.F. (1981) A demographic perspective on school desegregation in the USA, in C. Peach, V. Robinson and S. Smith (eds) *Ethnic Segregation in Cities*, London: Croom Helm.

Taylor, C. (2001) The geography of choice and diversity in the 'new' secondary education market of England, *Area*, 33, 4, 368–381.

Taylor, C. (2002) *Geography of the 'New' Education Market*, Aldershot: Ashgate.

Taylor, C. and Gorard, S. (2001) The role of residence in segregation: placing the impact of parental choice in perspective, *Environment and Planning A*, 33, 10, 1829–1852.

Thrift, N. (2002) The future of geography, *Geoforum*, 33, 291–298.

Thrift, N. and Waling, D. (2000) Geography in the United Kingdom 1996–2000, *The Geographical Journal*, 166, 2, 96–124.

Turner, B.L. (2002) Response to Thrift's 'The future of geography', *Geoforum*, 33, 427–429.

Valentine, G., Holloway, S. and Bingham, N. (2000) Transforming cyberspace: children's interventions in the new public sphere, in S.L. Holloway and G. Valentine (eds) *Children's Geographies: Playing, living, learning*, pp. 156–173, London: Routledge.

Warf, B. and Arias, S. (eds) (2008) *The Spatial Turn: Interdisciplinary perspectives*, London: Routledge.

Whatmore, S. (1997) Dissecting the autonomous self: hybrid cartographies for a relational ethics, *Society and Space*, 15, 1, 37–53.

Whitty, G. (2006) Education(al) research and education policy-making: is conflict inevitable?, *British Educational Research Journal*, 32, 2, 159–176.

Woolner, P., Hall, E., Higgins, S., McCaughey, C. and Wall, K. (2007) A sound foundation? What we know about the impact of environments on learning and the implications for Building Schools for the Future, *Oxford Review of Education*, 33, 1, 47–70.

Young, M. and Willmott, P. (1962) *Family and Kinship in East London*, London: Pelican.

9 Gaining a commanding voice

Sheldon Rothblatt

Introduction

I have been asked to comment briefly on the chapters written for this collection by way of being something of an offshore outsider. As an historian of universities, who has spent his career in departments of history or history of science (only occasionally teaching courses in graduate schools of education), I have limited first-hand knowledge of the state and condition of teacher training, or, for that matter, primary and secondary schooling. But insofar as the contributions deal with inter-institutional connections affecting a nation's provision for education, broadly and narrowly conceived, I can at least reflect on the relationships. I can identify the sources of tensions and salient political and social changes in the history of schools, schooling and teacher education on both sides of the Atlantic. Historians differ in their approaches to complex issues. Mine is rather to illustrate structural bottlenecks with some indication of causes. But indicating causes does not automatically suggest remedies. I cannot, however, deny that readers may find some furtive opinions lurking among the reflections.

The editors describe a Britain where members of the academic profession who work on education and learning in the schools may have lost a capacity for perspective, for engaging with the ghosts of yesteryear. Some of this may be a tendency within professions to focus on careers, forgetting the function of professions to further the common good. Some may be a loss of internal intellectual cohesion, partly, maybe largely, the consequence of government policies stressing educational goals that are narrowly utilitarian. This, of course, is an old quarrel in the history of education. It still produces much heat on my side of the Atlantic regarding the correct dimensions of a liberal education in schools and universities. But whether or not government is wholly to blame, some of the disciplines, it is suggested, have succumbed to the lure of markets and pots of gold.

There is a loss of public visibility, as it were. The argument of the editors continues to say that disciplines forming education are no longer mediating influences in public policy debates. They have lost whatever capacity they once possessed for elevating discussions and providing heft and weight to decision-making. In the hurly-burly of today's educational ferment, clear-headed, dispassionate analysis is both lacking and compromised.

The contrast is again with the ghosts of the past. The role of the disciplines today is far less assured in Britain than in the decades following World War II. Schools of education had proliferated, and intending teachers were solidly grounded in a core of 'foundation' disciplines such as those represented in this volume. The editors attribute the changes to neo-liberal funding policies begun by Thatcher governments but continued under New Labour.[1] These favor practitioner-led education, 'efficiency gains', 'rates of return' and market responses – in a word, a culture of 'accountability', which also means a culture of mistrust in established institutions shared by civil servants and the public. I will broadly comment on those dimensions that lie closest to my own understanding of educational issues, lower and higher, on both sides of the Atlantic.

The state of disciplinary confidence

The editors' pessimism is not fully shared by the contributors. They conclude that their primary disciplines, or, as in the example of comparative and international education, a field of enquiry or a 'knowledge domain', remain intellectually strong. The contributors have itemized some of the salient ideas, methods and research agenda that came out of the post-1945 expansion of higher education studies. From geography, new ways of looking at space in the learning process, with substantial contributions to the study of communities and neighborhoods. Psychology, the master discipline so to speak, has contributed to an understanding of the emotional well-being of children and the formation of social relationships in school environments. Psychology is now heavily invested in cognitive studies assisted by research in neuroscience. Sociology went through an extremely fruitful period in the 1950s and 1960s, providing insights on social mobility, selection, life chances and identity issues, engaging in the research that contributed to the founding of comprehensive high schools. In some respects sociology has given ground to the economics of education, which now include an attempt to quantify those aspects of education that are not conventionally regarded as economic, such as the levels of civic participation or crime. The relation of philosophy to education is probably the most general. Philosophy – *vide* the Faculty of Philosophy in the so-called Humboldtian German university – has always been the integrating discipline par excellence, the one whose abiding concerns are conceptions of the human condition and the dimensions of a just society.

History is Broad Church, its latitudinarian theology based on chronology. All human conduct and institutions are best appreciated when viewed in and over time. I am tempted to add what Balzac called the 'human comedy'. An ironic outlook, however, is not helpful to policy-makers. With respect to education, historians follow the curve of current interests, exploring gender, religion, school reform, the everyday experience of children and schools, popular education and the transmission of education to colonial areas. They are joined in this last endeavor by the proponents of comparative and international education, an active area of study at the moment. Ideally, and actually, all the disciplines work in tandem. Since education is the sum total of all human activity, the contributors agree that a multi-disciplinary approach ought always to be encouraged. This seems obvious, but whether teacher training today reflects this view, or whether the disciplines actually do cooperate, is an open question. And there exists the editors' warning that if a little learning is a dangerous thing, too much eclecticism leads a discipline away from a firm educational remit.

The record of professional activity is reported as good. New journals have been founded to promote sub-disciplines. The quality of submissions has probably improved. Subscriptions are reasonably steady. National and international networks and 'invisible colleges' are plentiful, while professional societies are numerous and active. Any number of educational research and policy centers has been established within universities. There is nothing surprising here. The pattern is a standard aspect of the history of academic professionalization. The lesson is that wherever academics are in charge of their own professional destiny, specialization increases. Each sub-interest must have its own journals, conferences and recognition, sometimes its own university program or department. But what is gained in detailed research is lost in information overloads. From the editors' perspective, the caveat is that precisely because academics control these activities, which are time-consuming career-building blocks, an education assignment is forgone.

The contributions of the various fields of science or mathematics to education, while suggested in relation to the medical sciences, are not mentioned in the volume, nor is political science, which has played some part in the schools topic called 'civics'. Nor are literary studies discussed, that is to say, literature as a repository of national experience as opposed to cognitive studies about how best to teach reading (or mathematics). The disciplines forming the body of the volume are those that are regarded as the social science core of teacher education.

Some concern is expressed by the editors and several contributors about whether the disciplines bearing on education will continue to attract able researchers, especially if the support of scholarly activity declines because of the rewards of practitioner-dominated curricula. The geographers, however, appear to be reasonably confident, even about 'a very messy subject' which they describe as being one of the largest social science disciplines in the UK. I do not sense any sentiment that the disciplines are in the doldrums or have reached a heuristic or intellectual impasse. This would accord with my own impression that the quality of scholarship and science within research-led universities is generally good, if often routine; but no single person is really able to appreciate more than a minute fraction of the work that goes on. I would certainly agree with the editors that not all theories and methods within the social sciences are worth the effort given to them. This is of course a matter of opinion. Individual scholars differ on the directions their disciplines are taking, deploring topics that are faddish or seem to be a response to market pressures, an 'interference' as it were with what is presumed to be the natural evolution of a discipline. But no remarks are offered along these lines. None of the contributors express a loss of confidence in their disciplines *qua* disciplines.

Fissures within disciplines relative to education

The contributors do, however, express dissatisfaction with the relationship of their mainstream disciplines to the sub-fields that focus on education. There is some sense that the education component of a discipline is secondary and consequently undervalued by the home department. This has career implications since the rewards of an academic profession are based on reputation. The psychologists here mentioned claim to be marginal to the core of their discipline, and the philosophers do not find institutional affiliations to be strong even if intellectually close. The economists, however, do not voice a similar sense of exclusion, possibly because of the common interest in quantifiable problem-solving and the market-related policies of both Labour and Conservative governments. The lesson is that in particular circumstances some academics sense a loss of influence, while others appear to gain, another illustration of the interior variety of higher education institutions even with regard to a supposed common antagonist.

Historical studies may be an example of a discipline that is not strongly represented in teacher education, or at least, I gather, not at present, but whether historians who research the history of education find themselves on the fringes of the discipline itself is a nice question. Historical activity goes freely in all directions. Locating a mainstream is difficult, although certainly historians are by no means immune from status-seeking, even if that should mean following trends and fads in what was once called 'the spirit of the age'. Oppositely and generously, instead of connecting academic ambition to a desire for recognition at almost any cost, Thomas Kuhn described an intellectual world of stasis. Paradigms, matrices or frameworks of inherited assumptions, 'normal science', guides research but needs to be overturned from time to time by bold innovators (Kuhn, 1970). Challenging an existing paradigm is always risky, even as the research ethic demands it.

Education schools struggle for respectability

If members of some disciplines indicate that colleagues do not value their work in the area of education, many of them also feel excluded or marginalized by schools or departments of education within their own institutions. There is a clearly expressed sense of a gap between the disciplines and teacher education or graduate programs in education. Words such as 'can' contribute or 'must' or 'should' contribute and references to fruitful 'potential' activity run through virtually all the contributions, exposing a belief that viable associations are either absent or weaker than expected. Schools of education, it is suggested, are not fully interested in the relevance of disciplinary departments.

But schools of education are entitled to make the same point about their standing with disciplines and their status within universities. Education as a separate field of enquiry and teaching has often been challenged as undemanding, insufficiently intellectual, lacking in rigor or breadth and unable to attract the ablest students. The historical circumstances are clear enough. The independence of the sometime normal school was lost when teacher training was made part of a university. The story is familiar and especially well documented by Geraldine Clifford and James Guthrie in their wry account of the history of American educational schools. In the earliest years of incorporation, the education schools found that the disciplines would only cooperate on their own terms, and their own terms frequently had little to do with the principal mission of teacher training or learning.

Whether teachers should primarily be prepared in a conventional academic way, by exposure to the values and subjects of a liberal education or by receiving pedagogical training more closely related to their vocation, was a persistent quarrel. If education schools lacked legitimacy from the perspective of the liberal arts, they also had not yet achieved standing as a profession. This was hardly an enviable situation. Rebuffed, education schools began to develop in-house disciplines. They hired their former students or obtained specialists from other education schools (Clifford and Guthrie, 1988). One other possibility was the joint appointment, a psychologist, for example, dividing time between an education program and a disciplinary department. This provided the advantage of familiarity with the needs of teachers. Significant drawbacks were work overloads – two halves always make more than a whole – and meeting the contradictory career requirements of multiple academic units.

A loss of professional independence, it is reasonable to suggest, becomes even stronger as mass schooling falls increasingly under central government. One response, the formation of teacher trade unions, provides a level of security, but professional legitimacy or academic status are not thereby guaranteed.[2] The establishment of national curricula in England, the frequent changes therein or in subject emphasis, continual alteration of the school-leaving examinations, different modes of gaining sixth-form exposure, to which we can add the disagreements over social issues that have characterized the dons, do not argue for much stability. This roller-coaster ride has arguably made the discipline/schools of education, the scholar/practitioner divide as great as at any time in a problematical relationship.

One other ingredient can be added to the mix. Education degrees and the credentialing process in the USA especially affect the sector of state schools. With a few exceptions – schools in affluent suburbs or the highly select specialized secondary schools of the City of New York – they possess far less

prestige than expensive private schools. These range from the famous pre-
paratory boarding schools of New England, possibly modeled on Thomas
Arnold's reforms at Rugby in the Victorian era, to local day schools. The
corresponding range in England includes the old select grammar schools and
the independent schools. The American teachers in these more privileged
environments are spared the difficulties confronted by those who work in
inner-city schools where poverty, crime and broken families are endemic,
and they are often recruited from liberal arts programs and not from educational schools. They are not required to sit 'methods' courses, so often
mocked as boring. Furthermore, from the beginning mass-access schooling
in the USA, as it must be in Britain, recruited by necessity from lower-status
families. Along with social work, school-teaching was a path of upward
social mobility. To some extent, schools of education that educate teachers
for public-sector schooling have never overcome the social stigma.

There is also another kind of boundary that affects most of the 15,000 or
so school districts in the USA. Burton Clark once explained that by and
large the social and intellectual gap between secondary schools and universities was greater than in other nations. Whereas teachers in a *lycée* or *Gymna-
sium* or British independent schools closely identified with higher education
and regarded their mission as preparing students for entry, American schoolteachers were pulled downwards into a system of bureaucracies, trade union
politics and lower occupational esteem (Clark, 2008). Even the community
colleges in California, central institutions for the promotion of upward educational mobility through student transfer, are not formally linked to the
higher education system. They fall under the authority of the office of the
State Superintendent of Education, just like schools. Further education institutions in Britain have similarly suffered from status ambiguity.

Given these substantial status difficulties, affecting the entire network of
teacher education, and with so much national frustration now expressed regarding high drop-out rates and low scores in standardized testing, it is hardly surprising that the most significant educational reform movements in the USA are
'charter schools' ('trust' schools in Britain) and the use of 'vouchers'. The first
are state-financed schools run by parents or educational companies, bypassing
the control of local authorities, and the second allows successful schools to
accept out-of-district pupils. Home schooling in the UK but especially in the
USA has grown rapidly as a means for bypassing the well-publicized problems
of local schools. Neil Smelser has written about 'primordialism' in Victorian
educational history (Smelser, 1991). Working-class parents resisted compulsory
primary schooling from a fear that control of their children's upbringing would
be sacrificed. The point seems relevant with regard to home schooling today,
except that the parents are primarily middle-class.

As the twentieth-century closed, and a new one began, these trends represented a direct repudiation of the original arrangements comprising mass
primary and secondary education. There is no logical reason why the educational disciplines cannot play a major role in developing a new configuration

of schooling, raising the esteem of public education. However, political and funding barriers are formidable, and I have no basis on which to assess whether substantial academic interest even exists.

Battles of the books

The divisions within disciplines regarding education, and the uncertain relationship between schools of educations and the disciplines, is not a unique academic phenomenon. The long history of universities is also a long narrative of intellectual rivalry and disciplinary quarrels, battles of the books, of which the most familiar is Jonathan Swift's parable of the spider and the bee, his humanist (the bee) attack on experimental science (the spider) in the late seventeenth century (Swift, 1950).

The reasons for the battles are various, but for a moment a short-cut response is probably sufficient. First, any new subject or new discipline requires financial support, so one part of the quarrel is over the allocation of resources. Second, over time subjects have a habit of claiming an identity with larger moral values. Thus Swift's humanist bee represents sweetness, light and tradition and is associated with classical learning, or, as re-stated by the Victorian poet Matthew Arnold, 'the best that has been thought and said in the world' (Arnold, 1993). Swift's spider represents the new technology of a 'modern' (his word) age. The spider's web, draped with dead flies, is the vision of a world filled with anger, destruction and self-aggrandizement. The spider claims his web is a unique artifice, his alone. It is not fanciful to see that the web will one day become the university's research ethic, although not in the savage terms expressed by Swift.

We can follow the battles of the books almost from the birth of the university itself. Paris had one system of logic, and quarreled with Orleans which had another. Arguments over the legitimacy of subjects or disciplines and rankings of their importance are a continuous feature of the history of universities. Some subjects were deemed worthy of inclusion in a university curriculum, others were banished to different institutions. The new liberal learning of Italy in the early modern period often went in search of academies and the patronage of ducal courts. Everywhere in Europe experimental science found a home in royal societies. As some disciplines spun off from others, or were created anew, they were forced to defend their stand-alone competence, and ultimately their adherence to a research ethic. To use examples from the history of Cambridge University, modern literature had to struggle for recognition from classics, history had to separate from constitutional law, anthropology from history, psychology from philosophy, economics from political science. Several subjects waited long for approval by Oxbridge. King's College summoned Edward Shils from Chicago in the 1960s to help establish sociology at Cambridge;[3] and Oxford had no professorial chair in the subject until the appointment of A.H. Halsey of Nuffield College, a contributor to this volume.

In Germany in the nineteenth century, novel sub-disciplines went in pursuit of new chairs, usually elsewhere, since they were not welcome in their first home (Joseph Ben-David, 1991).[4] This was true of the civic universities of Victorian England and has been true of the newer universities of Britain, which feature professorial appointments in subjects and sub-specialties unavailable or once unavailable in the traditional institutions. Vocational training, while sometimes pursued within universities and difficult to separate from professional instruction, found a more sympathetic home in alternative institutions such as polytechnics.

The only major national system where technological institutions gained more respect than universities was and remains France, with its select stratum of *grandes écoles*. French universities have been largely denied the prestige of a research mission (although individual professors find research opportunities) since research is the responsibility of outside organizations. A principle reason for the high standing of the great schools is the close relationship between this sector and state-building, an alliance that preceded Napoleonic technocracy but was enhanced by it.

Battles of the books are always with us, but the evolution of the university into the form Clark Kerr called a 'multiversity' (Kerr, 1963) provided a different way of accommodating diverse intellectual interests and knowledge domains. The multiversity is a house of many mansions. New subjects do not necessarily have to be banished to special institutions. But the irony of the multiversity is that while it appears to be the most open form of a higher education institution, accepting all kinds of subjects and programs apparently with ease, by that very same openness it also creates hierarchies of prestige. It does so through an immensely complex internal structure of sub-divisions: professional schools, departments, laboratories, faculties, research institutes, policy centers and, in a few universities, residential colleges for teaching students. Meiosis takes place for many reasons. Sometimes the reason is the refusal of existing faculties to accept a subject deemed illegitimate but political pressures dictate that room must be found somewhere (e.g. gender and ethnic studies). Sometimes the reasons are personal or individual.[5]

What is equally important, and especially relevant to the present discussion about education and its contributing disciplines, is that each division of the university has its own reference groups, communities and clients. Apart from the training of postgraduate students to follow in the footsteps of their teachers, the segments of a multiversity appear to have little in common. The late Tony Becher described the interior cultural world of universities as composed of 'tribes and territories', each tribe possessing a different reward system and varying views of what constitutes noteworthy scholarly assignments and research (Becher, 1987, 1989).[6] The situation is even more complicated when we add into the mix the partitions within single disciplines.[7] Historians and ethnographers have yet to systematically analyze the academic solar system to find the governing force that keeps the segments from spinning off in completely different directions since their tendency is centrifugal. Presumably this is a governance assignment, the task of trustees, senates, councils or congregations working together with central administration, or guild, collegiate traditions. The topic is huge.

The Matthew Effect

The closest a multiversity comes to having a bonding element is broad agreement on research as a career requirement. Until the late adoption of a research ethic with an emphasis on discovery, universities were places for undergraduate teaching and in some cases for professional training (the original purpose). Once the idea of original enquiry became the signature mission for a particular class of institutions, all of the interior life of the university was affected. Practitioner education was now pressed to join in the common endeavor to promote the advancement of knowledge, defined as a union of method and empirical investigation. While at first law and medicine did not meet this criterion, they had the advantage of being part of the university's birthright and were supported by influential outside interests. Furthermore, medicine could draw from the prestige of modern science, law from government. But the newer professional schools of business or social work or journalism or the library sciences or, in some instances, engineering and certainly education were under pressure to demonstrate a command of theory, methodology or 'pure science'. The performing arts did not escape. There too research on musical composition or the theory of art was required. Physical education was drawn into the health sciences. In newer universities in twentieth-century Britain, journalism was transformed into media and cultural studies.

A research mission separates one kind of higher institution from another, producing the gradations of prestige discussed by Martin Trow (1987). Research is also the main if not sole quality measured by the metrics, citation indices and global ranking scales that are much in the news these days (Tapper and Palfreyman, 2008; Wildavsky, 2009). Small wonder, then, that institutions without a research mission strive to obtain one. This has led to 'mission creep'. The upgrading of many polys to university standing in Britain is a recent phenomenon. But it certainly has happened repeatedly in the USA, although sometimes the binary line holds. In California, a second tier of state colleges and universities, where teacher education is principally located, has continued to press the state legislature for the financial and status privileges of the research universities, trying to gain what the sociologist Robert Merton called 'the Matthew Effect': to him that hath, more shall be given (Merton, 1973).

The ascent of research meant the descent of 'practice'. There was the higher learning and then everything else. Education schools in America could more readily conform to the new mandate if they became 'graduate schools' granting advanced degrees rather than retaining their strong training role as normal schools. The newer professions also did not have a client base with the money and standing of the older 'liberal' professions, and several, such as education and social work, were dependent upon government sponsorship. As nations entered the great period of mass-access education, policies were certain to fluctuate in keeping with new priorities and their budgetary implications.

The culture wars, transparency and loss of trust

The history of education schools, and, as it appears, the history of disciplines relating to the tasks of teacher education, indicate a continual struggle to gain acceptance and parity of esteem. There is yet another issue of legitimacy, if of more recent provenance. This one, however, affects all of academic life and not merely schools of education. Oddly, the contributors do not mention the political and ideological issues – the 'culture wars'[8] that have roiled the academy in both the USA and the UK, although the editors cite relevant remarks by Ron Barnett.

These involve both local or national issues (e.g. affirmative action and academic freedom) or international issues (e.g. the Middle East). The culture wars are more than academic tempests in teapots. They raise serious doubts about value-free research, especially with regard to what is being taught in lower and higher education. From a conservative perspective, Roger Scruton notes the paradox of a new, institutionalized humanist culture, 'relativist in favour of transgression and absolutist against authority' (Scruton, 2007, p. xii). Academic debates about the relativity of evidence have aroused the suspicions of policy-makers that the dons, by their own admission, are not always motivated by disinterested investigations. The converse is also true. Government policies are often ideologically motivated (as contrasted with 'problem-solving'), but that is scarcely surprising given the purpose of party politics. Academic values have certainly undergone many changes over time, but a belief in scientific modes of proof is supposed to elevate the scholarly enterprise. Ditto Max Weber's idea of the academic career as more than an occupation, in fact (with its religious overtones) a 'calling' (Weber, 1965).

If the academic community does not accept accuracy and objectivity as leading values, why should decision-makers pay heed to research results? Transparency has also become an issue. In an era of mounting expenses, how do research universities, obtaining their money from taxpayer (or private) sources, actually spend it? Any number of scandals in both America and Britain, to include dubious overseas outreach programs by British universities, have raised more than eyebrows. The current tendency of university leaders to assume the management style and the nomenclature of business organizations, along with the salaries that presumably attach thereto, adds to general confusion about the values actually existing in higher education. Campus heads are CEOs. Some of them (Berkeley) have a chief of staff. It is difficult for those who love universities to argue that they are dependable repositories of wisdom and guardians of the higher values. Trust and moral authority are at stake.

While a renewed market relevance may well be a major element in the promotion of policies supporting an emphasis on skills and vocational preparation, these also happen to be areas of the schools curriculum that are reasonably insulated from political partisanship, social activism, diversity issues, multi-culturalism (bearing several meanings), identity stereotyping and the furthering of an egalitarian agenda, all of which are present in the social science and humanistic disciplines. Professional schools and vocational education have a 'product' that can be measured in some way. A product can be made accountable. The task is nearly impossible with respect to teaching and research without immediate market relevance.

Schools are everybody's business

We may debate the question of moral authority and whether this entails a loss of trust, but it would also be hard put to notice whether any other institution possesses a greater degree of moral influence. Public disapproval of politicians is strong. Businesses, especially in today's economic difficulties, cannot claim to be ethical exemplars. Religions, at least the dominant religions of Europe and America, also do not qualify. Parish priests in the Roman Catholic Church have often violated their vows, and televangelists have a habit of disregarding all sorts of family values that they purportedly espouse. As for families, child abuse cases are newspaper items and divorce rates are high. Matthew Arnold looked for a metonym to replace the respect accorded to the Established Church, and he found it in a conception of high culture. But where is high culture in the media pop culture of today? And, what is more to the point, to what extent have universities contributed to the maintenance of high culture and models of civility? The branding phenomenon and the rankings game have revealed far more than at any other time just how much universities and academics are involved in the celebrity cultures of the present. Social historians have investigated moral slippage in the past, and the story easily becomes depressing. But what might have been concealed in the past is everyday news at present. We are more aware of the issues, and universities cannot possibly avoid intense public scrutiny.

Moral authority may be wishful thinking; and it may also be the case that moral authority in academia means the adherence to a professional ethic of disinterested enquiry, in which case we can still ask whether that particular mission still dominates academic thinking. I am puzzled by the fact that just as the culture wars are not mentioned by the representatives of the disciplines, neither is there a reference to any of the inherited ethics regulating academic activity and possibly uniting them.

Putting this omission aside for the moment, another way of looking at the connections between the university disciplines and the social institutions that are the subjects of their enquiries is simply to notice the unprecedented amount of competition for attention in a world dominated by an overload of information. I seem to recall one writer – it may have been Walter Ong – who mentioned that an overload of information was first noticed in or about the year 1800. The point is intriguing, but if the availability of information was becoming a problem in 1800, imagine what it is in the age of the Internet, broadband and what it pleases the pundits to call 'instant interconnectivity'. The amount of available information – reports, publications, commentaries, legislative activity and proposals regarding education – is overwhelming. Education is everyone's business, not only educators, but trade unions, professional associations, industries, parents and, today, think tanks, textbook publishers, social work agencies. Although their role is limited to the areas of their particular concern, the military, certainly in both America and Britain, are among the greatest providers of education, especially skills education, but also foreign languages and computer technologies. The list grows: in the USA there are religious groups troubled by secular or even anti-religious teachings about science. There are policing authorities eager to protect children from psychopaths or to prevent the horrific school crimes that make headlines. Worried about the transmission of diseases are those who want schools to engage in sex education. Wanting nothing of the sort and suspecting personal agenda are those on the other side.

Furthermore, in a consumer society, children are targets for the marketing of gadgets and seductive technologies, some of which can aid learning but others falling into the category of distractions. Children have been important aspects of a culture of consumption since the marketing revolutions of the later eighteenth century,[9] but it takes no thought to conclude that a much greater percentage of sophisticated attention is devoted to youth markets today.

The growth of mass schooling revealed the fact that schools were not just locations for the transmission of skills and cultural heritages, or preparation for employment. They were, as the geographers here say, 'places and spaces' for the creation of viable social relationships, life-adjustment skills, environments where all of being human was to be addressed. Social democratic principles, even in capitalist America, made the health of schools central to that conception of a just society.

I would argue that given the range of issues associated with schools, issues that are more than education conventionally defined, the opportunities for university-based research have never been greater. The opportunities are great, but the fault lines are equally great. In this kind of environment, fads and fancies are frequent. Many opinions clamor for a hearing. The academic search for originality that began in the nineteenth century may have reached a point where universities are generating more ideas about education than our over-burdened information cultures can assimilate. Too much information produces short attention spans. What appears to be the problem is

gaining a commanding voice. The one obvious way is to simplify complicated problems in order to offer easy digestives. But while politicians adopt
this approach, as do ideologues and radio talk-show hosts, we may hope that
academics will resist.

The dissemination of knowledge

Gaining a commanding voice is part of the very broad and interesting question of knowledge transfer. How ideas are transmitted from researchers to
practitioners is not merely an issue relating to education. It is a sub-set of a
larger issue of the communication of innovative ideas originating within
universities out into the broader reaches of society or into the agencies and
institutions that best make use of them. The adaptive process is in general
long, complex and expensive, involving many actors. The road from a discovery or an insight to an invention, to production and to marketing is
anfractuous. But as vexed and intricate as transfer may be in regard to specific scientific discoveries – for example, the laser and the use of the laser in
medicine and industry[10] – it would appear to be doubly complicated with
regard to schools. Where exactly are the entry points? Through central or
local government, politicians and civil servants, teacher unions and professional societies, parent associations, trusts and corporations with investments
in education, lobbyists, the media?

Among the contributors, the sociologists are the only ones to assay this
area, if just in passing. They suggest that teachers were their primary audience. By and large I suspect that schoolteachers are not regular readers of the
journals and specialist studies produced by disciplines and sub-disciplines. I
also have no substantial basis on which to judge how many teachers attend
meetings and conferences where leading approaches to learning and pedagogy are discussed, although I know from my own narrow experience that
annual gatherings of teachers do occur and that workshops and seminars are
available and possibly sometimes required by local authorities. Some upgrading of qualifications occurs in this way, along with part-time work for a
higher degree or credits useful in advancing careers. But the transmission of
the results of research from universities through teacher training and into
schools is, I imagine, not as systematic as the disciplines would hope,
although clearly some academics act as consultants to school districts and
boards. Once again I speculate that when their essential training is completed, most teachers are no longer in frequent contact with the institutions
responsible for generating new knowledge and testing existing assumptions.

The entry points for educational ideas are many but uncertain, and the
sources of innovation and co-operation are not unified. That is clear enough
from the contributions to this volume. I have listed some of the barriers: the
cultures of disciplines and peer approval; the social origins of schoolteachers,
status issues and the continuing ambiguous position of state schools of education; the lower standing of mass education relative to private education; and

the politicization of ideas and schools and school business. And education is particularly susceptible to shifts in purpose, community sentiment and public policies. No one doubts that schools are really the central institutions of a modern and democratic society. Being central, they are everybody's business.

That is a special problem for the educational disciplines.

Notes

1 Often put under the headings of global competition and privatization.
2 Academic teacher unions suffer from the same difficulty. It is often said that in the USA, academics within elite research universities and high-standing liberal arts colleges do not normally choose an industrial model of association, while those in lower-status institutions are more amenable. A similar observation can probably be made of Britain.
3 Personal knowledge.
4 According to Joseph Ben-David, the key element in this pattern was the highly decentralized character of nineteenth-century Germany. The *Länder* competed for prestige. Creating new chairs was part of the package, especially if market relevance existed.
5 An example provided by Andrew Abbot would be the Committee on Social Thought of the University of Chicago, created by the president Robert Maynard Hutchins in 1947 in order to house a body of intellectuals free from the narrower constraints of disciplinary departments. The Committee attracted names such as the sociologist Edward Shils, who had been marginalized by his home department.
6 He provides the following distinctions:

> [I]n fundamental-particle physics, solid-state physics, and molecular biology, discovery is a central notion. It is less obviously so in taxonomic studies of plant and animal life, whereas in mechanical engineering the concept is largely replaced by that of invention. Moving further afield, the term seems out of place in academic law; and in history, the discovery of new primary material, though it may be important when it occurs, is by no means crucial to the historian's task.

Diane Harley and her colleagues at the Center for Studies in Higher Education at the University of California, Berkeley are currently engaged in a massive project funded by the Andrew Mellon Foundation designed to update Becher, as it were. The analysis is comprehensive, concentrating on scholarly values in a digital environment. Astrophysics, archaeology, biology, economics, history, music and political science are the featured disciplines. Some materials can be viewed online at http://cshe.berkeley.edu/research/scholarlycommunication/index.htm.

7 We may be in the early stages of new subject hybrids based on cross-disciplinary collaboration, as notable in the medical sciences. These represent challenges to the customary disciplinary structure of multiversities; but the responses of the contributors to this volume suggest that the situation with respect to schools of education has not altered.
8 Probably an unfortunate phrase, since its origin is very likely Bismarck's *Kulturkampf* against the Roman Catholic Church in south Germany.

9 Historians speak about the 'invention of childhood', which occurred in England in the eighteenth century in conjunction with a proliferation of pertinent consumer items such as toys and children's books. The Newbury Prize dates from this period. The literature is substantial, but *inter alia* see Steward (1995).

10 Charles Townes, the Nobel Laureate who invented the laser, remarked in his autobiography that while he knew the laser would one day have wide applications, he could not foretell what those might be (Townes, 1999). In their study of knowledge transfer, the scholars assembled by Michael Gibbons concluded that university–industry communication was often facilitated by teams composed of both university and industry representatives working closely with one another from idea to production. See Gibbons (1994). This raises issues often associated with institutional autonomy and the freedom of researchers to select their own objects of enquiry.

References

Abbot, A. (1999) *Department and discipline, Chicago sociology at one hundred*, Chicago and London: University of Chicago Press.

Arnold, M. (1993) *Culture and anarchy and other writings*, ed. S. Collini, Cambridge: Cambridge University Press.

Becher, T. (1987) The cultural view, in Burton R. Clark (ed.) *Perspectives on Higher Education, eight disciplinary and comparative views*, Berkeley: University of California Press.

Becher, T. (1989) *Academic tribes and territories, intellectual enquiry and the cultures of disciplines*, Milton Keynes: Open University Press.

Ben-David, J. (1991) *Scientific growth, essays on the social organization and ethos of science*, ed. G. Freudenthal, Berkeley: University of California Press.

Clark, B.R. (2008) *On higher education, selected writings, 1956–2006*, Baltimore: Johns Hopkins University Press.

Clifford, G.J. and Guthrie, J.W. (1988) *Ed school, a brief for professional education*, Chicago and London: University of Chicago Press.

Gibbons, M. *et al.* (1994) *The new production of knowledge: The dynamics of science and research in contemporary societies*, London and Thousand Oaks, CA: Sage.

Kerr, C. (1963) *The uses of the university*, Cambridge, MA: Harvard University Press.

Kuhn, T. (1970) *The structure of scientific revolutions*, Chicago and London: University of Chicago Press.

Merton, R.K. (1973) The Matthew Effect in science, in *The Sociology of Science*, Chicago: University of Chicago Press.

Rothblatt, S. (2006) *Education's abiding moral dilemma, merit and worth in the cross-Atlantic democracies, 1800–2006*, Oxford: Symposium.

Scruton, R. (2007) *Culture counts, faith and feeling in a world besieged*, New York: Encounter Books.

Smelser, N. (1991) *Social paralysis and social change: British working-class education in the nineteenth century*, Berkeley and New York: University of California Press.

Steward, J.C. (1995) *The new child: British art and the origins of modern childhood, 1730–1830*, Seattle: University of Washington Press.

Swift, J. (1950) *Gulliver's travels, the tale of a tub, the battle of the books*, New York: Modern Library.

Tapper, T. and Palfreyman, D. (2008) *Structuring mass higher education: The role of elite universities*, New York: Routledge.

Townes, C.H. (1999) *How the laser happened: Adventures of a scientist*, New York: Oxford University Press.

Trow, M.A. (1987) The analysis of status, in Burton R. Clark (ed.) *Perspectives on higher education, eight disciplinary and comparative views*, Berkeley: University of California Press, pp. 132–164.

Weber, M. (1965) *Politics as a vocation*, Philadelphia: Fortress Press.

Wildavsky, B. (2009) How America's mania for college rankings went global, *The Washington Monthly* (September/October).

10 Disciplines of education

The value of disciplinary self-observation

Edwin Keiner

Introduction

At present education research seems to be experiencing a widespread crisis, created by demographic pressures, the effects of a global market on scientific knowledge, the pressures of neo-liberal managerialism and the competition of public and private research organisations, as well as the increasing importance of EU funding criteria and regulations that give education research a new shape. These are significant pressures which affected the responses of the authors in this book, and which have shaped my overall view of the contemporary value of this book.

However, has there ever been a history of education and education research which is free of self-perceived crises (Keiner and Tenorth, 2007)? The idea of progress and enlightenment is systematically inherent in education, science and research as is the experience of its failure. The educational focus upon individual upbringing and societal reform, and the perception of the present world as imperfect, necessarily leads to disappointments when the usefulness of education research results and the success of educational interventions are evaluated. Indeed, since education research started to become institutionalised at universities from the beginning of the twentieth century onwards, it not only contributed to changing the world via education but also began more and more to contribute to its own disenchantment about its value and effects. With this in mind, the chapters in this volume can be perceived both as a reaction to 'external' pressures and as a consequence of 'internal' self-reflection. The chapters are part of this constant process of disenchantment and 'rationalisation'.

However, the disciplinary self-observation the chapters represent might be rather dangerous. Today, political systems demand 'applicable' and 'useful' knowledge in order to justify decisions scientifically and, at the same time, hide their own weaknesses and produce 'cover' for politically justified decisions. From this point of view, scepticism, doubt and questioning – constitutive for modern science and research – is perceived more and more as ineffective, a non-productive outcome of the academic discipline. Other concepts, i.e. usefulness, accountability, applicability, prognostic capacity, efficiency, power, impact of knowledge, evidence-based research, have gained in importance. This has also meant that new beliefs could enter the academic arena: belief in management according to economy, belief in learning instead of education, belief in applied rather than basic research, belief in decoupling research and teaching, belief in market-driven competition according to benchmarks and performance indicators, and belief in high-quality and useful outcomes of research, measured by using de-contextualised organisational correlates. These new concepts and beliefs have generated new contexts for research in new alliances between universities and business, and new 'quasi-research institutions', sometimes linked to universities, which are all mobilised by national EU funding policies. These shifts have led to a struggle over the power of definition and the application of criteria for research quality. Attempts at governing education research via policy, administration and management can only refer to infra-structural conditions. They aim at securing and improving the 'quality' and 'excellence' of research and research products (publication) without being able to define and justify the respective criteria of high (or low) quality. In this respect, then, disciplinary self-observation may gain in importance as an instrument to productively contribute to this struggle. The definition of scientific quality is a matter to be decided by the self-governing disciplinary community itself. The discipline analytically and systematically defines the quality of research on the basis of a (content-based) discipline's systematic procedures and/or the discipline's experts, the peers.

Our concern to analytically and empirically strengthen and reconstruct education research sufficiently, however, is confronted with the problem of a rather heterogeneous discipline, both in epistemological and sociological terms. This problem increases when different nations and research cultures are considered and attempts at comparison are made (Keiner and Schriewer, 2000; Hofstetter and Schneuwly, 2002); for example, is it correct to denote the German 'Bildungsforschung' as 'educational research', and the German 'Erziehungswissenschaft' as 'education research'? Is, then, the term 'education research' sufficient to also denote the French 'science de l'éducation'? Though English-language publication and citation indices (using primarily English references) are dominant, we lack sufficient cross-linguistic translations and signifiers which can express different meanings of the term.

Against this background, this volume of chapters on the disciplines of education is an important attempt to observe and assess education research 'from within' and to analyse and compare different disciplinary structures within diverse intellectual and research cultures: it is useful in its aspiration to discern different disciplinary shapes and to discuss and to define our differing expectations of research quality.

The following sections take the significance of the chapters for granted and, taking an outsider's point of view, acts as a commentary addressing their issues from several directions. First, it looks at scholarly associations of education research on a German and a European level and their contribution to disciplinary self-observation. Second, it asks how education research is conceptualised as a unit to be investigated. Third, it suggests some distinctions which probably could help to comparatively relate education research experiences in the UK to other (European) countries and cultures. Fourth, it offers one possibility in using comparative aspects in order to investigate different education research cultures and their consequences when dealing with crises. Fifth, it discusses the problem of 'disciplinary autonomy' and the degree of self-governance as a possible aspect of comparative observation and issue of education research policy. Finally, it considers 'Europe' as a possible future for integrated research upon education research. Although *Disciplines of Education* primarily addresses education research in the UK (see also Lawn and Furlong, 2007), many of the recent problems discussed in the chapters are much more widespread and not only restricted to the UK.

Observation and organisation of education research

From a very German point of view, education research (Erziehungswissenschaft) in Germany can be perceived as a rather stable and disciplinary-framed enterprise – in spite of competing reference disciplines also researching on educational issues (sociology, psychology, philosophy), in spite of the currently dominant paradigm of empirical, social sciences-oriented educational research (Bildungsforschung) which blurs disciplinary boundaries, and in spite of a cut of 26 per cent in professors between 1995 (1,133 professors) and 2006 (843 professors). The stable situation of German education research is indicated in several ways. First of all is the importance of the German Association of Education Researchers (Deutsche Gesellschaft für Erziehungswissenschaft (DGfE)) which covers 70–80 per cent of education research personnel at universities. These personnel amount to a total of 843 professors with an average of 2.73 assistants per professor in 2006. The rather stable disciplinary situation is indicated by a remarkable internal differentiation in partial or sub-disciplines (also mirrored by the sections and commissions through which the DGfE is structured), and by the third-party funds (€59,000 on average per professor in 2005) which increasingly approach the respective amount gained by psychology (€80,000), politics (€64,000) and social sciences (€59,000).

The council of the DGfE has taken several self-observation initiatives in order to examine the discipline's history, structure and developments; it has also installed several advisory boards, which have worked out analyses and policy statements relevant for the discipline's profile.

For example, out of the DGfE a new organisation emerged in 2002, the Convention of Educational Faculties at German Universities (Erziehungswissenschaftlicher Fakultätentag (EWFT)), which is related to the Convention of German University Rectors (Hochschulrektorenkonferenz). The EWFT addresses organisational and infrastructural questions about universities and higher education policy, which distinguishes it from the academic and scholarly focus of the DGfE. The EWFT meets twice a year and consists of delegates from about 60 universities.

Within the DGfE, a Research on Education Research Commission (Wissenschaftsforschung) was established in 1978. Finally, the DGfE created a key instrument to make education research visible in the educational professions and public policy and to contribute to a self-reliant and realistic self-awareness of the discipline's strength and weaknesses: the Data Report on Education Research (Datenreport Erziehungswissenschaft), published biannually since 2000 (recent issue: Tillmann *et al.*, 2008). The report contains information about Bachelor's and Master's programmes in education and teacher education; number of students, their social background and motivation; the relation between university degrees in education and the labour market; about staff, research performance, younger researchers, gender distribution, etc. To a large extent it uses official statistics or other quantitative data to display problems and productivity of education research. It serves as a kind of observatory which not only informs the discipline about itself, but also uses indicators to compare its situation with other disciplines.

European education research is rather different. Since a big, but erratic, 1970s survey (West Germany, France, Italy, Yugoslavia, Soviet Union, Sweden, UK) (Malmquist and Grundin, 1975), education research in Europe has not had systematic, comparative observation and analysis. Empirically and comparatively, little is known about European scholarly discourses and research practices, which are often locked in national, disciplinary and practical specialities, or focused upon big European key topics, for example, on education and learning or the future of the knowledge society. Nor, in spite of the large-scale studies carried out by the EU and the OECD, are we well informed about knowledge production, distribution and reception within particular European countries and cultures, and we are far from agreeing a range of common criteria for assessing and evaluating research quality. Nor have we knowledge about new forms of organisations in education research beyond the traditional universities and research institutions. Networks, joint ventures and hybrid constructions are taking over mediation and 'knowledge management' functions in global and European mutual adjustment processes. The degree and impact of the coupling/decoupling of the relation between these new intermediate organisations and traditional research and governance, as well as their impact on research practice and professionalism, has barely been studied.

One important new factor, created by the national education research associations, which is contributing to knowledge about the processes of Europeanisation and to an emerging European Education Research Policy Area, is the European Education Research Association (EERA), its annual European Conferences on Education Research (ECER) and its *European Education Research Journal* (EERJ). It works as academics across Europe experience how 'doing Europe' in education research unlocks their own particular national and cultural views and creates productive friction. On the other hand, the empirical and organised self-observation of how they are 'doing Europe' appears rather under-developed. So, it would be useful to know more about education research in the UK whose scholars are active in the EERA and constitute about 25 per cent of all ECER participants.

Social composition and cognitive texture of education research

As Lawn and Furlong observe in their opening chapter to this volume, in looking at education research in the UK, one can find a distinction between sociological and epistemological perspectives. In a social dimension, education research is based on social roles, status, staff and infrastructural conditions, one of the concerns of this book. In a cognitive (that is, knowledge) dimension, education research is based on the characteristics of scientific networks of communication, on the publication and reception of processes and products. The self-regulating flow of a communication process is generated, continued and reproduced in the frame of regular conferences, study groups, clusters, invisible colleges, professional associations or scholarly societies. Additionally, it aims at generating knowledge that conforms to specific requirements, that is, to thematic pertinence, conceptual integration and methodological quality. It is characterised through epistemic logic, method and justification, through theory and analysis, and refers to truth and consistency within a critical medium. This analytical distinction is necessary in order to be able to relate both perspectives and – in a possible further step – to relate this relationship to other (European) research cultures in a comparative view.

However, it also raises fundamental questions regarding the definition of the subject we are observing – first of all: what counts as education research from a sociological perspective and from an epistemological perspective? Additionally, we could ask whether our own disciplinary point of observing education research counts as education research or not. One might reject such questions as 'very German' or fruitless. However, some diagnoses about the situation of education research in the UK seem to start from the assumption that it was the impact of new modes of governance, based on neo-liberal trends and new managerialism, that affected the disciplinary structures, universities and education research. This explanation does not seem to be sufficient and does not take into consideration the contribution of education research itself.

How did it happen that managers of structures and organisations subordinated and controlled producers of scholarly knowledge? Or, alternatively, why could scholars and researchers in education not resist the power of managerial control? To understand this problem, it makes sense to suggest two further analytical distinctions which might lead to new empirical and theoretical insights.

Education research, higher education and the university

Universities include both education research and teacher education within their domain, yet these operations are both different and entangled. Teacher education works closely with the educational professions and their future needs, and while teaching is part of the education system, it distributes and provides knowledge in the mode of teaching and mediating. Its ideal point of reference is the scholarly informed, well-educated good teacher who is able to develop and improve educational practice. Students as well as educational professionals expect to be provided with professional knowledge that is relevant to solve educational problems and improve education; they expect 'useful' knowledge.

Education research, on the other hand, primarily addresses the scientific community which does not work in the teaching and mediation mode, but in the mode of reflection, analysis and research. Its ideal point of reference is theoretically and methodically proved knowledge; it aims at understanding, interpretation and explanation; it asks answerable questions, for example, why is improving educational practice so difficult? The distinction between education research and teacher education is based on different 'logics' of knowledge application: the first refers to 'true' or verifiable knowledge, the latter to 'useful' or applicable knowledge. Thus, research and teaching constitute different spheres of reflection on educational issues, according to different modes of knowing and seeing.

However, we should remember that education research has and should have direct impact on university teaching and teacher education. Not every good teacher is a good researcher, and well-assured knowledge might be more useful for teacher education than brand-new, irritating research findings. This also means that the university can be conceived of as an organisation serving a double and conflicting function: it contributes to the education system by producing the 'good teacher' and to the science domain by producing proved knowledge, for example, about the problem of producing the 'good teacher'. This might be regarded as a more continental European point of view, but the assumption of Lauder *et al.* (this volume), that 'the focus on teachers may have been a key factor in the separation of the discipline from "mainstream" sociology', is generalisable and indicates this two-fold function of the university.

Teacher education as a part of the educational system is organised mostly in universities. Research is also dependent on the infrastructure provided by the university (positions, staff, libraries, laboratories, etc.), but its core feature is not organisation but networking and communication, including its publications. In this analytical respect, disciplinary networking and communication is independent from organisation. 'Organisation' means the infrastructural conditions and 'input' resources (universities, faculties, personnel, funds, etc., but also politically defined directions and rules) that education research is based on. 'Communication' refers to the scientific community in education as 'discipline'; its self-organised conditions and 'outcome' of knowledge production, reception and distribution; its publications and references; its main topics and methodologies; and its associations and research networks.

This communicative space is not necessarily identical with the organisational space, but includes educational practitioners and administrators as well as researchers from other disciplines and nations. The degree of overlapping of these spheres remains an empirical question (Keiner, 1999, 2002).

From an historical point of view, intellectual disciplines emerge from the disjunction of organisation (university) and communication (scholarly network). The emergence of modern research universities from the sixteenth century cannot be understood without this disjunction, which also led to the decline of mandarins (Ringer, 1990) and the differentiation of generalists and specialists (Harwood, 1992). It is noteworthy that the usefulness of this distinction – between the university as an organisational service infrastructure and the discipline as an autonomous communicative structure – is supported by several contributions in this book. Oancea and Bridges, describing recent developments in British philosophy of education, show how scholarly communication remains stable despite the interests of particular universities. Crozier, regarding psychology of education, makes a similar point. However, although these authors affirm the relative independence of 'communication' from (university) 'organisation', they opt for a close connection between research and practice, which re-introduces the notion of the university or the 'audience'. It is Goodman and Grosvenor, the educational historians, focusing on scholarly journals and conferences, who consequently limit their focus on interdisciplinary and international historical education research, and, thus, escape from the trap of arguing as researchers/scholars and as teachers simultaneously.

Research cultures: comparative aspects

The process of disjunction between organisation (university) and communication (scholarly network) to some extent has been moderated by diverse cultures of communication and degrees of organisational and disciplinary rigidity across different countries. Therefore the social profiles and cognitive textures of European disciplines in education vary according to the different national contexts and research cultures they emerged from. These variations can be seen in different types of research orientation, use of methods, theoretical key concepts, links to contributing disciplines (sociology, psychology, philosophy, etc.), conceptualisations of the relationship between theory and practice, modes of trans-national exchange of knowledge, etc., as well as in the different types of organisational infrastructure. Additionally, the degree of self-reflection varies across different education research cultures.

According to Wagner and Wittrock (1991) we find three different patterns of theoretical and social formation in the social sciences and the sciences of education in the context of the establishment of the nation state.

1   The model of *comprehensive social sciences* (France and francophone cultures) is characterised by inter- or trans-disciplinary traditions of social sciences within the tradition of Emile Durkheim, with a high degree of originality, comprehensiveness and multi-faceted scholarship, hardly caring about disciplinary structures and self-reflections. However, regarding education research there appears to be a weak and insufficient organisational infrastructure in order to be able to follow these modes of thinking and reasoning.

2   The model of *formalised disciplinary discourses* (Germany, Austria, Switzerland, Belgium) with a high intensity of self-reflecting discourses on its own disciplinary status and profile. In these cultures, the theory–practice relationship is expected to be a crucial issue.

3   The model of *pragmatically specialising professions* (Anglo-Saxon countries), which comprises more pragmatic academic cultures focusing on particular practical issues. Research themes and groups emerge and stabilise according to economic, social and political needs. One could expect criticism addressed to (research) policy and governance which urges researchers – for example, through funding – to focus on politically relevant, useful and applicable research topics rather than on systematic, basic/fundamental research.

Table 10.1 presents an overview over main characteristics. The different modes of communication and self-control are also expected to lead to different modes of coping with crises (see Table 10.2).

Against this background it is also to be expected that the intensity of self-reflective discourses on education as an intellectual discipline is very high in cultures based on traditions of 'formal disciplines' (Germany, Austria, Switzerland, Belgium). In contrast, in academic cultures characterised by inter- or trans-disciplinary traditions (France) the degree of self-reflection on education is expected to be rather low. When education research in more pragmatic academic cultures is considered (Anglo-Saxon countries), research on education research itself is occasional and non-systematic (except in case of research performance measurement according to the 'research market'); it emerges as a by-product of research on particular educational issues or as a reaction to external public and political pressure. It is necessary to note that these expected patterns of degrees of disciplinary self-reflection are not high or low status, or more or less advanced. However, it might be very interesting to historically investigate the degree of intensity of self-reflective discourses in the UK and to ask the question, why this issue is on the agenda now, and whether it is at the centre or the periphery of the entire recent disciplinary discourse in the UK.

Relative disciplinary autonomy

One could say that the different modes of coping with crises reflect and depend on the degree of coupling or decoupling of organisation and

Table 10.1 Models of theoretical and social formation in the social sciences and education research

	Comprehensive social sciences	Formalised disciplinary discourses	Pragmatically specialising professions
Cultural references	France and francophone cultures	Germany, Austria, Switzerland, Belgium	Anglo-Saxon, English-speaking countries
General profile	Pro theoretically and empirically based sociology. Contra disciplinary segmentation and professions-related specialisation	Pro disciplinary and systematic structure of knowledge. Claims thematic, theoretical and methodological autonomy	Pro non-dogmatic division of labour without intricate meta-theory. Aims at serving needs of knowledge and qualification of 'professions' and at solving societal problems
Profile of education research	Part of a comprehensive social science; interdisciplinary, sociological and technological research field	Disciplinary autonomy through demarcation. Emphasis on German hermeneutics mode *Geisteswissenschaften* (arts and humanities), qualitative research as reflection	Combination of practical know-how, experience and empirical research. Varied and flexible inter-disciplinary and practical connections
Subsequent problems	Weak and unstable institutionalisation	Disciplinary isolation and marginalisation; theory–practice relationship as continuing problem	Weak theoretical justification and systematic array; knowledge depends on market supply and demand

Source: Adapted from Wagner and Wittrock (1991).

Table 10.2 Different modes of communication and self-control in the social sciences and education research

	Comprehensive social sciences	Formalised disciplinary discourses	Pragmatically specialising professions
Strategies of relief	Integration and cross-linking of research questions and projects with other research groups and disciplines	Further disciplinary differentiation	Addressing up-to-date problems; strengthening the capacity of solving practical and political problems

communication, university and discipline. The more the university as an administrative or managerial structure aims at meeting external goals (e.g. 'excellence', whatever this might be), the more the disciplinary communication structure and even the possibility to choose research topics are out of the control of the scientific community. Even in Germany, the traditional home of strong disciplinary cultures, the organisation (universities as well as research institutes) more and more has taken control. The organisational location gains in importance, whereas the communicative realm (transcending local fixations by nature) loses importance. The reason for this shift we find not only 'outside', but also 'inside' the discipline, and, in spite of a high 'external' neo-liberal influence, the education research community contributes to the fact that it feels under pressure. It is our own weakness not to be able to define the quality of research and knowledge independent from organisational structures. So, it is also important to remember the distinction between teacher education and education research. Teacher education necessarily needs an organisational structure, which its teaching procedures, curricula and syllabuses are embedded in. However, education research does not! Instrumentally it uses the infrastructural conditions, the possibility of getting its research monies administered, but the very core of research – its ideas, questions, results, interpretations – are beyond or transversal to organisation. Organisation needs a location, and communication does not.

If the education researcher (as a researcher) focuses too much on university teacher education, he/she takes the risk of falling under regulation and control. If we long for more independence and autonomy, we have to stress research and its analytical, theoretical and methodological qualities. Therefore it could be – in line with the view of the editors of this book – useful to remember the question of 'autonomy' of a scientific field of study and its specific 'logic' of work. From an epistemological point of view one could say, according to Bourdieu (1998, p. 19; Keiner, 2002), that the degree of the autonomy of a field is defined according to its ability to break external expectations or requests into a specific form: 'The decisive indicator of the degree of the autonomy of a field is its breaking strength, its translation power.' Scientific fields generate knowledge that is basically characterised through 'epistemic logic', 'method' and 'justification', through 'theory' and 'analysis', and refers to truth and consistency in the medium of criticism. This episte-mological part of a discipline should be considered as important as the socio-logical part.

Against this background, it might be interesting to consider the different modes of self-control, which are able to define good, excellent or insufficient knowledge. In other words, it is the battle about the definition of the 'quality' of education research. What counts as good research, and who defines what counts as good research? Just as teacher education knows what a good teacher is, education research has to know what good education research knowledge is – and what it is not. It is necessary to state that talking about quality necessarily means talking about differentiation, even exclusion.

All over the world this problem is solved via finance, the regulation of funding organisations and the role of peers. Yet we can expect the issue of research quality to be treated differently in different countries. In the franco-phone culture, I assume, the quality problem to a large extent is dealt with by a differentiated hierarchy, which regulates and structures epistemological issues in a social mode; this might result in some relief regarding justifica-tion of quality and might enable intense inter- and trans-disciplinary research. In Germany, the solution of the quality problem is structured according to a modernised medieval guild, where doctoral degree, habilita-tion and professorship still mark the 'normal' academic career, especially in social sciences, arts and humanities. This is in line with the regulations of the German education research association, which restricts access to full membership to those who obtained a doctoral degree and additionally asks for a recommendation from two other members from the education research community. The English-speaking world seems to establish semi-organisations, according to limited social problems, or creates networks and hybrid structures in order to force flexibility of reaction. One could also find a more paternalistic structure when looking at journals or publishers who control larger or smaller fenced fields.

Europe as Utopia?

When looking at the analyses of pressure under which education research is working at the moment, within organisations and markets, Europe appears as a new field of communication into which, at least temporarily, education researchers and disciplinary scholars could escape. In this respect the EERA, the association of many national education research associations, is a good source: there has been an increasing number of conference participants from all over Europe, and, on average, UK scholars represent abut a quarter of them.

For the last ten years there has been a continuing debate within EERA about research quality, on quality indicators, on increasing the quality of the papers and about rejection rates. EERA expects delegates to pay special attention to Europe and Europeanisation as it assumes that the ECER is the place where European education research issues are discussed (rather than nationally relevant research subjects). An investigation based on all proposals for ECER 2006 (Geneva) and 2007 (Ghent) shows that 39 per cent of papers are indifferent in addressing subjects beyond the national, 50 per cent have only one nation in mind, and 10 per cent focus upon two or more nations (see Table 10.3).

So, a sound and methodologically reflected comparative perspective analysing European diversity is rather visible, and one of the most striking findings was the degree of reference to the European space. The EERA is a European enterprise with its own quality criteria reflecting its focus on Europe, and although network convenors use a focus upon Europe as a peer-review criterion, it is still a quality issue for the networks.

Obviously the ECER is primarily a European forum to present education research knowledge originating from national cultures. At one level, paper presenters at EERA can be represented as international and as European researchers, both valuable and useful labels in the science community. More radically, being accepted at ECER can be taken as an indicator of research quality: a sign in the presenter's CV of an international scholar. The presenter converts an internationally less accepted epistemological label (nationally restricted research) into a higher accepted social label (internationally open researcher): it serves as a code, an institutionalised capital (Bourdieu), cheap to buy and dear to sell. That means that this interest to obtain a European marker could be motivated more by sociological than by epistemological reasons.

One also could assume that the education research discourse on the European level mirrors the discourse on the national level. This also seems to be wrong. Regarding the methodological tradition and self-descriptions of education researchers from the UK one could expect a high share of empirical research presented at ECERs. However, the proposals from the UK show an unexpected high share of theoretical and discursive research methods. Are our expectations or the self-descriptions wrong? Or do we observe a segmentation of national research profiles according to conference milieux? Could we

Table 10.3 ECER 2006 and 2007: reference to nation/
country within proposals

Units of comparison: nation	N	%
No nation	846	38.8
One nation	1,106	50.8
Two nations	69	3.2
More than two nations	158	7.2
Total	2,179	100

Table 10.4 ECER 2006 and 2007: proposals' reference to Europe or the process of European-isation

Explicit reference to Europe/Europeanisation	N	%
None	1,757	80.6
Some	198	9.1
Medium	102	4.7
High	57	2.6
Very high	64	2.9
Total	2,179	99.9

assume that those education researchers who are quite accepted, powerful and dominating within their respective countries prefer communication within their own country (and present their empirical research there), whereas those education researchers who feel probably less powerful and marginalised within their respective countries discover Europe as the new field to gain in power and acceptance, imagining the future in a new education research area?

Integrated research on education research

For all the above reasons, more research, an advanced disciplinary self-observation, is necessary. This book contributes to knowledge about how education research in the UK works: its indicators we should use for comparative purposes, its distinctions should guide our theoretical efforts and its questions we should ask to better understand the diversity of distinctions and theoretical perspectives we are all used to using. In view of the inspiring chapters in the book, the plea for more comparative research on (European) education research is not combined with a pessimistic view or a defeatist attitude.

In contrast, the analytical and conceptual capacity and, so, power that education research has to offer results from being self-aware and insisting on its limitations as a scientific field, and that its work of generating knowledge is necessarily framed by its epistemic logic, method and justification, theory and analysis. Political relevance and importance are not the basic – or even the second or third – criteria for education research products' quality. It is the theoretically and methodologically framed observation (including observing whether and how our research products become relevant in the political/policy context) that characterises research quality. In my opinion, this should be the background against which education research could broaden and strengthen its self-observation as research on education research which is – in view of European diversity – comparative by nature. Disciplinary self-observation may gain in importance as an instrument to productively contribute to definitions of scientific quality and education research could become stronger by engaging in this activity and defending its products.

References

Bourdieu, P. (1998) *Vom Gebrauch der Wissenschaft. Für eine klinische Soziologie des wissenschaftlichen Feldes*, Constance: Universitäts-Verlag Konstanz.

Crozier, M. and Friedberg, E. (1993) *Die Zwänge kollektiven Handelns. Über Macht und Organisation*, Beltz Athenäum: Frankfurt am Main.

Harwood, J. (1992) *Styles of Scientific Thought: A Study of the German Genetics Community, 1900–1933*, Chicago: University of Chicago Press.

Hofstetter, R. and Schneuwly, B. (2002) Institutionalisation of Educational Sciences and the Dynamics of Their Development, *European Educational Research Journal*, 1(1), 3–26.

Keiner, E. (1999) *Erziehungswissenschaft 1947–1990. Eine empirische und vergleichende Untersuchung zur kommunikativen Praxis einer Disziplin*, Weinheim: Deutscher Studien Verlag.

Keiner, E. (2002) Education between Academic Discipline and Profession in Germany after World War II, *European Educational Research Journal*, 1(1), 83–98.

Keiner, E. (2004) Educational Research between Science and Policy [part of the roundtable 'OECD Examiners' Report on Educational Research and Development in England'], *European Educational Research Journal*, 3(2), 511–516.

Keiner, E. (2006) The Science of Education: Disciplinary Knowledge on Non-Knowledge/Ignorance?, in Smeyers, P. and Depaepe, M. (eds) *Educational Research: Why 'What Works' Doesn't Work*, Dordrecht: Springer, pp. 171–186.

Keiner, E. and Schriewer, J. (2000) Erneuerung aus dem Geist der eigenen Tradition? Über Kontinuität und Wandel nationaler Denkstile in der Erziehungswissenschaft, *Schweizerische Zeitschrift für Bildungswissenschaften/Revue suisse des sciences de l'éducation/Rivista svizzera di scienze dell' educazione*, 22(1), 27–50.

Keiner, E. and Tenorth, H.-E. (2007) Die Macht der Disziplin, in Kraft, V. (ed.) *Zwischen Reflexion, Funktion und Leistung: Facetten der Erziehungswissenschaft*, Bad Heilbrunn: Klinkhardt, pp. 155–173.

Lawn, M. and Furlong, J. (2007) The Social Organisation of Education Research in England, *European Educational Research Journal*, 6(1), 55–70.

Lawn, M. and Keiner, E. (2006) The European University: Between Governance, Discipline and Network – Editorial, *European Journal of Education*, 41(2), 155–167.

Malmquist, E. and Grundin, H.U. (1975) *Educational Research in Europe Today and Tomorrow*, Amsterdam: European Cultural Foundation.

Ringer, F.K. (1990) *The Decline of the German Mandarins: The German Academic Community, 1890–1933*, Middletown, CT: Wesleyan University Press, University Press of New England.

Tillmann, K.-J., Rauschenbach, T., Tippelt, R. and Weishaupt, H. (eds) (2008) *Datenreport Erziehungswissenschaft 2008*, Barbara Budrich: Opladen and Farmington Hills.

Wagner, P. and Wittrock, B. (1991) States, Institutions, and Discourses: A Comparative Perspective on the Structuration of the Social Sciences, in Wagner, P., Wittrock, B. and Whitley, R. (eds) *Discourses on Society: The Shaping of the Social Science Disciplines*, Dordrecht: Kluwer, pp. 331–357.

11 Disciplines of education and their role in the future of educational research

Concluding reflections

John Furlong and Martin Lawn

Introduction

In our introductory chapter, we used the metaphor of the ghost to explore the relation between the disciplines of education, their material bases in universities, their recruitment and career patterns and the major shifts taking place again in the university sector. Was there, we wanted to know, still a place for the disciplinary shaping of education research or had their analytical power largely been replaced by routinized method and atheoretical empiricism? Were the educational disciplines still relevant to contemporary education enquiry and, if they were, what was their current state?

Our interest in such questions arose first and foremost from our sense that, during our working lives in university and college education, education disciplines had shifted in relative power in the academy and between themselves, that recruitment had waxed and waned but that, at the same time, publication output had vastly increased. We therefore felt that there was a need for a retrospective look at the current situation to make sense of it for future advantage. Looking forward, we were also aware that a great shift of people, resources and ideas is about to take place in UK universities: the massification of universities is perhaps halting, its stratification is perhaps increasingly being accepted; the loss of a significant age group, who entered in the first widening of university access as disciplinary specialists, who are retiring. This is within the context of tightening audits, forceful knowledge economy objectives and greater cross-border work of contemporary universities. These tendencies created the core problematics of the book as we considered the place of disciplines in education today.

Our primary focus, and that of most of our contributors, has been the UK, though with some additional reflections from the USA and Europe. Of course we recognize that not all universities internationally share the same structures and material bases for disciplinary-based work in education. However, we would suggest that, despite diverse histories internationally, there are today global influences that, by discourse, economic lever or new university mission, create a common ground for analysis in many parts of the world.

So now, at the end of this project, what have we learned about the disciplines of education and their future contribution to education research? In the main, the other contributors to this book present interesting and constructive disciplinary pasts; they also envisage useful and creative futures. These authors' close identification with their disciplines is perhaps inevitable, a reflection of our selection of them as creative and valuable representatives of their different fields. After reading this book, therefore, the reader might be excused for being focused primarily on the creativity and resilience of these disciplines in education, rather than on the challenges they face in contemporary higher education.

But is that the whole story? We think not, and in this final chapter we therefore want to reflect on what we have learned about the current and future contributions of the disciplines of education; we do so in terms of five main themes. First, we consider what we have learned about the nature of disciplines per se. Then we review what we have learned about the contribution that the disciplines can potentially make to the study of education – substantively, methodologically and epistemologically. We then consider whether there is indeed a crisis in the current position of the disciplines in relation to education, in the UK and more broadly. Next we look to the future, outlining major policy shifts at an international level that could further alter the position of the disciplines. Finally we ask what those working with and committed to the educational disciplines should do in order to help shape their own future.

The nature of disciplines

In our opening chapter we discussed the nature of disciplines, and particularly the extent to which they represent a body of knowledge, a tradition, or the extent to which they are better understood as 'a project', a subject of political struggle. What this volume confirms is that, in the anglophone world, and particularly in a diverse field like education, disciplines do become a 'project'. That may be different in other subject areas such as economics, where there would appear to be greater agreement about theories, topics worthy of investigation and methods. And in the field of education itself, it may well be different in other parts of the world where there are different intellectual traditions. Keiner, for example, in his chapter distinguishes the 'comprehensive social sciences' model of France and francophone cultures and the 'formalized disciplinary discourses' model of Germany, Austria, Switzerland and Belgium from the dominant model of the anglophone world which he characterizes as a 'pragmatically specialising professions' model.

Educational enquiry in the anglophone world, Keiner reminds us, is built on an enduring and unstable compromise – a compromise between a commitment to make both an intellectual and a practical contribution to the advancement of the field. It is this unstable compromise that was behind the long struggle to establish education as a legitimate field of study within universities in the first place. While there were major universities which took a leading role in promoting education in the first half of the twentieth century, for example, Manchester, Edinburgh and London, they were exceptions. Oxford, for example, did not appoint its first professor of education until 1989. The late-twentieth-century growth in university education – the growth of the polytechnic/new universities sector and their absorption of teacher-training colleges – created further tensions. Across the sector as a whole, a new intellectual and practical compromise has had to develop through which universities accept (or more frequently tolerate) a tension between different missions – between a commitment to the study of education and a commitment to the practical training of teachers.

Throughout the anglophone world, therefore, 'struggle' is a fact of life for the discipline of education as a whole within the university sector as well as for the sub-disciplinary fields we are considering here. Within this volume, that struggle is perhaps most vividly illustrated in the case of sociology. Lauder *et al.* describe the changing fortunes of the sociology of education over time – the early close encounters with policy-makers in the 1950s and 1960s, the turn to teachers as a key audience in the 1970s and 1980s and the 'falling from grace' in the late 1980s with the explicit intervention of the Thatcher government to challenge the contribution of educational theory in general and sociology in particular in the education of teachers. 'The politics of position' is also apparent in psychology's story told by Crozier, although as a story it is far more positive than that of sociology, in no small part ensured by the over-riding institutional position of the British Psychological Society (BPS) which accredits courses and qualifications in many of our universities. Economics' position, as described by Dearden *et al.*, is different again; they describe a disciplinary perspective that in institutional terms is marginal; economics of education has very few centres of teaching and research in the UK but its influence in terms of policy has increased dramatically recently – in many ways it became the leading intellectual influence on educational policy in the UK under New Labour. The historian's narrative, built around moments of insecurity and curiosity, expresses the struggle for existence and engagement

What we have learned (or perhaps reminded ourselves) therefore is that far from representing stable bodies of knowledge, with widely supported theories and methods and clear patterns of induction and reproduction over time, the disciplines of education are complex and unstable intellectual traditions; they do not have sharp boundaries and their legitimacy has to be argued for in constantly changing institutional conditions and in changing relationships with different audiences.

The enduring contribution of disciplines to the study of education

Reading the various contributions to this volume it is clear that each area we have considered can present a strong claim to making a significant contribution to the public understanding of educational processes – substantively, methodologically and conceptually.

Substantively our contributors provide evidence that, on many occasions in the past, disciplinary-based perspectives have had a major influence on national policy as well as on day-to-day practice in classrooms: sociology's past work on 'origins and destinations' that was influential in the move to comprehensive education in the 1960s and 1970s; the contribution of economists to more recent debates on the expansion of higher education with their work on human capital theory and 'rates of return'. And there is no shortage of suggestions of future educational problems to which disciplinary-based research might contribute. For example, Crossley and Watson argue, convincingly in our view, that comparativists have a major contribution to make in the context of the increasing globalization of educational policy. It is they, they argue, who have the expertise to interrogate the increasing popularity of international 'policy borrowing' and the rise in the significance of cross-national studies of student achievement that are today driving many governments' educational thinking. Another example is psychology, where Crozier suggests that, in the future, we might expect significant advances in research in cognitive development, in neuropsychology and in understanding the influence of the social and cultural context on development. Even history is able to point to useful interventions in current policy fields, for example in school building.

Substantively, we can see that each field is capable of arguing strongly for its present and continued relevance. But our contributors have also laid claim to important methodological and conceptual expertise as well. Economists, Dearden *et al.* argue, take a particular theoretical perspective and therefore may be more focused on incentives and other related issues in trying to distinguish between benefits and costs of educational policies. Furthermore, from a methodological perspective, economists, they argue, bring a wide range of quantitative tools to bear on their research, providing a range of methods that can be applied in non-experimental settings. As Lauder *et al.* note, it is the economists' quantitative skills, still sorely lacking in much other educational research, that have helped them eclipse sociology in many policy debates. In geography, Taylor argues for the importance of the concept of 'scale' in understanding the relationship between different 'spaces and places' where learning takes place. And Oancea and Bridges make strong pleas that questions of a philosophical nature are central to every significant debate in the field of educational theory, policy, practice and research. In philosophy, they argue, analysis, argumentation and critique are given central, systematic and comprehensive attention. Philosophy is also connected with practice and policy through nurturing democratic conversation about education and supporting practical deliberation at all levels and on all aspects of educational practice. Again, each disciplinary perspective has argued clearly for their distinctive methodological and/or conceptual contributions.

In our introduction we quoted Bridges (2006) who suggested that disciplines offer at least three different things: *differentiation* between different kinds of enquiry, *coherence* in terms of internal consistency and the '*systematic*' or rigour of enquiry – 'the discipline' of disciplines. What our contributors have demonstrated is that by building communities that share certain epistemological assumptions, that recognize a common agenda of issues to be addressed, these communities can provide contexts in which these different attributes can be realized among widely distributed scholars working on the problems of the day.

Disciplines of education are therefore seen by their protagonists as offering a serious and necessary contribution to the study of education as part of social science. And this is certainly the view of the Economic and Social Research Council (ESRC) (the UK's leading social science funding body) which assumes a methodological strength and a substantive contribution in applications which can only be delivered through a discipline-based proposal. The European Research Council also assumes a disciplinary base for all research proposals but then also demands a trans-disciplinary perspective as a dimension of all projects as well. Both the UK and Europe's most prestigious funding bodies accept that it is through disciplinary-based work that research of the highest quality is achieved.

Yet for all of the acclaimed benefits of disciplinary-based work, we know that, in reality, such research represents only a very small part of what is produced by scholars today. The vast majority of education research has only a tangential relationship to disciplinary-based work. As we have repeatedly stated, such research often seems to be based on the residue, on the ghosts of disciplinary-based methods and concepts, but used in ways that are often cut off from wider debates. But does this matter? Is it only research that is part of a particular disciplinary 'canon' that has value? Unfortunately, given the primary purpose of this collection, this is not a question that any of our contributors have addressed directly. Certainly some of our contributors warn against the dangers of conceptual and methodological 'borrowing'. Crozier, for example, warns against educational researchers borrowing from psychology without a full appreciation of the theories they are using. At the same time he warns against 'mainstream' psychologists applying their research to educational settings about which they have little real insight. Taylor makes a similar point about geography.

But is this type of territorialism sufficient? We think not: in our view, the field would benefit by further conceptual work here, exploring the *indirect* influence of the disciplines in research in education. Not all educational research can or should be 'pure' in terms of disciplinary background; there are many questions in education that need to be addressed that do not fall neatly into any one particular disciplinary 'box'. It may, though, be possible to distinguish between strong disciplinary and weak disciplinary framed research. Here perhaps the line is drawn in terms of purpose (the anglophone compromise again): is the research intended to produce normative improvement or is it intended to produce analytical explanation? It is clear that the disciplines are widely regarded as essential for analytical explanation. A key question, though, becomes: are disciplines necessary to the study and development of a field of practical action, and if so, in what ways? If they are, if at least some ghosts are important, then the influence of the disciplines runs much wider and much deeper than is conventionally acknowledged.

The current state of disciplines of education

The disciplines of education may be important but what have we learned about their current position, in the UK and beyond? On the surface it would seem that they are strong; our contributors report a great deal of activity. As Rothblatt comments in his reflective contribution: 'I do not sense any sentiment that the disciplines are in the doldrums or have reached a heuristic or intellectual impasse.' Yet clearly this is not the whole story.

In our opening discussion of the nature of disciplines, we drew on the work of Barnett (1990) to suggest that it is valuable to distinguish between disciplines' epistemological and their political or sociological dimensions. The epistemological dimensions of disciplines focus on questions of theory, of method, debates about the nature of evidence and how it should be represented and defended; their sociological position examines the means through which they are established within the field. We also noted Kuhn's (1962) assertion that for intellectual progress to be made, one needs both relatively close agreement on theories and methods of enquiry and sufficient institutional certainty so that newcomers can be inducted into the discipline. This distinction between a discipline's sociological and epistemological dimensions provides a useful heuristic in considering their current health.

Interestingly, the chapters in this volume have helped to refine our understanding of the sociological position of disciplines by demonstrating that there are at least three different but interrelated dimensions that are important. First, there is the *institutional dimension* – the extent to which disciplines are institutionalized through established courses, qualifications, dedicated lectureships and professorships and established procedures for the induction and promotion of new recruits. The story that most of our contributors described was of the continued tension between the academic and vocational mission of education faculties and the progressive whittling away of such institutional structures as did exist in earlier periods.

Most academics working within university education departments are funded through government sources directly, supported for their contribution to initial teacher education and training, or CPD (continuing professional development) in England through the TDA (Training and Development Agency for Schools) and elsewhere in the UK through higher education funding councils. They have been appointed for their practical and professional competence rather than their academic expertise. Unlike other social sciences, they are experts in applied and practical issues in education but apprentices in education research.

Because of the funding base, there are today relatively few dedicated professorships or lectureships in UK universities (or indeed elsewhere in the

English-speaking world) that are tied to particular disciplinary fields; most disciplinary professors are not employed as such – they are employed because of their competitive research excellence. And outside educational psychology, where bodies such as the BPS hold sway, there are very few designated courses and qualifications that are formally linked to the disciplines of education. As a result, lecturers who, through their personal research, develop strong disciplinary commitments are unlikely to have consistent opportunities to teach their discipline.

The only real exception to this institutional story is the gradual realization of graduate schools in many universities. Although they have existed for some time in semi-virtual terms, that is as a registration and administrative system, they are now becoming more than that. Graduate schools are increasingly viewed as vital to departmental and faculty survival, particularly in our larger and more powerful universities: they attract international students and highly skilled research staff and are closely associated with strong research identities and disciplinary strength. Scotland has shown that it is possible for university departments (especially in the sciences) to 'pool' their resources, academics and strategies to achieve critical mass and research prominence. The establishment of UK national or regional graduate schools in social science would benefit the disciplines of education enormously.

Even so, the opportunities for home-based students remain extremely limited (just 4 per cent of doctoral students received ESRC scholarships in the last Research Assessment Exercise period) and those who do undertake a disciplinary-based doctorate often find it extremely difficult to find established positions; such positions as do exist are frequently taken by those with initial training in a parent discipline – psychology, sociology, history (Mills *et al.*, 2006). As a result, an able doctoral student in education would not be well advised to pin their colours too definitely to a disciplinary mast if they were keen to follow an academic career in the UK.

A second sociological dimension, and source of potential power, concerns *audience*. Here the contributors to this volume tell a more mixed story. The historians, for example, seem to focus primarily on other historians of education in university departments of education; internationally, there would seem to be a ready audience for historical work within this specialist community. To some degree the focus on such 'internal' audiences is true for all of the other disciplines too; however, some have other important audiences as well. For the economists, for example, it is clear that policy-makers are vitally important. Given the relatively small number of students and academics studying economics of education at the present time, their survival is perhaps more than in any other area we have considered dependent on this very important external audience. Psychologists have a rather different primary audience – those studying BPS-validated degrees and professional qualifications where certain sorts of curriculum are mandated. Sociology's audience, we are told, has varied historically; it moved from policy-makers in the 1950s and 1960s to teachers in the 1970s and 1980s; since then its audience has been curtailed, primarily drawn from subject specialists also interested in the sociology of education with very little cross-over to mainstream sociology. Philosophy, we are told, is relevant everywhere – it is 'all that'. But in reality its penetration into mainstream educational thinking remains sporadic; despite its evident power, its audience is largely a specialist one, however lively its community.

If the institutional structures are weak and audiences, beyond other specialist academics, are highly variable, then we might ask how these disciplinary sub-fields survive at all. What we have learned through the contributions to this volume is that disciplinary perspectives can be maintained sociologically in other ways too – particularly through different forms of *academic networks*. Here our contributors were able to tell a much more positive story. Stimulated by the demands of research audit through publication and the development of a low-cost, global academic publishing industry that can cater to increasingly niche audiences, our contributors described numerous examples of thriving specialist journals (there are currently 650–700 English-language educational research journals internationally). Each sub-disciplinary field would also seem to have its own lively learned societies and well-supported specialist academic conferences. Sociologically we have learned that such academic networks are now the main arena through which the disciplines of education are 'lived'.

Sociologically speaking, therefore, the current position of the disciplines of education is at best mixed – there are strong networks but largely internal audiences and a relatively weak institutional position. What of their epistemological position? Given the intense period of epistemological self-doubt that the entire academy has been through in the last 20 years, what is striking about all of our contributors is their lack of self-doubt. All confidently claim to be vitally important in their contribution to the development of educational thinking, policy and practice (however defined). Again as Rothblatt says, 'None of the contributors express a loss of confidence in their disciplines *qua* disciplines.' None address the highly complex issues that arise because of the anglophone compromise between studying 'what' and studying 'how'. In their aspirations, it would seem, the disciplines hope more to live in continental Europe than in the English-speaking world; they aspire to a world where academic knowledge is valued in and for itself, untroubled by 'use value'. Perhaps that is why, as Keiner suggests, so many British academics flock to European conferences and leave the normative cultures of their UK meetings behind!

But despite their confidence, to us it would seem that all is not well in these disciplinary communities in that they are very small and largely cut off from their 'parent' disciplines and, indeed, from each other. Only geography sketches out what a symbiotic relationship between education and geography would look like – perhaps rather easier than in the other cases because such a relationship is at this stage of development largely theoretical. All of the other relationships seem problematic in different ways – psychology warns of the dangers of psychologists undertaking educational research without due regard to the day-to-day complexities of educational realities; sociology describes the earlier period of seamless collaboration between sociology and the sociology of education, followed by a period of progressive distancing; the philosophers talk of developing a better relationship with mainstream philosophy as an important aspiration; while the historians seem to find strength in international links. Of course, this is not the whole story. There are some sub-sections of these disciplines that do have a much closer relationship with the parent discipline – the field of education and work-based learning would be a case in point where communities of sociologists, economists and sociologists of education work together across fault lines on a regular basis. However, such examples are rare except on an individual basis. How the disciplines of education relate to their parent disciplines is problematic and it can be viewed across university sites where the distancing of education from other social science departments is manifold.

As a result of this isolation, the education disciplines perhaps lack the critical mass to argue about their fundamental assumptions and purposes; perhaps that is why they are so confident. In our opening chapter we referred to Bridge's discussion of the conceptual and epistemological conflicts experienced within the sociology of education in the 1970s and 1980s – conflicts between ethnographers and neo-Marxists, between critical theorists, postmodernists and social relativists. Lauder *et al.* tell the same story in more detail in their chapter. But while such conflicts were real and often painful, they were evidence of a very lively academic community with sufficient size and sufficient links to a parent discipline to sustain such debate. We would look in vain for similar lively debates among any of our education disciplines today, held together as they are with relatively small and perhaps comfortable networks.

Disciplines in education in the twenty-first century

Next we look to the future, outlining major policy shifts at the European/ UK level that could further alter the position of the disciplines.

It is perhaps natural that a book based largely on UK work assumes a commonsense position and interior view on it. It would be an error, however, to ignore the determining and shaping effects of European research policy on the substance and form of education and its disciplines in the UK. As a result of European research policy, universities, the main source of organizational support for the disciplines of education, are set to change substantially in the coming years.

The shaping of European research policy takes place through the European Research Area, its policy strategy, funding and organization. The Research Area is viewed as an active arena, that is, it is audited to allow information about its integrating effects to be judged; for example, on the speed of university reforms, the growth of research funding, the mobility of researchers between specified countries and aspects of knowledge-sharing across borders. The way that universities will organize their research to achieve funding will shift from an individual scholar mode to teams, from disciplines to domains or cross-cut areas of work, and into a concentration on powerful research institutions. Many of our leading universities already recognize that research is no longer an isolated activity and that the emphasis is shifting from individual researchers to teams and global research networks. Scientific problems tend to go beyond traditional disciplinary structures; cutting-edge research is increasingly being conducted at the interface between academic disciplines or in multi-disciplinary settings. Universities' research environments are more competitive and globalized with greater interaction (EC, 2006, p. 3). So, European policy is focused on altering research cultures, organization and careers. Concern about the inhibiting effects of research clusters and their bordered cultures of research has been growing in EU policy for several years. As the European Commission argues, 'New ways are needed to address the asymmetry between relevant scientific and societal problems and the disciplinary structures underpinning the University' (EC, 2005, p. 14). Inter-disciplinarity (furthering expertise through common developments), trans-disciplinarity (interaction leading to radical epistemological rethinking) and increased cross-border research mobility are therefore needed to overcome 'traditional disciplinary clustering' (EC, 2006, p. 31).

This direction of travel is reflected in current (2010) proposals to consolidate or cluster specialist university Doctoral Training Centres in the UK (following plans from the ERSC Training Board). The creation of the Centres will be produced under forms of competition, with uneven spread of provision and a likely dominance of research universities. In most cases, the disciplines of education will become part of a general social science centre, working in an inter-disciplinary way. The aspiration, according to the ESRC, is to promote 'exciting new interdisciplinary research, particularly through the deep integration of social science' (ESRC, 2009, p. 25).

The training of postgraduates will, therefore, in the future take place across a range of social science disciplines, and will involve inter-disciplinary and discipline-specific research methods training, alongside core-skills training. The definition of research training, and so of research identity, will be an inter- and trans-disciplinary definition, and no longer defined by the discipline or sub-discipline alone.

Researcher mobility across Europe will also have a reshaping effect, breaking down local and national cultures of research. The expectation is that more students will undertake different degree-level work especially in the UK from across Europe. They will move in countries and between countries, within degree cycles and between degree cycles, and within organized mobility programmes (like Erasmus) or as 'free movers'. The purposes, definition and organization of disciplines of education, while not the main focus of what is happening, will be significantly affected by these developments.

Conclusion: shaping our own future

The organization of social science/education research is therefore changing, and the UK will reflect these changes in its own infrastructure and policies. European funding streams, like the Framework programme, seek inter-disciplinary proposals, and the European Research Council demands trans-disciplinary proposals, built on disciplinary foundations. Disciplines of education in the UK have to recognize that a common field of employment, research and training is being created in the EU, and it is being reflected in new communicated subjects (in journals) and even new journals, and new sources of funding. A key question for those working in faculties of education is whether or not it will be they who will have the opportunity to engage in these new initiatives or whether it will be others, with perhaps more systematic disciplinary training but perhaps with less engagement with education as a field of practice, that will be best placed.

However, it is not clear whether educational researchers in the UK often recognize and engage with this new situation. Too often it would seem that, despite the creative endeavour and analytical strengths of the disciplines, most are unaware of each other and of the challenging and changing circumstances of their operation. The latter is viewed more often as a private trouble and not a public issue. However, we have come to recognize that there are at least three ways in which those involved and committed to the disciplines of education could improve their position – ways in which they could, at least to some degree, help to shape their own futures.

What this volume has shown us above all is the importance of networks, journals and conferences of learned societies as the life blood of the disciplines. These are activities that are within our own hands; it is academics themselves who make these things work. And it is therefore these networks that can be formed or reformed in order to strengthen the position of the disciplines – opening them up to new collaborators and audiences.

The first imperative, we believe, is to open up the disciplines of education much more than at present to their 'parent' disciplines: sociology of education needs closer links with sociology; history of education with history, etc. As we have noted, most of the academic communities represented by our contributors are very small. Oancea and Bridges estimate that there are fewer than 100 academics working in education departments in the UK who publish in the field of philosophy of education; Crozier, using 2001 RAE data, estimates that there are about 200 academics publishing in psychology journals; numbers of sociologists and historians, economists and geographers are likely to be even smaller. We also know that many of these disciplinary specialists work in relative isolation in their own institutions, perhaps inevitable given the lack of disciplinary-based teaching that is available in many university departments of education.

While it would seem that these disciplinary communities are managing to thrive in terms of supporting international journals, lively conferences and learned societies, there are real disadvantages of being small and largely closed. As we argued above, there is a particular danger in terms of the flourishing of lively debate about theories, methods and epistemologies. In the UK, the parent disciplines are much, much larger – psychology has over 3,000 academics, economics around 1,500 and sociology around 1,100. As a consequence, these communities support widely differing approaches to their disciplines; inevitably they provide richer and more challenging communities in which to pursue fundamental questions about research.

The current 'isomorphic closure' of educational disciplines from their parents is also unhelpful in terms of the recruitment and induction of new academics. We know that education faculties are net importers of disciplinary specialists (Mills *et al.*, 2006) but, too often, once an individual has made that transition, they find it hard to move back; their reputation, their networks as well as their commitments become focused on education alone.

We would suggest that much could be achieved if our leading journals and leading learned societies took on these issues as a matter of priority. The *Oxford Review of Education*, in which we published earlier versions of chapters in this volume, was specifically established to explore the links between those in education and the broader academy (in Oxford and beyond). But very few other journals have this in their remit; too often editorial boards and mission statements encourage closure rather than openness. The same is true of our learned societies and professional associations; very few see forging links between their specific membership and those working in the parent disciplines as a core activity.

Developing better networks of this sort does not mean that the essential purposes of faculties and schools of education or of economics or sociology or history should change; they will remain wedded to their particular institutional position and markets; in education the 'eternal compromise' of being both theoretical and applied will continue to be a reality. But it is suggested that the academy themselves could establish new forms of cultural activity that move across these boundaries in ways that would strengthen us all.

For example, were such intellectual links to exist, it would be much easier for collaborations between those in departments of education and those in parent disciplines. It would be much easier for those with a disciplinary background to move back and forth between different departments, bringing the insights of the disciplines to the field of education and the realities of educational practice to the parent disciplines. More importantly, given the current direction of travel of European research policy that we outlined above, if educationalists are to be represented at all in this new world of multi-disciplinary and trans-disciplinary research centres, then such opening up is going to be essential. Failure to do so could mean that educational issues are increasingly addressed by disciplinary specialists without contributions from the field of education itself.

The second imperative is to open up the disciplines of education to more applied work. Probably 75 per cent of those researching in the field of education do not consider themselves to be disciplinary specialists and over 60 per cent of funded research in education in the UK comes from government sources, where disciplinary-based work is not prioritized – given these realities, opening up the disciplines of education to this more applied world would seem to be an essential step if they are to continue to survive, especially in today's harsh economic world. Again our learned societies, and particularly the British Educational Research Association, should perhaps take a lead here.

But before that can happen we, as a community, need to develop a much clearer understanding of what the contribution of the disciplines can and should be to applied work. Not all educational questions are first and foremost disciplinary questions; the applied field of education has its own policy and practice priorities which researchers need to address. Yet our educational disciplines do have a vitally important contribution to make conceptually, in 'framing' educational problems, and in providing powerful methodologies with which to study educational problems in a rigorous way. But how do we distinguish the good-quality use of disciplinary perspectives for applied work from poor-quality use? As we argued above, the field would benefit from some further careful work here – of an empirical as well as a philosophical nature.

Given the reality of the current political economy of research, particularly in the anglophone world, if they are to survive, the disciplines of education need to make their case as important contributors to applied work. It will, in our view, be increasingly difficult to sustain an argument that their contribution is only in terms of 'pure' research. A careful analysis of what their contribution can and should be could do much to increase the quality of applied research (Furlong and Oancea, 2006). It would also potentially strengthen the position of the disciplines within the academy by demonstrating that their influence – conceptually, methodologically and in terms of the education and training of new academics – is perhaps much broader and much deeper than at first sight it might appear to be.

Our final 'opening up' concerns the relationship between the disciplines themselves. What is increasingly clear, particularly in applied work, is that however powerful the contribution of the disciplines of education in the 'framing' of educational problems, any such framing is in itself inevitably only partial. As European research and university policy now explicitly recognizes, there is an urgent need to address complex social problems, and education will always be one of these, through multi-disciplinary and even trans-disciplinary perspectives.

This issue is to some degree touched on by Lauder *et al.* in their discussion of the role of 'redemption' as a sentiment and 'domain assumption' within the sociology of education. As such, the idea of redemption has guided much of sociology's commitment to asking questions about who gets what out of education in terms of 'origins and destinations'. Such questions have been and remain powerfully important for a society to ask about itself and it is the sociology of education more than any other discipline that has continued to prioritize these questions. But what Lauder *et al.* also learn, by highlighting this domain assumption, is how partial it is in answering a genuinely *educational* (rather than sociological) question about educational opportunities. In educational terms, as these authors seem to imply, we need to ask much broader questions than merely ones of distribution; we also need to ask questions about the *moral purposes* and about the *quality* of education that different members of our society get. And these issues are not ones that sociology as a discipline is particularly well equipped to answer on its own. These are questions perhaps better addressed by philosophers, when they consider what constitutes education for 'the good life'; they are better answered by psychologists working with subject specialists, when they are asking what constitutes 'good subject pedagogy'. The strength of our disciplinary perspectives – their ability to 'frame' educational issues in ways that can promote rigorous analysis – is also often their weakness, in that they can limit the questions that we can ask about complex educational issues: limited questions give limited answers.

There is therefore an urgent need for those in the disciplines of education themselves to develop opportunities to work collaboratively on key educational issues of the day. Again, our own learned societies, journals and conferences could take a lead here. Developing this sort of experience within the educational community would mean that we would be far better placed than we are at present in facing the challenges of European policies that will increasingly shape our world.

In conclusion we need to return to the idea that disciplines are always a political project. To engage with a discipline is to struggle to occupy a field of study and so to gain meaning within it. In this sense it is, in all its sub-areas of engagement and identity, a field of contestation, taking place through its forms and means of communication. What we hope we have demonstrated in this volume is that the disciplines of education remain vitally important to the current and future advancement of education – both as an intellectual and as a practical activity. All of our disciplines of education have a very positive story to tell; they remain vital and engaged academic communities. But they are also very fragile institutionally; they could quite easily disappear in the complex array of national and international policies that are currently sweeping our university system. Academics themselves therefore need to recognize that in their disciplinary lives they are indeed engaged in a political project to occupy a field of study. But they also need to recognize that in the contemporary world they can't do this alone. They need to work with each other, they need to work with applied researchers and they need to work with their 'parent' disciplines. If they open themselves up in these ways, then they can perhaps ensure that, in the future, they will be more than merely ghosts, spectres from an earlier, more straightforward period in our collective intellectual history.

References

Barnett, R. (1990) *The Idea of Higher Education*. Buckingham: SRHE/Open University Press.

Bridges, D. (2006) 'The disciplines and discipline of educational research', *Journal of Philosophy of Education* 40(2), 259–272.

Council of the European Union (2008) 'Presidency conclusions', Brussels: European Council, 13–14 March 2008.

ESRC *Strategic Plan 2009–2014*. Swindon: ESRC.

ESRC (2009) *Postgraduate Training and Development Guidelines: For the Accreditation of Doctoral Training Centres*. Swindon: ESRC.

European Commission (2004) *The Europe of Knowledge 2020: A Vision for University-based Research and Innovation*. Conference Proceedings, Liege, 25–28 April 2004.

European Commission (2005) *European Universities: Enhancing Europe's Research Base*. Luxembourg: Office for Official Publications of the European Communities.

European Commission (2006) 'Delivering the modernization agenda for the universities', Brussels: Communication to Council, 10 May 2006, 208 Final.

European Commission (2009) *Students and Higher Education Reform: Survey among Students in Higher Education Institutions, in the EU Member States, Croatia, Iceland, Norway and Turkey*, analytical report.

Furlong, J. and Oancea, A. (2006) 'Assessing quality in applied and practice-based research in education: a framework for discussion', *Review of Australian Research in Education, No 6: Counterpoints on the Quality and Impact of Educational Research*.

Kuhn, T. (1962) *The Structure of Scientific Revolutions*. 1st. edn, Chicago: University of Chicago Press.

Kuhn, T. (1977) *The Essential Tension*. Chicago: Chicago University Press.

Mills, D., A. Jepson, T. Coxon, M. Easterby-Smith, P. Hawkins and J. Spencer (2006) *Demographic Review of the Social Sciences*. Swindon: ESRC.

Contributors

David Bridges is an Emeritus Professor at the University of East Anglia and Professorial Fellow in the Faculty of Education, University of Cambridge. He has contributed extensively to the literature in philosophy of education, especially on philosophy and educational research. He is Honorary Vice President of the Philosophy of Education Society of Great Britain and he founded and was for eight years co-convenor of the Philosophy of Education Network of the European Educational Research Association.

Phillip Brown is a Distinguished Research Professor in the School of Social Sciences at Cardiff University. He has written, co-authored and co-edited 13 books, the most recent being *Education, globalization and social change* with Hugh Lauder (Oxford University Press, 2006) and *The mismanagement of talent: employability and jobs in the knowledge economy* with A. Hesketh (Oxford University Press, 2004). *The global auction: the broken promises of opportunity, jobs and rewards*, written with Hugh Lauder and David Ashton, was published by Oxford University Press, in March 2010.

Michael Crossley is a Professor of Comparative and International Education and Joint Director of the Research Centre for International and Comparative Studies at the Graduate School of Education, University of Bristol. He was Editor of *Comparative Education* from 2004–2010 and was Chair of the British Association for International and Comparative Education (BAICE) from 2002 to 2004. He is the founding Series Editor for the *Bristol Papers in Education: Comparative and International Studies*. His main research interests relate to theoretical and methodological scholarship on the future of comparative and international education; research and evaluation capacity and international development co-operation; and educational development in small states. He is an Academician of the Academy of Social Sciences.

W. Ray Crozier is currently a Visiting Fellow at the School of Social Work and Psychology, University of East Anglia and Honorary Professor, School of Social Sciences, Cardiff University. Previously he was Professor of the Psychology of Education at Cardiff University and Professor of Psychology at the University of East Anglia. He is a Fellow of the British Psychological Society.

Lorraine Dearden is a Professor of Economics and Social Statistics at the Institute of Education, University London (IOE) and Research Fellow at the Institute for Fiscal Studies. She is Director of the Economic and Social Research Council's (ESRC) National Centre for Research Methods (NCRM), ADMIN (Administrative Data: Methods Inference and Network) NODE based at the IOE.

John Furlong is a Professor in the Department of Education at the University of Oxford; he was Director of the department from 2003 to 2009. Originally trained as a sociologist, he has spent much of his academic career working on issues of educational policy; he has particular interests in research policy, educational research capacity and the role of universities in the professional education of teachers. He is a past president of the British Educational Research Association and was a member of the 2008 RAE panel. He is an Academician of the Academy of Social Sciences.

Joyce Goodman is a Professor of History of Education at the University of Winchester. She is author of numerous articles and books on women and education. Current research includes work on girls' secondary education and empire, women's trans-national organisations and intellectual co-operation. She is the President of History of Education Society UK and a former Editor of the international journal *History of Education*.

Ian Grosvenor is a Professor of Urban Educational History at the University of Birmingham. He is author of numerous articles and books on racism, education and identity, the visual in educational research, the material culture of education and the history of urban education. Current research focuses on new ways of conceptualising and presenting the educational past through consideration of issues relating to space, design, technology, the visual in education, artefacts and identity formation. He is Managing Editor of the international journal *Paedagogica Historica*, Secretary General of the European Educational Research Association and a Fellow of the Royal Historical Society.

A.H. Halsey is an Emeritus Professor of Sociology, Oxford University and Emeritus Fellow of Nuffield College, Oxford, formerly BBC Reith Lecturer, adviser to Secretary of State for Education and author of many books and articles on the sociology of education. He is a Fellow of the British Academy.

Edwin Keiner is a Full Professor of Foundations of Education at the Friedrich-Alexander-University of Erlangen-Nuremberg, Germany. He is the Chair of the Foundations of Education section and of the commission Research on Education Research (Wissenschaftsforschung) within the German Association of Education Research (DGfE). His research areas include comparative history, the sociology of education and education research in the context of processes of Europeanisation.

Hugh Lauder is a Professor of Education and Political Economy at the University of Bath. His publications include *High skills: globalization, competitiveness and skill formation* (Oxford University Press, 2001); *Capitalism and social progress* (Palgrave, 2001) and *Trading in futures: markets in education* (Open University Press, 1999). He is also the Editor of the *Journal of Education and Work* and a member of the ESRC (UK) Virtual College. He has served as an adviser to central and regional government agencies in the UK. His research interests include the relationship of globalisation to national labour markets and educational systems in relation to higher education.

Martin Lawn is a Professorial Research Fellow at the Department of Education, University of Oxford and previously at the Centre for Educational Sociology, University of Edinburgh. He is an ex-Secretary General of the European Educational Research Association and a member of its Council. He works in education within historical sociology and political sociology, and has published on the histories of education and educational sciences and on European networking. He is an Academician of the Academy of Social Sciences.

Stephen Machin is a Professor of Economics at University College London, Research Director of the Centre for Economic Performance at the London School of Economics and Director of the Centre for the Economics of Education. He is one of the Editors of the *Economic Journal*. Previously he has been visiting Professor at Harvard University (1993–1994) and at the Massachusetts Institute of Technology (2001–2002). He is an elected Fellow of the British Academy (since 2006), President of the European Association of Labour Economists (from 2008) and is an independent member of the Low Pay Commission (since 2007).

Alis Oancea is a Research Fellow at the University of Oxford Department of Education. She has two doctorates, including one from Oxford University, and is an elected member of the Executive Council of the British Education Research Association. She has published extensively in the fields of philosophy of research, research policy and governance, research assessment and post-compulsory and lifelong education. Recent publications include *Assessing quality in applied and practice-based research in education* (Routledge, 2007) and *Education for all: the future of education and training for 14–19 year olds* (Routledge, 2009).

Sheldon Rothblatt is an Emeritus Professor of History at the University of California, Berkeley. He was educated at Berkeley and King's College, Cambridge and holds an honorary doctorate from Gothenburg University. He is also a Fellow of the Royal Historical Society of Britain and a Foreign Member of the Royal Swedish Academy of Sciences. His research is on the study of universities from the perspective of cultural history.

Chris Taylor is a Senior Lecturer in the School of Social Sciences, Cardiff University. He has written extensively on education from a geographical perspective, and published in geographical, sociological and education journals. This research includes the impact of marketisation and school diversity, participation in higher education and the opportunities for out-of-school learning.

Anna Vignoles is a Professor of Economics of Education at the Institute of Education, University London (IOE) and Research Fellow at the Centre for Economic Performance, London School of Economics. She is Co-director of the ESRC's NCRM, ADMIN NODE based at the IOE.

Keith Watson is an Emeritus Professor of Comparative and International Education and a former Director of the Centre for International Studies in Education Management and Training at the University of Reading. He is a former Editor of the *International Journal of Educational Development*; a past President of the British Comparative and International Education Society (CIES); and former Chair of the United Kingdom Forum for International Education and Training (UKFIET). Keith Watson has published widely in the field, on issues ranging from education and language policies to educational policy, planning and administration.

Index